KT-454-775

# FAMILIES, HOUSEHOLDS AND SOCIETY

Graham Allan
and
Graham Crow

palgrave

© Graham Allan and Graham Crow 2001

All rights reserved. No reproduction, copy or transmission of this publication may be made without written permission.

No paragraph of this publication may be reproduced, copied or transmitted save with written permission or in accordance with the provisions of the Copyright, Designs and Patents Act 1988, or under the terms of any licence permitting limited copying issued by the Copyright Licensing Agency, 90 Tottenham Court Road, London W1P 0LP.

Any person who does any unauthorised act in relation to this publication may be liable to criminal prosecution and civil claims for damages.

The authors have asserted their rights to be identified as the authors of this work in accordance with the Copyright, Designs and Patents Act 1988.

First published 2001 by
PALGRAVE
Houndmills, Basingstoke, Hampshire RG21 6XS and
175 Fifth Avenue, New York, N.Y. 10010
Companies and representatives throughout the world

PALGRAVE is the new global academic imprint of St. Martin's Press LLC Scholarly and Reference Division and Palgrave Publishers Ltd (formerly Macmillan Press Ltd).

ISBN-10: 0-333-69306-X hardcover
ISBN-10: 0-333-69307-8 paperback
ISBN-13: 978-0-333-69306-3 hardcover
ISBN-13: 978-0-333-69307-0 paperback

This book is printed on paper suitable for recycling and made from fully managed and sustained forest sources.
This book is printed on paper suitable for recycling and made from fully managed and sustained forest sources.

A catalogue record for this book is available from the British Library.

Library of Congress Cataloging-in-Publication Data
Allan, Graham, 1968–
    Families, households, and society/Graham Allan and Graham Crow.
      p. cm – (Sociology for a changing world)
    Includes bibliographical references and index.
    ISBN 0-333-69306-X
      1. Family–Great Britain.    2. Home–Great Britain.    3. Households–
Great Britain.    I. Crow, Graham.    II. Title.    III. Series.

HQ614 .A55 2000
306.85'0941–dc21                                                    00–034516

Printed in Great Britain by the MPG Books Group, Bodmin and King's Lynn

In memory of **Donald Allan**, 1913–99

A man of his time

# Contents

# List of Tables and Figures

## Tables

**Figures**

# Acknowledgements

We would like to acknowledge the help we have received in the various stages of writing this book. We are grateful to Mary Maynard, Jane Ribbens McCarthy, and an anonymous referee for their comments on earlier drafts of the book. Staff and postgraduates in the Department of Sociology and Social Policy at the University of Southampton have continued to provide a supportive and stimulating environment in which to work. We would like to make special mention of Sheila Hawker and thank her for the many discussions we have had about household practices in general and stepfamilies in particular. The undergraduates taking the courses we teach have also helped to clarify our thinking about the best ways to make sense of changing family and household patterns. We would like to thank Catherine Gray at the publishers for her encouragement and patience throughout the project. Finally, members of our own families have contributed to this book in many ways, not all of which they will recognize.

GRAHAM ALLAN
GRAHAM CROW

The authors and publishers are grateful for permission to reproduce the materials contained in the following tables and figures: Tables 2.1, 2.6, 2.7, 6.1, 6.2, 6.3 *Marriage, Divorce and Adoption Statistics*, Office of National Statistics, ©Crown Copyright 1971–1997; Table 2.2 *Population Trends*, Office of National Statistics, ©Crown Copyright 1996, 1998; Table 2.3 *Birth Statistics*, Office of National Statistics, ©Crown Copyright, 1976, 1986, 1998; Table 2.4 *General Household Survey*, Office of National Statistics, ©Crown Copyright, 1990; Tables 2.5, 4.1, 6.4, 6.6, 6.7, 6.8 and 6.9 *General Household Survey*, Office of national Statistics, ©Crown Copyright, 1998; Table 4.2 *General*

*Household Survey*, Office of National Statistics, ©Crown Copyright, 1997; Table 5.1 *New Earnings Survey*, Office of National Statistics, ©Crown Copyright, 1999; Table 5.2 *New Earnings Survey*, Office of National Statistics, ©Crown Copyright, 1975, 1985, 1999; Table 5.3 *National Census*, Office of National Statistics, ©Crown Copyright, 1981, 1991; Table 5.4 C. Vogler and J. Pahl, 'Money, power and inequality within marriage', *Sociological Review*, ©The Editorial Board of Sociological Review, 1994; Table 6.5 A. Marsh, R. Ford and L. Finlayson, *Lone Parents*, Office of National Statistics, ©Crown Copyright, 1997; Table 8.1 and 8.2 *Annual Abstract of Statistics*, Office of National Statistics, ©Crown Copyright, 2000; Table 8.3 *Social Trends*, Office of National Statistics, ©Crown Copyright, 1997; Table 8.4 J. Ginn and S. Arber, 'Patterns of employment, gender and pensions', *Work, Employment and Society*, ©Cambridge University Press, 1996; Table 8.5 and 8.6 S. Arber and J. Ginn, 'In sickness and in health: care-giving, gender and the independence of elderly people', published in C. Marsh and S. Arber (eds), *Families and Households*, ©Macmillan Press Ltd, 1992; Table 8.7 H. Qureshi and A. Walker, *The Caring Relationship*, ©Macmillan Press Ltd, 1989; Figure 6.1 G. Crow and M. Hardey, 'Diversity and ambiguity among lone-parent households in modern Britain', published in C. Marsh and S. Arber (eds), *Families and Households*, ©Macmillan Press Ltd.

# 1 Changing Families, Changing Households

Patterns of social change make it necessary for us periodically to take stock of the ways in which we make sense of the world. Within everyday life our understandings of 'families' and 'households' are often taken for granted, but closer examination reveals a good deal of uncertainty about their character and how they are changing. But changing they certainly are. Most obviously, the last quarter of the twentieth century saw major shifts in the demographic constitution of families and households, especially in aspects of their formation and dissolution. As a consequence, there is now far greater diversity in people's domestic arrangements than occurred earlier in the century. Living patterns are less and less adequately captured by conventional models of 'the nuclear family'. Against this background of change, the exploration of what we mean by 'family' and 'household' has considerable importance.

The use in sociological analyses of terms which have everyday meanings can create difficulties. Yet, necessarily many of the concepts used in sociology to understand social relationships are also used in everyday characterisations of that world. This becomes problematic because in common usage the terms themselves are imprecise, signifying a range of different meanings. This is particularly evident in examining family life. To ask questions about the ordering of family ties and how domestic relationships are altering requires that we draw on terms which have a significance within the culture being examined but which are generally poorly defined.

Consider, for example, the concept of 'family'. Everybody knows what 'family' means; it is a term we use routinely, normally without any need for reflection or self-awareness. Yet it is

1

also a term which in everyday usage signifies a range of different relationships, practices and emotions. At times 'my family' can mean my partner and children; at other times, it may be taken to include my children's children too. Alternatively, its reference may be my own natal family, my parents, brothers and sisters, or it may signify a wider range of kin including, for instance, aunts and uncles. It may also mean a much smaller group, for example, just a married or cohabiting couple living alone. Often the meaning intended is clear enough from the context in which the term is being used. However, in writing sociologically about family issues there is a need for greater precision in the deployment of terms.

The problematic nature of conventional concepts for analysing different aspects of family life has come more to the fore over the last twenty years as a result of the demographic changes which have been occurring within the family realm. Details of these changes will be provided in Chapter 2. Here it is sufficient to recognise that increases in, for instance, cohabitation, births outside marriage, the level of separation and divorce, and the number of lone-parent and stepfamilies have all resulted in old certainties about family and household arrangements being questioned. The different changes there have been – summarised by Lewis and Kiernan (1996) as the increasing separation of sex, marriage and parenthood – have highlighted the imprecise boundaries around our everyday conceptions of 'family'. They have also informed new understandings of how families and households operate, as discussed in the chapters that follow.

Until the 1980s, it was quite common within sociology to talk about the 'family cycle'. Inherent in this notion was the idea that people typically followed a similar family pathway. From living with parents and siblings in their natal nuclear family, they left home, married, usually had a relatively small number of children, and then once these children became adult, lived out their lives until one or other spouse died. Of course, there was far more to family life than this simplistic model suggests. The changing socio-economic conditions under which families lived ensured this, but this broad pathway was one which most people followed. It allowed sociologists and other analysts to look at patterned change over the life course and to emphasise the similarities there were in people's experiences.

No longer is this the case. There remain many similarities in people's family experiences, but there are also now many differences (McRae, 1999). These differences may not occur randomly, but they are not entirely predictable either. Instead of 'family cycle', with its notions of routine stages, each one tidily following the last, the concept of 'family course' is far more appropriate (Finch, 1987). This latter term allows for variations in how people's family lives develop and in the family commitments they generate over time. Although some people do follow 'conventional' pathways, many people's experiences are far more complex, with cohabitation, divorce and remarriage all complicating the sets of family relationships in which they are involved. Moreover, even if their own family course is relatively straightforward, they are likely to experience the impact of these changes indirectly, through the more varied patterns generated by children, friends or siblings.

These demographic shifts in family formation and dissolution have been significant in framing contemporary understandings of family and domestic issues. No longer is 'the family' so readily seen as a static social entity – a view which was always suspect. Instead the complexities of what was previously subsumed under 'the family' have become the focus of much more popular and research attention. Thus, it is now recognised that a distinction needs to be made between family and household activities. As will be discussed more fully below, many domestic activities are household-based, that is, they arise through people sharing a home. They are not of themselves family activities, though frequently, of course, it is family members who are involved. But equally, other members of that same family may live elsewhere, depending on what 'family' is taken to comprise.

## Families and households

There is, thus, a need for greater precision about how the terms 'family' and 'household' are used in sociological analysis, though often they merge into one another in sociology as much as in everyday life. The essential distinction is not particularly complex, but if we are to generate satisfactory analyses of the organisation of domestic life, it is one about which we need to be clear. Moreover, as we shall see later, conceptually distinguishing between 'family' and 'household' encourages some significant questions to be posed about topics which might otherwise be overlooked.

Despite the differences there are, what holds the diverse notions of family together is the theme of *kinship*: that is, family is essentially about the solidarities which exist between those who are taken to be related to one another through ties of blood or marriage (Schneider, 1968). Competing ideas exist about how these relationships are best ordered (Finch and Mason, 1993), though broad cultural beliefs about the solidarity of 'family' are pervasive. While a variety of discourses exist around the family – think here of the different images of 'family' used in advertising, or political rhetoric, for example – most emphasise the boundaries to be drawn between those who are 'family' and those who are not, between those who do and those who do not 'belong' to this collective. In other words we can recognise the existence of powerful ideologies imbued with notions of the proper ordering of family ties and a strong sense of inclusion and exclusion.

In reality, however, specifying who belongs to families is no longer as straightforward as it was. There have always been instances of people who are not kin being treated as though they were part of the family. Usually, however, it was recognised by all that these were fictive or 'honorary' kin ties and that the people involved were not 'really' family. What has made for more complex kinship issues in recent years has been the radical increase in patterns of cohabitation, divorce and remarriage (Allan, 1996). Consider, for example, when a cohabitee is regarded as 'family'. Almost certainly, this will happen at different speeds and in different ways for different people in the 'family'. For instance, those cohabiting for a period of time may see themselves as family, be regarded as such by each other's siblings, but not by their respective 'parents-in-law'. Equally it is not always clear when people stop being kin. People defined as kin through marriage – a sister-in-law, for example – are likely to continue to be seen as kin after the death of the intermediary sibling/spouse, but it is much more questionable whether they are after a divorce. There is little research evidence on this, but often it seems that kin relationships are regarded quite differently once a marriage is terminated (Finch and Mason, 1990).

Importantly, stepfamilies raise all sorts of difficult questions about what 'family' means. The perceptions of the different people involved can vary a good deal. The couple, whether married or cohabiting, are likely to see themselves as part of a new family, while the children involved may resist this notion strongly, emphasising the absence of familial bonds in the new unit. Similarly, other family members outside the immediate household may have different views and perceptions about the 'family-ness' of the newly-formed stepfamily. Finch and Mason's (Finch, 1989; Finch and Mason, 1993) research suggests that such variation is quite common and that the degree to which different individuals are treated as 'family' will be a consequence of the personal relationships which have developed between them. Thus the fact of divorce does not necessarily mean that family links are severed between, say, mother-in-law and daughter-in-law (Finch and Mason, 1990). Nor does even quite prolonged cohabitation necessarily lead to step-children or other kin fully accepting the partner as part of the family. The basis of kinship is rooted in marriage and biological connection, but the ties which are honoured and the solidarities which develop are socially defined.

Because of this greater complexity, recognising that ideas of 'family' and 'household', while overlapping, frequently refer to different social entities and involve different processes, has become much more important. Issues of solidarity, cooperation and conflict are often different in practice between the two categories and, as importantly, raise separate conceptual and analytical questions, for example, following marital separation, cohabitation or remarriage, membership of 'family' and 'household' can be different, at least as far as children are concerned, even when 'family' is defined in its narrowest sense of parents and offspring. The household represents one focus of activity but family relationships constitute a different, albeit overlapping one. This can be seen quite clearly when the notion of 'household' is examined. Although definitions of 'household' vary, essentially what they all refer to are social groupings which typically share a range of domestic activities in common. These include sleeping in the same dwelling as one another, having most meals together, and normally sharing in a common domestic economy and household budgeting (Anderson, Bechhofer and Gershuny, 1994; Harris, 1983; Morris 1990a, 1990b). Clearly these activities do not require that those involved share any kinship link with one another. Indeed many households now consist of single individuals or of individuals who are unrelated (Social Trends, 1998). Many student households are of this latter type.

Empirically, of course, the majority of households do contain family members living together, though not usually in the standardly-conceived conventional nuclear form. In the 1991 census, only a quarter of all households consisted of a male and a female adult together with dependent children. And, of course, an increasing proportion of these entailed a stepfamily rather than a first-time family. However, the patterns of household practice which arise are quite varied, making the definition of household more complex than it first appears. Thus what it means to share a common housekeeping is not clear-cut. How much sharing is necessary? How frequently do you need to sleep in a household to be a member of it? What proportion of meals must be shared? When do those whose work or study regularly takes them away cease to be members of the household? Can people be members of more than one household? Definitionally all of these questions can be resolved, albeit in a somewhat arbitrary fashion. What they indicate though is the complexity of social arrangements that can be subsumed within the idea of a household.

Thus while 'families' and 'households' often overlap empirically, from a sociological perspective it is useful to keep the two concepts separate, as different questions arise from considering each of them. A focus on family matters, for example, brings to the fore the character of the solidarity and conflict developing between people who are linked through kinship. It directs attention to such issues as how parents socialise children; how love is expressed within marriage and between the generations; and how care provision is influenced by prospects of property inheritance. Focusing on households tends to emphasise a different set of concerns. These include, *inter alia*, the division of responsibility and workload between household members; the extent and character of the strategies which households develop for coping with the contingencies they face; and the ways in which resources are distributed within households between different members (Allatt and Yeandle, 1986; Hutson and Jenkins, 1989; McKee and Bell, 1986; Morris, 1990b; Pahl, 1984).

In theory there is nothing which stops such questions as these being posed within a 'family' framework, and indeed at times they have been. For instance, over the years some family sociologists have focused on systematic differences in the distribution of money and other resources between family members, especially husbands and wives (see, for example, Brannen, and Moss, 1991; Brannen and Wilson, 1987; Delphy and Leonard, 1992; Pahl, 1989). The point though is that more frequently such issues have tended to be disguised by assumptions which are rooted in normative, if not idealised, values about the collective identity of families. Thus, for example, it has often been assumed that if family income is sufficient to meet the needs of those in the family, then poverty is not an issue. However, research has shown that the distribution of these resources between household members is often skewed to such a degree that some within the household may be living below subsistence level while others live well above it (Graham, 1987a).

Approaching such issues from a household rather than a family perspective does not rule out such assumptions. However, it sensitises the researcher into asking the right kind of questions rather than confusing kinship issues with ones of domestic organisation. Just as families and households overlap empirically, so conceptually the questions to be asked of them also have much in common. Nonetheless, being aware of the distinctions between the two makes it more likely that the framework in which questions are posed is appropriate. In turn, this will encourage better descriptions and explanations of the activities in question, as the basis of each type of relationship can be recognised more readily. These issues – empirical and conceptual – should become clearer in the chapters which follow.

There is a more general point here. Just as the demography and character of family and household relationships have been altering significantly over the last twenty years, so too have our understandings of the significance of these changes, both at a popular and an academic level. Certainly, within sociology and social policy a different range of questions is now being asked about the solidarities of both households and families than was the case, say, in the 1960s or 1970s. Where once functionalism largely provided the framework of enquiry – in particular, a concern for the ways in which family life was modified to mesh best with the 'demands' of the changing economy – now other theoretical frameworks have emerged which focus on different issues.

## Understanding change

It has been the rise of feminism and women's studies, together with the concerns of late- or post-modernity, which have had most impact on the ways that family and domestic life have recently come to be interpreted. The changes in domestic arrangements and personal relationships, which will be discussed more fully in the next chapter, are clearly indicative of a wider tolerance of alternative family and household formations than that which existed in the past when a more prescriptive social control was exercised. Yet, the greater freedom there is now for individuals to make 'life-style' choices involving the construction of their personal, sexual and domestic relationships is linked to the wider social transformations of late modernity in which increased priority is given to 'the self as a project' (Giddens, 1991; 1992). Similarly the changes there have been in the politics of gender have opened up fresh areas of enquiry about familial organisation as well as having an impact on the character of that organisation. What are now recognised as important questions, about, for example, the distribution of resources within marriage, the incidence of family abuse, and the gendered character of caring, were largely absent from family sociology until feminist perspectives brought into focus issues that were previously obfuscated.

In previous periods, family sociology was hampered by the adoption of approaches which were either excessively descriptive and atheoretical or influenced by broad theories embodying overly general functionalist assumptions. The respective problems of 'abstracted empiricism' and 'grand theory' (Mills, 1970) have taken longer to be recognised in the sociology of the family than in many other branches of the discipline. However, growing recognition of the shortcomings of such approaches has highlighted the need for theoretical reflection, not least about the concepts with which we try to make sense of family relationships. In turn, this development has sharpened awareness of the excessively abstract and over-general nature of functionalist frameworks of analysis which, by treating family forms as things shaped by external forces, allowed little scope for individual agency or variation from the norm. The prescriptive character of distinguishing between 'normal' and other family forms has also come to be seen as a problematic feature of conventional accounts of family life which it is important to avoid.

The reassessment of how best to approach the study of domestic life has involved rethinking what Morgan (1996) calls 'family connections'. Once the assumption is dropped that family relationships are simply a dependent variable which changes in response to macro-social forces (most obviously industrialisation), the way is opened up for family members to be credited with a more active role in shaping domestic life. Thus one significant current of recent thinking has focused on the importance of individuals and their active consideration of how they connect with others around them in their intimate relationships. A second strand of thinking has been concerned less with individuals than with the implications of treating families and households as units of analysis with distinctive interests, strategies and dynamics into which individuals fit with varying degrees of ease or difficulty. Thirdly, it is possible to identify innovatory lines of thinking which attempt to explain the links between family forms and wider social forces in which causal influences do not all run from the latter to the former but suggest instead more of a two-way relationship. Each of these interconnected theoretical developments warrants discussion.

The need to explain as well as to describe the growing diversity of family arrangements in societies like contemporary Britain has generated a great deal of interest in Beck's idea of individualisation (Beck, 1992, 1997; Beck and Beck-Gernsheim 1995). Beck suggests that people in affluent societies are no longer materially constrained to conform to the conventional gender roles associated with the nuclear family, and that this opens up the possibility of greater individual choice over how a person lives her or his own life. In particular, Beck notes, it is no longer typical for women to be committed to 'compulsory housework and support by a husband' (1992, p. 104) because of the educational and labour market opportunities which have opened up for them. The male breadwinner model of family organisation is now merely one of several possibilities. Modern social structures like those of the welfare state encourage the emergence of 'the individual as *actor, designer, juggler* and *stage director* of his own biography, identity, social networks, commitments and convictions' (1997, p. 95, emphasis in original). Beck and Beck-Gernsheim (1995) treat the rising proportion of single-person households as one indicator of the process of individualisation, but regard other trends like the growth of cohabitation, divorce and remarriage as further evidence of the increasing extent to which people are choosing (or, in some cases, being forced) to depart from traditional norms of family life. In turn, the possibility of choice increases potential conflict between individuals over the contributions each makes to the domestic division of labour, and over the nature of family relationships more generally.

The theory of individualisation highlights the uncertain character of many of the developments taking place in contemporary family life. Beck and Beck-Gernsheim argue that in this uncertain environment, 'love acquires a new significance as the very heart of our lives' (1995, p. 49) as people search for stability and meaning in their personal relationships. What Giddens (1992) refers to as the transformation of intimacy involves the attachment of heightened meaning to the emotional side of intimate relationships which makes them unstable precisely because so much is expected of them. Yet, as individuals become more reflexive about the nature of their intimate relationships so the fragility of these relationships is exposed. Individuals' concerns with self-identity lead them to treat intimate relationships as ones which are maintained for the satisfactions which they deliver to the partners as individuals. Thus, in its 'pure' form, a modern intimate relationship is said by Giddens to be 'continued only in so far as it is thought by both parties to deliver enough satisfactions for each individual to stay within it' (1992, p. 58). In such circumstances, romantic notions of love as fixed and permanent are increasingly brought into question.

The ideas of Beck and Giddens concerning individualisation and the transformation of intimacy place much greater emphasis on individuals' aspirations and choices than is to be found in conventional family sociology. What such ideas offer is an explanation of diversity and change in family life in which family members are creative agents, actively constructing their relationships rather than simply adopting pre-set roles. For Giddens, 'Personal life has become an open project' (1992, p. 8) in which individuals experiment as part of the conscious pursuit of arrangements which suit their particular needs and ambitions. Such ideas offer potentially powerful explanations of the increasing divergence from the traditional nuclear family, but some caution is necessary when evaluating them. To begin with, the ideas are somewhat speculative, as both Giddens and Beck acknowledge. The evidence on which they are based is quite limited and open to different interpretations. Jamieson (1998), for example, has noted how several commentators do not share Giddens's optimism about the changes underway. This issue is linked to a second concern: the degree to which it is appropriate to generalise. However far the process of individualisation has gone, marked differences remain between individuals along lines of class, ethnicity, religion, sexuality and gender, and these have a significant bearing on their ability to negotiate how their family lives are constructed (Smart and Neale 1999).

A third criticism of approaches giving analytical priority to individuals concerns the collective nature of much family life. Smart and Neale point out that these accounts are selective in their treatment of children and strangely muted about the significance of wider kin such as grandparents in family relationships, with the result that 'The field of intimacy seems very empty of players' (1999, p. 19). A rather different picture emerges once the individual is located more explicitly in her or his set of relationships, of which the partner relationship is only one (albeit often the most important). For example, research conducted by Jordan, Redley and James (1994) into middle-class couples with children highlights the importance of 'family' as a reference point in people's accounts of who they are and what they are trying to achieve. What stands out in these accounts is how actions are framed in terms of prioritising family responsibilities in ways which place limits on what is reasonable for an individual to seek for her or himself. Jordan and his colleagues observe that when they were being interviewed, 'men and women required themselves to show how they had put the family first' (1994, p. 32). Put another way, the sense of self which an individual has is frequently hard to separate from their sense of the family unit to which they belong.

A good deal of attention has been devoted recently to the problem of how best to understand what is meant by 'family'.

Jordan and his colleagues found that among their respondents 'the definition of "the family" was usually one in which partnership and parenthood were given much greater priority than other kinship relationships' (1994, p. 38), a finding consistent with other research (Finch, 1989; Finch and Mason, 1993). Family obligations extend to wider kin, but they are most significant where family members live in the same household. Within families, substantial differences exist between members' perceptions of what 'family' means. The continued existence of gender differences in this respect has been well-documented; and perceptions also vary with age (Scott 1997). As a result, contributions to and expectations of family life remain gendered and age-specific to significant degrees, although precisely why is a matter of continuing dispute. It is possible to argue that men's concentration on income-earning and women's on home-making may benefit a family unit more than equal participation in these spheres would. In line with this, attempts have been made to use the concept of family strategies to explain differential involvement in work outside and inside the home. However, as Cheal (1991) notes, family interests and individual interests should not be presumed always to coincide; indeed where they are seen to diverge, the contested meaning of 'family' is thrown into sharpest relief.

Historical research, such as Hareven's (1991), suggests that the synchronisation of individual and family interests is a perennial problem, but one which changes in different historical circumstances. In some periods, explanations framed in terms of economic necessity carry a great deal of force, while in others they are less convincing. Modern family relationships are in a state of flux as the balance of household members' involvement in paid and unpaid work shifts, but attention has focused increasingly on the emotional as well as the economic dimensions of these changes. Hochschild (1990, 1996, 1997) has argued that the growth of women's involvement in the labour market makes sense only once their dissatisfaction with the devalued status of housework and childcare is taken into account. For women, employment provides 'a source of security, pride, and a powerful sense of being valued'; they are attracted by the sense that 'the "male" world of work seems more honourable and valuable than the "female" world of home and children' (1997, p. 247). The search for greater emotional satisfaction has contributed to women's declining preparedness to accept the role of full-time housewife. However, efforts to restructure what Hochschild calls 'the work-family balance' (1996, p. 28) may in practice have the undesired effect of speeding up the pace of family life and intensifying tensions between household members. Daly's suggestion that the increasing pace of life generates 'centrifugal families' (1996, p. 205) whose members are held together only with increasing difficulty conveys a similar notion.

Numerous competing meanings of the term 'family' and the wide range of actual social arrangements it entails has led sociologists to speak of 'families' in the plural rather than privileging one particular set of arrangements as 'the family' (Bernardes 1997). Morgan's observation that 'notions of "family" are rarely static but are constantly subjected to processes of negotiation and re-definition' (1999, p. 18) echoes this view, but also suggests that it is useful to ask whose definitions are being deployed. While definitions of 'family' may vary both within and between different family groups, the definitions with which people operate are not freely chosen. The role of state agencies in the promotion of particular understandings of family life and the discouragement of others has been the subject of increasing interest to researchers in recent years, not least because of growing awareness that there is considerable variation in the family policies pursued in different countries. Duncan and Edwards (1997a) have shown the existence of important international differences in how state bodies relate to single mothers, for example, while Brannen (1999) has made the same point in relation to policies concerned with children. Such policies do not determine the content of family relationships in a straightforwardly causal fashion but they do operate as a framework which makes certain outcomes more likely than others.

The identification of social policies which exert pressure on people to conform to particular conceptions of family relationships makes the existence of diversity in family arrangements all the harder to explain. The declining significance of nuclear families and the growth of what Simpson (1994; 1998) terms 'unclear' families cannot be treated as the direct effect of social policies which have a bearing on family life, since these retain strong associations with conventional family patterns (Silva and Smart 1999). Nevertheless, many of the most important policy developments which there have been are concerned with financial flows into and out of households, and Simpson has this point in mind when he argues that 'Consideration of the arrangements which couples themselves devise or otherwise have imposed upon them requires that we re-think the way that kinship articulates with economy' (1998, p. 49). Major changes have occurred in the relationship between families and the wider economy since the 1950s (the period in which the nuclear family is widely believed to have been the dominant family form), and the influences have been in both directions.

It is, of course, impossible for the state or any other political agencies to recreate so-called 'traditional' forms of family life in contemporary society. Family relationships are too embedded within the wider social and cultural formation for this to be realisable. At this level, change within society cannot be engineered. Yet the state is not powerless to influence the character of family life and the nature of the relationships that develop between people who are linked by kinship. If it is to be successful in this though, it needs to do so in ways which are sympathetic to the global changes occurring which influence the understandings individuals have about the character and possibilities of family life. Thus, for example, it would simply not now be feasible to attempt to impose a family form which reaffirmed or strengthened men's traditional domination of women. Nor would it be possible to return to notions of childhood in which parents could hold absolute power over dependent children. As Giddens (1998) rightly emphasises, the shifts there have been in cultural understandings of moral and appropriate family relationships have been ones which emphasise democracy allied to individual rights and collective responsibility. There is no prospect of imposing a family system in which male or any other form of autocracy rules.

Precisely because of the increased democratisation of family relationships, there is little prospect of the state being effective in changing family life through 'strengthening' marriage, if by this is meant a wider acceptance of the sanctity of marriage as a lifelong relationship. The dominant view that unhappy marriages should be ended is now too powerful an element within the ideology of family life for this to be altered. However, if the contingent character of marriage is now widely recognised, this is not so for relationships between parents and their children. These are not seen as contingent or matters of choice in the same way. Thus the state is able to emphasise the rights that children have to a continuing parental relationship and the obligations of biological parents to care for and support their children, irrespective of the parents' own relationship.

Given the cultural understandings that now exist of marriage and partnership – a term whose rise itself indicates the change in understanding there has been in these matters – and of childhood as a phase of development, it is no coincidence that the focus of much political debate around family matters is concerned with developing policies that endorse the responsibilities of both parents towards their biological children. There are, of course, tensions within this concerning the rights of adults to avoid conflict with previous partners and to engage in new relationships (Neale and Smart, 1997). Yet we have seen in efforts to develop divorce mediation and conciliation services, to generate standard policies of financial responsibility towards children following separation, and to foster co-parenting, how the state, in Britain and elsewhere, is attempting to promote specific notions of family responsibility in the light of changed circumstances. However, the state is likely to be effective in this only to the degree that these policies are broadly in tune with the character of family practices generated by emergent socio-economic conditions.

With the level of change occurring in families and households, it is not surprising that numerous explanatory frameworks have been developed. Family sociology has come a long way since the era when functionalist approaches were dominant. The proliferation of different perspectives has opened up all sorts of new ways of looking at family relationships. At the same time, choosing between these different theoretical approaches highlights the difficulties inherent in trying to make sense of patterns of domestic life. As well as problems of definition, there is little consensus between different theorists about what constitutes appropriate evidence in support of one position or another. Facts and figures cannot alone resolve disputed questions, since these tell us only that 'there is both continuity and diversity in family life at the end of the twentieth century' (Silva and Smart, 1999, p. 4). It is also important to recognise that debates over the relative significance of continuity and change necessarily involve comparisons between the present and the past, about which we know less than we might think (Harris, 1994). In this sense any statements about families, households and social change are bound to be provisional and open to different interpretations.

## Plan of the book

In the next chapter, we are going to explore some of the major changes recently occurring in family and household life and, in particular, in family and household formation and dissolution. These changes, far more radical than was ever predicted, can be read simply as modifications in demographic patterns. Yet they represent much more than this; they reflect a change in family practices, in Morgan's (1996) sense: that is, underlying them are changes in the understandings people have about the character of familial commitment and the appropriate ways in which household and family relationships should be ordered. In this chapter, we will compare the changes occurring in Britain with those happening elsewhere in the western world. Internationally, there are certainly marked similarities in the ways in which family life is altering. Yet alongside such globalising trends, each society carries the influence of its own economic, social and legal heritage which colours the ways contemporary patterns develop. For this reason, in the chapters that follow the principal concern will be with understanding the changes currently shaping British family life. However, many of the shifts in practice and ideology analysed are mirrored to differing extents elsewhere.

In Chapter 3 we focus on young people becoming independent and leaving the parental home. From one perspective this represents the formation of a new household, albeit sometimes a temporary one. But equally it marks a new stage in the course of an existing family/household. It involves the growing independence of the younger generation from the older, and the consequent need for their relationships to adjust accordingly. Commonly, this process is viewed as a relatively straightforward one: the young person moves from the parental home to set up their own household, often for reasons to do with higher education, occupational mobility or marriage plans. In reality, as the chapter explores, the processes are more varied and complex than this: for example, surprisingly often – from a conventional viewpoint – young people move back into the parental home after a period of living away. Such diverse patterns raise questions about the meaning of independence as children become adult.

Chapters 4 and 5 are concerned with aspects of partnership and marriage. Chapter 4 concentrates on the earlier phases of partnership, focusing in particular on the personal and cultural significance of romantic love, the growth of cohabitation and the early years of marriage. It highlights the ways in which couple/family formation has altered in recent years, but also points to some of the continuities there are, especially in the ways in which responsibilities are assigned. This point is developed further in Chapter 5 which is concerned with later phases of marriage, in particular, when there are dependent children present. It examines how gender inequalities in the labour market and elsewhere pattern the decisions which couples (in theory) come to about how their domestic economy and marital relationship are best organised, and analyses the consequences of these patterns for resource distribution within households and the exercise of power, including the use of force, within marriage.

Chapter 6 examines the significant growth in lone-parent families. It begins by looking at the impact that rising levels of divorce have had on family and household relationships. Drawing on recent research, it emphasises that divorce needs to be seen as a process rather than an event and that the 'history' of a divorce is important in explaining its consequences. The chapter then turns to consider the social and economic circumstances of lone-parent families more generally. It highlights the argument that while there are many differences in the experiences of lone-parent households, there is also much in common between them. In particular, the great majority are female-headed and many are materially deprived in comparison to two-parent households. The chapter explores the consequences of these patterns for the lives of those involved.

The topic of Chapter 7 follows quite directly from the changes explored in Chapter 6. The chapter examines how stepfamilies – or reconstituted families, as they are sometimes called – differ from 'natural' or 'first-time' families. Although people in stepfamilies often portray themselves as being just 'ordinary families', the relationship dynamics in these families are frequently more complex than those occurring in 'natural' families. Of course, there are important differences between stepfamilies as well, reflecting their different histories. While fully recognising this, the chapter will focus on the implications for family relationships of the complex patterns of solidarity stepfamilies encompass.

Chapter 8 is concerned with the familial and household relationships of older people. As well as providing details of the material circumstances and household composition of older people in contemporary Britain, it considers their involvement with their families and, in particular, their (adult) children. The chapter assesses arguments about the decline of family solidarity and the neglect of older people by their kin. It argues that such views misrepresent the significance of independence for older people and overestimate the degree to which support is needed by the majority of people over retirement age. The final section of the chapter focuses on the minority of older people with significant disability, and examines the extent to which they routinely do receive family support and who the kin are who provide it.

As well as summarising the arguments of the previous chapters, in the concluding chapter we also seek to build on the earlier analyses by highlighting the processes which work to unite and differentiate families and households. The chapter traces how recent developments have seen important continuities in certain aspects of domestic life alongside fundamental changes in others, with different pictures emerging depending upon which models of family and household relationships are privileged. The active part played by individuals in shaping their domestic lives through negotiating roles within their families and contributing to household strategies has to be set against awareness of structural factors, including social policies, which are beyond the control of individuals but which shape the contours of domestic life.

# 2 Family and Demographic Change

As discussed in Chapter 1, there is now far more variation in the patterns of family life which people develop than there used to be, at least as far as recent eras are concerned (McRae, 1999). Popular understanding of this variation is rooted in the notion that family life has become increasingly detached from other considerations, be these social or economic. Individuals and families are now more able to exercise choice and personal volition over domestic and familial arrangements than previously, their options no longer being as constrained by social convention and/or economic need. In other words, family matters are also seen as increasingly *personal*, in a number of linked senses. First, the family is routinely viewed as a key site of personal achievement and identity. Ideologically, it is constructed as one of the primary social locations in which people are most free to express themselves and find personal fulfilment, even if reality for many does not match these ideals.

Secondly, family life is taken as personal in the sense of being private, set apart from the more public, more formal and impersonal activities typically occurring outside the domestic realm. Central here are notions of family and home life becoming increasingly privatised and less community oriented as industrialisation developed. Those outside the family are seen as having little right to interfere, though where the boundaries around 'the family' are drawn is, as suggested in Chapter 1, itself a more complex issue than has traditionally been assumed. And thirdly, within contemporary society, we associate family life with personal choice: that is, we tend to view our family experiences as ones which we are active in constructing and which consequently reflect our own personal desires, wishes and needs. Rather than

500400 85

simply being given or following an institutionalised script, family relationships are, to a greater degree than previously, culturally perceived as emergent personal constructions, recreated and re-negotiated over time, and thus reflecting the individual commitment and agency of those involved.

Yet while this broad cultural discourse of the privately constructed organisation of family life is powerful, it is evident that individual families and individual family members do not, and cannot, simply generate their own discrete patterns of relationships independently, nor act in a social or economic vacuum. In a famous passage, Marx argued that people make 'their own history, but they do not make it just as they please' (Marx, 1934, p. 10). When he wrote this, Marx was certainly not thinking about the organisation of family and domestic life. Yet for each of us the family represents a very clear example of this principle in action. While we may perceive ourselves as actively constructing our family relationships, fully playing a part, for better or worse, in the ways they develop, these relationships are all in reality enacted within the constraints imposed by the configuration of other social and economic relations within which our lives are embedded.

As with all social relations, agency and structure go hand in hand. Individuals are important in developing their own modes of behaviour, their own ways of responding both individually and, as with families, collectively. But the way such behaviour is formulated is also strongly influenced by the broader social and economic contexts within which such behaviour is set. These contexts pattern and shape the choices individuals make. In consequence, many of us end up making broadly similar decisions about the appropriate organisation of our domestic and family relationships. We see 'love,' for example, as the key criterion for the selection of long-term partners; we order our homes in broadly similar fashions to others; we come to similar decisions about the domestic division of labour; we raise our children in congruent ways.

Of course, there are variations in all these matters, variations which often themselves need to be understood as part of the interplay of agency and structure. And moreover there is nothing inevitable about the commonalities which exist. They are not determined in any simple fashion, either by nature, economics or social convention. But the very fact of their existence indicates that the decisions which each individual, each couple and each family makes are not quite so freely taken as contemporarily dominant ideologies about the private character of the domestic and family sphere suggest. As we shall see more fully in the chapters which follow, while people are active in constructing their home and family life, material and social factors also constrain their choices. It also needs recognising that families are not social units in which all members have an equal say. The way in which domestic life and family relationships are constructed reflects the different social and economic positions of the individuals who make them up. Some individuals (men more than women, adults more than children) usually exercise more power and control than others.

The range of external factors which impinge on family life is extensive. Many of the traditional debates within the sociology of the family were concerned with exploring these connections: for example, analyses of the transformations which modernity engendered in family life were a major focus of mid–twentieth century family sociology (Litwak, 1960a; 1960b; Parsons, 1949; see Harris, 1969; 1983). Debates about the ways in which the changing employment structure altered the division of labour and the allocation of resources within households also have a long history. Changes in the material standards of homes, in consumption patterns, in expectations of childhood, in the demands on family support made by educational, health and other bureaucracies, have all had an impact on the character of domestic and family relationships.

Yet while there are many commonalities in the ways in which people construct their family life, there is nothing 'set' about the family as such. Indeed, in an important sense, there is no such thing as 'the family'. There are many different families; many different family relationships; and consequently many different family forms. Each family develops and changes over time as its personnel develop and change. Importantly, as Hareven (1978; 1982; 1991) has argued, such change occurs at a variety of related levels. To begin with, there is the obvious change which occurs within individual families and individual households through the passage of time. However conventional or unconventional people's family careers are, each family group inevitably alters as its members age and generate altered forms of dependence and solidarity. Routinely, over time these involve the creation of new households and the changed membership of older ones. Children become mature and independent of their parents. They form sexual partnerships, set up their own homes and start their own families. Less predictable events will also influence family relationships. Divorce, unemployment, infirmity in ageing parents or disability of other household members will all have an impact on the development of family relationships and responsibilities.

Equally the character of family relationships alters historically as socio-economic structures outside the household are transformed. This has been alluded to above. Essentially, the family remains a key institution within social life, crucial to reproduction and consumption, if not production directly. But the ways in which the family/household complex articulates with other social institutions, the part it plays within the overall social formation, are not unchanging. Its patterning is influenced by the broader sets of relationships within which members of the family, and hence the family as a unit, are embroiled. At this broad historical level, a picture is sometimes presented of family life changing rather little, in particular, with regard to core activities and functions. Families, for example, care for and socialise children; much sexual expression occurs within a marital framework; for most people throughout most of their life, day-to-day reproduction occurs within families; and so forth.

Yet, as soon as such claims are made, it becomes apparent that they are, at best, partial. Children certainly receive much socialisation within families, but the socialisation they receive is not the same across different generations. The ideologies of childhood, the expectations there are about children's care, the obligations of different categories of adults to them, have all changed significantly, making the experiences of contemporary childhood quite different from those of children two or three generations ago. Patterns of reproduction and consumption within families and households have also changed dramatically over the last hundred years. The family may still be the key unit of consumption within society, but what is consumed, who has what rights over that consumption, and how resources are distributed within domestic units is by no means fixed. Today's families do not order these activities in the same ways that families did previously, and nor will the generations which follow do so in ways common today.

And bridging these two levels of change – the personal and the historical – is a third level, the cohort or generational level: that is, changes which may or may not at some later date be understood as part of wider historical shifts arise through the different experiences and behaviour of each new generation. These changes also reflect individual decisions and choices, but they are more than this. They are part of a patterned change which embraces a large number of people and need to be understood as collective rather than individual. Thus at one level, emerging conceptualisations about how familial relationships should be formulated can be seen as generational. Current ideas about, for example, cohabitation, marriage and divorce, and the emphasis there is on intimacy and love as personal commitment, can be understood as an element within a generational shift expressing fresh aspirations as to what normal family life should be like. Equally though, they can be viewed as personal choices to do with the individual construction of intimate worlds, and yet again, as elements within a longer-term, socio-historical shift in ideologies about personal relationships (Beck and Beck-Gernsheim, 1995; Giddens, 1992; Hawkes, 1996). Similarly, the changes which have occurred in childhood which were discussed briefly above are changes which can be readily understood at all three levels. They are not just individual decisions about the organisation of personal life: they also represent a broader cultural shift concerning the moral ordering of family relationships. Importantly, the period since the mid-1970s does, with hindsight, appear to be one in which cohort or generational change has been particularly marked, as the rest of this chapter will demonstrate.

## Changing demographic patterns

Family life is never static. Changes are occurring at different levels all the time. However, there can be no doubt that in Britain and in other Western countries, the period since the mid-1970s has seen very significant shifts occurring in a number of key aspects of people's family and household experiences. In particular, patterns of household and family formation and dissolution have altered in ways which are quite different from the trends which dominated the first three-quarters of the twentieth century. For most of this earlier period, changes were gradual and followed a clear path. However, during the 1970s radically different trends began to emerge. The chapters which follow will contain detailed analyses of the implications of these changes; here the aim is to provide an overview. The principal focus will be on Britain, but, where appropriate, international comparisons will be made as the changes are ones which are affecting developed countries generally, albeit to differing degrees and over different time spans. In other words, many of the social and economic transformations which lie behind these demographic shifts are part of broader, more global transformations impacting on a range of different societies.

*Divorce*

One of the changes which has received much attention in Britain, as elsewhere, has been the rise in divorce rates over the last thirty or so years. This has indeed been quite spectacular, as is shown in Table 2.1. In the early 1960s, there were approximately 30,000 divorces per year in England and Wales. This represented a little over 2.5 divorces for every thousand marriages (Marriage and Divorce Statistics, OPCS). By the end of the decade, the numbers had risen significantly, with the increase leading to pressure for legal changes in divorce procedures. The 1969 Divorce Reform Act not only introduced new grounds for divorce – the period living apart from one another of itself became a justification for divorce – but, more importantly, became a key element within dominant definitions of what divorce represented. In turn, it also redefined people's perceptions of what was acceptable within marriage. Specifically, the Act's emphasis on the 'irretrievable breakdown of marriage', rather than on the breaking of a legally enforceable marital contract, reflected the changed understanding there was about the nature of marital commitment (Gibson, 1994).

The trend that developed in the early 1970s as a result of the 1969 Act continued over the next 25 years, as Table 2.1 shows. The early 1980s saw a period of relative stability with the divorce

**Table 2.1** *Divorce: decrees absolute (England and Wales)*

| Year | Numbers | Rate per 1,000 married population |
|------|---------|-----------------------------------|
| 1931 | 3,668   | 0.4  |
| 1951 | 28,265  | 2.6  |
| 1964 | 34,868  | 2.9  |
| 1969 | 51,310  | 4.1  |
| 1972 | 119,025 | 9.5  |
| 1981 | 145,713 | 11.9 |
| 1991 | 158,745 | 13.4 |
| 1995 | 155,499 | 13.6 |
| 1996 | 157,107 | 13.9 |
| 1997 | 146,689 | 13.0 |

*Source*: Marriage, Divorce and Adoption Statistics.

rate for England and Wales staying at close on 12 divorces per 1000 marriages. However, in the years since 1985, the numbers of divorces and the rate of divorce have again increased, though somewhat more slowly and with fluctuations. Thus in 1996, there were over 157,000 divorces, with the rate per 1000 marriages reaching 13.9. While there was a decline in divorce in 1997, probably due to fewer marriages being solemnised during the 1990s, even if the rates stabilise at around this level, some 40 per cent of marriages will end in divorce (Haskey, 1996a). However, if divorce rates continue to increase as they have been doing, divorce, far from being an unusual ending to marriage, will in fact become the norm. Moreover, there is no reason for believing that the underlying trend in divorce rates will be reversed. Indeed, contemporary understandings of marriage – what can be expected from this relationship, what is acceptable and what is unacceptable – reflect these changes, in turn fuelling heightened divorce levels. These matters will be addressed more fully in Chapters 4 and 6.

Increases in divorce rates are not peculiar to Britain. There have been increases throughout the Western world. Historically the United States has had a comparatively high divorce rate. Nonetheless, the rate of divorce still doubled between 1960 and

1997, when there were nearly 1.2 million divorces (FASTATS, 1999; Kamerman and Kahn, 1997). In Canada, the divorce rate rose from less than 38 per 100,000 population in 1951 to over 270 per 100,000 population by 1991. Similarly, in many countries in Europe divorce rates have shown very significant increases since the mid-twentieth century, but especially since the 1970s; for example, in Belgium, the divorce rate doubled between 1970 and 1990, while in France and Holland it increased by a factor of three (Goode, 1993). Current projections for most northern European countries are that around a third of all marriages will end in divorce (Prinz, 1995). As would be expected, the divorce rates in countries with a high Roman Catholic population are lower than others, though in these countries too the rates have recently been rising.

### Lone-parent households

The heightened incidence of divorce has contributed significantly to other changes in household and family demography. In particular, it has been an important element within the increasing numbers of lone-parent households. In Britain in 1971, there were estimated to be some 570,000 lone-parent households. By 1986, this number had increased to over 1,000,000, and by 1996 to an estimated 1,600,000. This represents nearly a threefold increase in twenty-five years. And as with divorce, the increases may well continue, at least if social and economic policies concerned with lone parenthood remain as they are. However, as Table 2.2 shows, it is not just higher levels of marital breakdown which have generated the increases in the number of lone-parent households. There has also been a very significant rise in the number of never-married women who are lone parents. Whereas there were fewer than 100,000 lone-parent households headed by never-married women in Britain in 1971, by the early 1990s this had risen to nearly 500,000 – an increase from 15 to 35 per cent of all lone-parent households. Currently around one in five dependent children live in a lone-parent household.

Similar changes have been occurring in most other Western countries: for example, in the USA the numbers of lone-parent households increased from under 4 million in 1976 to over 10 million in 1991. However, there are significant ethnic differences in the routes into lone-parenthood (de Acosta, 1997). Over

**Table 2.2**    *Lone parents: numbers (Great Britain)*

|  | 1971 | 1986 | 1992 | 1996 |
|---|---|---|---|---|
| Single | 90,000 | 230,000 | 490,000 | – |
| Separated | 170,000 | 190,000 | 300,000 | – |
| Divorced | 120,000 | 410,000 | 430,000 | – |
| Widowed | 120,000 | 80,000 | 60,000 | – |
| All lone mothers | 500,000 | 910,000 | 1,280,000 | – |
| All lone fathers | 70,000 | 100,000 | 120,000 | – |
| All lone-parents | 570,000 | 1,010,000 | 1,400,000 | 1,600,000 |
| Number of dependent children in lone-parent households | 1,000,000 | 1,600,000 | 2,300,000 | 2,800,000 |

*Source*: Haskey, 1996b; 1998.

half of all Afro-American lone-parent mothers have never been married, while white lone-motherhood more frequently stems from marital breakdown. The pattern for Hispanic lone mothers lies in between these two. In Australia, the number of lone-parent households stood at 183,000 in 1974 but rose to 424,000 by 1994 (McHugh and Millar, 1997). In Eire the increase has been even more rapid, though starting from a very low base. In 1981 there were fewer than 30,000 lone-parent households, but by 1991 there were over 90,000 (McLaughlin and Rogers, 1997). In France the numbers of lone-parent households have grown less quickly, but the overall trend is still clearly upward, with a 60 per cent increase between 1968 and 1990, from 720,000 to over 1.2 million (Lefaucheur and Martin, 1997).

As Table 2.2 demonstrates, lone parenthood remains very largely the preserve of women. In Britain since the early 1970s, approximately 90 per cent of all lone-parent households have been female-headed, with the proportion increasing slightly in the 1990s. A very similar picture is found in other developed countries (Duncan and Edwards, 1997). As discussed in Chapter 6, while there is diversity between different lone-parent households, there are also very significant commonalities, the most important of which concerns the relative poverty which many experience. This is undoubtedly a direct consequence of

**Table 2.3**   *Births to unmarried mothers % (England and Wales)*

|  | 1976 | 1986 | 1998 |
|---|---|---|---|
| % of all births | 9.2 | 21.4 | 37.8 |
| % of mothers aged 20–24 | 10.8 | 28.2 | 59.7 |
| % of teenage mothers | 28.7 | 69.0 | 89.1 |
| % of births to unmarried mothers where father's name is registered | Not known | 66.2 | 79.2 |
| % of these births where mother and father give the same address | Not known | 70.4 | 76.9 |

*Source*: Birth Statistics.

the great majority of these households being female-headed, often by women who have few opportunities to earn reasonable incomes because of their childcare responsibilities, their own lack of qualifications and the gendered inequalities of the labour market.

The increased numbers of mothers who are not and never have been married reflects a clear change in social expectations and conventions (Babb and Bethune, 1995). Whereas a little more than a generation ago, unmarried pregnancy generally led to marriage prior to the birth, the situation now is quite different. The changes here have been quite remarkable in a very short period of time, as Table 2.3 highlights. In the mid-1970s, only about 1 in 10 births were to unmarried mothers. Twenty years later this proportion had increased to over one in three. More importantly, whereas around a quarter of teenage mothers were unmarried in 1976, by the mid-1990s this figure had increased to nearly 90 per cent. This certainly indicates that the social controls being exercised over teenagers who become pregnant have altered dramatically. It would appear that parents and others are no longer putting daughters (and to some extent sons) under pressure to marry. In addition to the greater availability of abortion, there is now far less stigma attached to giving birth outside marriage; it no longer places personal and family honour at risk as it previously did. The changes occurring are captured in the language used to characterise such events. Terms like 'shot-gun wedding', 'illegitimacy'

**Table 2.4**  *Percentage of women cohabiting with future husband prior to their marriage* (*Great Britain*)

|                              | 1965–9 | 1975–9 | 1985–9 |
| ---------------------------- | ------ | ------ | ------ |
| First marriage               | 5      | 20     | 50     |
| Second or subsequent marriage | 66     | 84     | 86     |

*Source*: General Household Survey, 1990.

or 'bastard' are no longer common, reflecting the changed conventional understandings of these matters.

*Cohabitation*

In some respects though, the first part of Table 2.3 is misleading. Underlying the trends in unmarried births is a further trend which is just as radical. As the last two rows show, quite a high proportion of unmarried mothers – currently around 60 per cent – are living with the father of their child at the time of the birth. This in turn reflects a much broader trend in patterns of cohabitation, for while reliable data are scarce, there is no doubt that significant changes are occurring. These changes represent a much freer attitude towards sexual expression, as well as altered notions about appropriate routes into coupledom and marriage.

Table 2.4 provides data on women's cohabitation patterns with their future husbands prior to their marriage. The changes that there have been are easy to recognise. In the late 1960s, only 5 per cent of first-time brides lived together with their future husbands before their wedding. By the late 1980s – the last period for which these particular data were collected – this was becoming the majority pattern with 50 per cent doing so. Recent data on people's addresses at the time of their marriage confirm this trend (Marriage and Divorce Statistics, OPCS). However, there are significant ethnic differences in this. In particular, it would appear that very few people from an Asian ethnic background currently cohabit (Berrington, 1994; Heath and Dale, 1994).

But as well as becoming the dominant form of engagement, cohabitation is now a far more widely accepted form of union (irrespective of whether there are explicit plans to formalise it through marriage), no longer carrying the moral overtones it once did. Language again reflects changed moral understandings with people now rarely being described as 'living in sin'. Table 2.5 indicates the changes there have been. The numbers of unmarried women aged between 18 and 49 cohabiting have more than doubled since the late 1970s, with the increase being particularly notable among never-married women. (The proportion of widows cohabiting has increased a great deal too, but their numbers in this age range are very small.)

The trend towards higher levels of cohabitation is not unique to Britain. Indeed in some societies, in particular in Sweden and Denmark, cohabitation has long been a common practice (Andersson, 1998). However, other northern European countries, including Austria, Germany, France and Holland, have similar patterns to Britain with rises in cohabitation first occurring in the 1970s. Southern European countries, with a stronger Roman Catholic tradition, followed more slowly though rates had increased substantially by the 1990s (Hantrais and Letablier, 1996; Kiernan, 1996; Kiernan, 1999). Cohabitation has also increased rapidly in the USA (Cherlin, 1992). Graefe and Lichter (1999) report that only slightly over 500,000 couples were cohabiting in 1970 compared to 3.5 million in 1993. Australia and Canada have also seen equivalent rises in cohabitation (Baker and Phipps, 1997; Carmichael and Mason, 1998; Ravanera and Rajulton, 1996), so that now throughout the Western world, cohabitation is becoming a normal prelude for marriage, and for a growing number of

**Table 2.5**  *Cohabitation rates for unmarried women aged 18–49 % (Great Britain)*

|  | *1979* | *1985* | *1996* |
|---|---|---|---|
| Single | 8 | 14 | 28 |
| Widowed | 0 | 5 | 5 |
| Divorced | 20 | 21 | 31 |
| Separated | 17 | 20 | 7 |
| All unmarried | 11 | 16 | 26 |

*Source*: General Household Survey, 1998.

people an alternative form of union (Hantrais and Letablier, 1996; Kiernan, 1996).

*Marriage*

While cohabitation rates have been increasing, marriage rates have been declining. The relationship here is not a direct one, for, as discussed above, cohabitation has become an accepted form of engagement and so often acts as a precursor to marriage rather than a replacement. Certainly trends in cohabitation are influencing age at first marriage. Throughout most of the twentieth century, this generally declined, reaching a low of just over 21 for women and 23 for men in the late 1960s. From that time on though, there has been a steady increase in people's age at first marriage, as demonstrated in Table 2.6. In 1997, the median age for first marriage stood at nearly 27 for females and over 28 for males. This reflects changed cultural conceptions about the 'right' age to marry, fuelled by such factors as increased educational opportunities for females especially and greater premarital sexual freedom. Most noticeably the number of teenage brides has decreased very significantly, from nearly a third of all first-time brides in 1974 to less than 5 per cent in 1997. Similar trends have been apparent elsewhere. In North America and in much of Europe, there has been a postponement of marriage with first-marriage age increasing by some 3 years since the 1970s (Andersson, 1998; Baker and Phipps, 1997; Kamerman and Kahn, 1997; Kiernan, 1996).

The question of whether cohabitation is replacing marriage in a significant fashion is a much larger one. Arguably there are

**Table 2.6**   *Median age at first marriage (England and Wales)*

|  | Males | Females |
|---|---|---|
| 1965 | 23.5 | 21.3 |
| 1975 | 23.6 | 21.4 |
| 1985 | 24.9 | 22.8 |
| 1990 | 26.1 | 24.5 |
| 1997 | 28.6 | 26.7 |

*Source*: Marriage, Divorce and Adoption Statistics.

increasing numbers of couples forming long-term unions who see marriage as constraining and harmful to the relationship they are seeking to achieve together. For these people, cohabitation does represent a conscious alternative to marriage. For others However, marriage retains much of its symbolic significance, even though they may cohabit with one or more partners before marrying. In these cases, marriage still represents the public acknowledgement of a personal, long-term commitment. Here, cohabitation tends to be seen not so much as an alternative to marriage, certainly not in ideological terms, but more as a stepping stone towards it. Nonetheless the number of marriages being solemnised each year is in decline. In the decade between 1965 and 1975, there were on average nearly 400,000 marriages a year in England and Wales. By the mid-1990s, this had reduced to under 300,000 despite the larger number of second marriages. To express this more precisely, between 1981 and 1991 marriage rates per thousand unmarried men and women fell by some 25 per cent and 30 per cent respectively (Haskey, 1995).

Another way of looking at these changes in the demography of marriage is to examine the proportion of people who have ever been married by a given age. Data on this are shown in Table 2.7. It can be seen from this that there has been a steady decrease in the percentage of people married at different ages.

**Table 2.7**   *Proportion of people ever married at given ages % (England and Wales)*

| Year of birth | 1941 | 1951 | 1961 | 1971 |
|---|---|---|---|---|
| Men, aged | | | | |
| 20 | 6.3 | 9.8 | 5.7 | 1.7 |
| 25 | 60.5 | 58.5 | 38.2 | 16.8 |
| 30 | 83.0 | 78.0 | 61.5 | – |
| 35 | 88.8 | 84.5 | – | – |
| Women, aged | | | | |
| 20 | 28.0 | 30.6 | 20.2 | 6.7 |
| 25 | 80.4 | 77.4 | 57.7 | 32.1 |
| 30 | 90.7 | 88.1 | 74.3 | – |
| 35 | 93.8 | 91.3 | – | – |

*Source:*Marriage, Divorce and Adoption Statistics.

Whereas over 60 per cent of men aged 25 in 1966 were married, this had fallen to under 17 per cent of those aged 25 in 1996. Similarly, for women the equivalent figures were 80 per cent in 1966 and less than 33 per cent in 1996. While some of this is due to people marrying later, lifetime marriage rates also appear to be falling: that is, even by middle age, significantly fewer of the generation born in the 1960s and 1970s will have married compared to the cohorts of the 1940s and 1950s (Haskey, 1995). In a similar vein, Hantrais and Letablier (1996) report from their comparative study of European family policies that marriage rates were falling in many European countries by the mid-1970s and in virtually all by the 1990s (also see Jensen, 1998). In America too, first-marriage rates have been declining in a similar fashion (Kamerman and Kahn, 1997).

*Stepfamilies*

A final change to consider is the growing incidence of step-families. While it is generally acknowledged that stepfamilies are more complex than 'natural' families, they have only recently begun to attract much popular or academic interest. Moreover, in comparison to lone-parent families, stepfamilies have generated little debate within policy circles, no doubt in part because remarriage is so frequently viewed as a 'solution' to the dilemmas of lone-parenthood rather than as a family form which generates its own issues. Indeed there appears to be reluctance even among many stepfamilies to acknowledge that their experiences are likely to be different to those of other family forms, many preferring to present themselves as just 'ordinary' families, a point made strongly by Burgoyne and Clark (1984) in their pioneering study of stepfamilies in Sheffield and by Ribbens, Edwards and Gillies (1996) more recently.

   It is difficult to ascertain how many stepfamilies there are because of the diversity of 'reconstituted' household formations. Thus, while stepfamilies certainly embrace those cases where dependent children live with one of their natural parents and a new spouse, they can also include cohabitees; non-residential parents living with new partners; and adult rather than dependent children. A stepfamily may also involve more than one set of stepchildren as well as half-siblings born to the new partnership. The picture becomes even more complex with serial cohabitation and/or divorce. These matters will be considered at greater length in Chapter 7.

For present purposes, it is simplest to focus on the number of dependent children who are living in their main household with a natural parent and a married (or long-term cohabiting) step-parent. Using this narrow definition of stepfamily, current estimates are that some 7 per cent of all dependent children in Britain are living as stepchildren (Haskey, 1994a). Other children will be living in these households though they are not themselves stepchildren, while, as indicated, many other children living in lone-parent households will have a step-parent in a different household. In America, Bumpass, Raley and Sweet (1995) estimate that around 30 per cent of all children will live in a stepfamily for some period. In Britain, the estimates for this are much lower – around 12 per cent (Haskey, 1994a). While it is impossible to estimate with any degree of accuracy how many people there are who consider themselves to be part of a stepfamily, there can be no doubt that the numbers have been growing significantly over the last twenty years as divorce, unmarried motherhood and remarriage become more common.

## Conclusion

The focus in much of this chapter has deliberately been on recent demographic changes. Other social and economic changes though have also been important in shaping people's domestic experiences: for example, aspects of economic restructuring over the last twenty years, including high levels of unemployment, greater job insecurity and reduced employment opportunities for school leavers in many localities, have all had an impact on family relationships. In the process, they have generated new divisions between families, over and above those linked directly to the types of demographic factors discussed above. Other changes, like the development of Britain as a more ethnically mixed, multicultural society, the increasing proportion of elderly people in the population, and altered understandings of, amongst other things, gender, sexuality, marriage and childhood, have also fostered the emergence of divergent patterns of family experience.

While such changes as these are not going to be addressed further at this point, they do highlight the inappropriateness of conceptualising family life as though it were static. They also indicate the care which needs to be taken when analysing differ-ent facets of family organisation and experience. It is to these issues which we now turn. In the next chapter, we are focusing on the position of young people in families and households, and the character of the dependencies in which they are involved. In the two chapters which follow this, we examine partnership and marriage and, in particular, the ways in which these ties are currently constructed and managed.

# 3 Leaving Home: Becoming Adult

In Chapter 1, we emphasised that families and households are not static. Change is routine and occurs at a variety of different levels. Some changes are easily adjusted to, others are far more consequential. In this chapter we address a series of changes which have a profound impact on household organisation and family solidarities: children becoming adult and leaving home. The traditional model of this is of a relatively unproblematic transition from parental home to life in an independent household. In practice, enormous diversity exists in how leaving home is managed, affecting parents as well as children. It is rare to find instances of young people experiencing the growth of autonomy in their lives as a smooth linear process. Far more common are complex and contradictory patterns in which the achievement of independence in one sphere of life may well involve compromises in others. Studying how and when young people leave home thus has the potential to reveal a great deal about the nature of families and households in contemporary societies.

The transition to adulthood takes many forms. For different social groups, in different historical periods and for different societies there exist significant variations in the age at which it is considered appropriate to leave home, as well as the destinations for which young people leave. According to Jones (1995, p. 23), it was during the 1950s and 1960s that transitions 'appear to have been at their most condensed, most coherent and most unitary. Many young adults, especially those from working-class families, typically left home, married and started families within a short space of time'. This situation contrasts with what Jones refers to as the 'protracted transitions' of earlier historical periods and the 'extended transitions' (1995, pp. 21 and 23) of more recent

36

decades, and further confirms the point made elsewhere in this book that the decades following World War II were peculiar rather than normal, comparatively speaking. It is thus somewhat ironic that the 'condensed transitions' of that period have come to take on the status of a norm from which other patterns are judged to be deviations, particularly as, even then, a significant degree of diversity was observable. As various studies have shown, not all young people during the 1950s and 1960s followed the path of leaving their parental home by their mid-twenties in order to get married and set up a household of their own. To take just one example, Rosser and Harris (1965) found 40 per cent of couples in Swansea starting married life in the household of their parents or parents-in-law, only later progressing to a home of their own. Despite such evidence, the model of the condensed transition has become a crude yardstick against which other patterns are often compared.

The dependent status of children in modern societies has been widely recognised. The dependence of children is most obvious in their relationships with their parents upon whom they are physically, economically and emotionally dependent. In other spheres of life too (such as schooling) children are denied the autonomy and independence which characterise adulthood. The centrality of dependence in the construction of modern Western childhood makes the transition to adulthood problematic since 'dependency must be shrugged off in favour of an individualistic, knowledgeable independence' (Hockey and James, 1993, p. 69). Because it is the intermediate stage between childhood and adulthood, youth is inevitably a period of ambiguity and contradictions, reflecting the difficulties of moving from a situation of dependence to one of greater self-reliance. The renegotiation of family and household relationships which this process entails is complicated by the uncertainties and disagreements which surround the rights and responsibilities of young people as they pass through this phase. A blunt distinction between dependence and independence fails to capture the complex realities of situations such as those where young people's wages are insufficient to support full independence, or where unemployment necessitates continued economic support from their parents. In circumstances like these, young people are neither passively dependent nor self-referentially independent, but are located in an intermediate situation, in which the responsibility for their welfare is shared and subject to periodic renegotiation.

The growing complexity of young people's experiences of leaving home reflects changes in broader social and economic arrangements which previously had more certainty about them. The model in which steady employment and independent housing are treated as predictable outcomes of the transition to adulthood has less relevance in a society in which unemployment and homelessness are resurgent social problems. Changes in patterns of education and training have also served to complicate the transition from school to work (Land, 1996). Wyn and White (1997, p. 112) refer to their country's early school leavers as 'Australia's "outsiders"', and the strengthening link between disadvantage and lack of educational qualifications is evident in other countries. Equally, patterns of marriage (or marriage-type relationships) and parenthood have been complicated by a greater diversity in young people's household situations than was characteristic of earlier generations (Berrington and Murphy, 1994; Mansfield and Collard, 1988; Wallace and Kavatcheva, 1998). The more general expression of this point is that in societies in which marked social inequalities exist along lines of social class, gender and ethnicity, it is unsurprising to find these factors being reflected in the contrasting trajectories of different groups of young people as they move towards adulthood and fuller citizenship (Jones and Wallace, 1992).

## Variations in the transition to adulthood

The norm in contemporary Western societies is for young people to leave home at some point between the ages of 16 and 25, although the processes involved in this transition are often drawn-out (Kerckhoff, 1990). The commonest view among Brannen *et al.*'s (1994) 16-year-old respondents was that adolescence signified an intermediate stage between childhood and adulthood in which they are denied the opportunity to do many things (such as voting or buying alcohol) but which also protects them from adult responsibilities such as financial independence. Overall, their status could be described as 'not quite adult'. Yet even among 16-year-olds there is considerable diversity to be found, with as many as a quarter of Brannen *et al.*'s respondents regarding themselves as adult. The reasons for this are diverse, as the researchers note: 'In one case, a young woman mentions giving birth and deciding to bring up her child without a partner. Others describe feeling grown up because they have experienced family bereavement (in two cases the death of the father)' (1994, p. 29). Greater participation in paid work was also found to be influential to the emergent sense of being free to make their own decisions, even if full economic independence was still some way off for most young people aged 16. The study also found that the parents of the 16-year-olds were making adjustments in their approach to family relationships, and were mindful of the long-term shift towards greater negotiation over permissible behaviour. These points are echoed in Hutson and Jenkins's (1989) study of people slightly older, though their research also illustrates the point that adulthood may take longer to come than many 16-year-olds anticipate.

An important reason why young people's experiences of becoming adult follow different courses is that there is no one starting point. By the age of 16, many young people have acquired at least a modicum of economic self-sufficiency from their parents by taking paid work, either full-time or part-time. While earnings may not be high, especially from Saturday or other part-time jobs, they do help young people to gain a degree of independence from their parents while still living at home (Hutson and Cheung, 1992). Overall, different levels of participation in employment and education result in considerable diversity in the financial situations of 16-year-olds. While only a minority have no independent income of their own through work, equally the majority remain a long way off achieving full economic independence from their parents. At 16 and for some years after, 'children leaving home are more prone to steep falls in income than other groups, mainly because they no longer necessarily share in their parents' income' (Taylor *et al.*, 1994, p. 94). Limitations on young people's economic resources inevitably operate to curb their power within and beyond the household, a situation which is likely to be particularly marked for those young people who have no independent income of their own, and conversely less pronounced for those earning a full wage.

Jones (1995) has observed that economic viability may not be the prime consideration in leaving home and it is a view supported by other researchers (Liddiard and Hutson, 1990). Among the groups of young people who tend to leave at an early stage are those from poor or overcrowded homes, those subjected to physical and emotional abuse, and, Jones adds, those leaving care homes. In Jones's analysis of young people in Scotland, 10 per cent of the young men who left home before the age of 17 did so because of family problems, and for young women the figure was almost 30 per cent. Such a course of action was found to carry with it the serious risk of homelessness; one in four of the young people who left home at age 16 or 17 because of family problems (broadly defined) went on to experience periods of being homeless. Jones (1995) found young people (especially young men) from stepfamilies particularly likely to leave home early. As she notes, divorce and remarriage can generate significant problems for some young people, although the conflict and stress associated with stepfamilies may to some extent reflect their poor economic standing rather than relationship tensions. This said, young people from lone-parent households were found to be only slightly more likely to leave home early in comparison to young people with both parents at home.

Reference to leaving home 'early' needs to be set against the background of the majority of young people not leaving home permanently until they have reached their twenties. However, there is great variation around this norm, including marked gender and class differences. Sons on average spend two years more at home compared to daughters, of whom the majority will have left by the age of 21 (Berrington and Murphy, 1994; Jones, 1995). Similarly the middle class 'live away' from home at a younger age, but the working class leave home more permanently at a later age. Much of this difference can be attributed to the greater likelihood of young people from middle-class backgrounds entering further and higher education, while working-class young people are more likely to leave home for marriage (Berrington and Murphy, 1994; Jones, 1995). Statistically speaking, it is working-class men who are the last to leave home. A further factor influencing age of leaving home is employment, although this is not a straightforward correlation. Indeed, local employment opportunities may be so poor as to make leaving home in search of work the best option. On a larger scale, the region in which young people grow up also has an important bearing on their trajectories (Roberts, Parsell and Connolly, 1991). Ainley (1991, p. 105) identifies a significant 'area effect' when comparing the preparedness of young people to move away from places like Liverpool and Swindon. Cultural factors also contribute to the complexity of the overall picture. Distinct ideas about leaving home are held by members of certain ethnic minority groups in Britain (Brannen *et al.*, 1994), while there is also significant cross-national variation both within and beyond Europe (Jones, 1995; Wallace and Kovatcheva, 1998).

The complexity of the patterns which emerge out of variations in the age at which young people leave home is further compounded by differences in their destinations. The distinction between living away from home (in order, for example, to continue in the educational system) and leaving home to set up an independent household is an important one. In the former case, the parental home continues to serve as a base for young people who are 'living away from home'. As Jones (1995) notes, students are far from being the only category of young people to whom this applies; young people living with friends or relatives, or in hostels or barracks are in a similar situation. Thus, for a range of young people, leaving home is better understood as a process rather than a single event, involving as it does a combination of periods with parents and periods elsewhere in a transitional phase which may be of several years' duration.

Leaving home to set up an independent household may also take a variety of forms. Conventionally, this process is understood to revolve around the creation of a new family through marriage, but independent households other than 'partnership homes' (Jones, 1995, p. 113) have become increasingly common in recent times. A distinction can be drawn here between independent households made up of young people who have decided to pool their resources ('peer independent households') and single independent households in which a young person lives on their own (or, if they are lone parents, with dependent children). Among the 19-year-old Scots studied by Jones, over three-quarters of the young men and two-thirds of the young women were living in the parental home; intermediate, peer and single households were all more numerous than partner households for young men, while only a quarter of the young women living away from their parents' home were living with a partner. There is thus no automatic connection between leaving home and forming a new family, a point further reinforced when it is recognised that Jones's figures for those living at home include young people who have returned after earlier leaving. Put another way, the conventional pattern of leaving home to get married is now the exception rather than the rule. Differences in tenure types are a further element in the heterogeneity of young people's housing situations.

The contrasting contexts in which young people become parents also serve to illustrate the absence of uniformity in transitions to adulthood. A young single woman can become a parent without necessarily leaving home. Several researchers have reported that a significant proportion of single mothers continue (or return) to live with their parents following their child's birth, at least for some period of time (Haskey, 1991; Holme, 1985; Phoenix, 1991; Allen and Bourke Dowling, 1999). Among new parents living with partners, there is again no single pattern in the way events unfold, with cohabitation and/or marriage sometimes preceding and in other cases following conception or the birth. Even though her sample of young mothers was relatively small, Phoenix nevertheless found great diversity among them:

> A minority of women … were married or cohabiting when they conceived. But some women's marital status changed over the course of the pregnancy and after birth. Some single women married, or began to cohabit, while a minority of cohabiting or married women moved into single or separated status.

Her general finding that 'Relationships with male partners did not always fit neatly into the three categories, married, cohabiting or single' (Phoenix, 1991, p. 119) necessitated use of the further category of 'semi-cohabitation' in which women lived with male partners on a regular basis for part of each week, and are in some other arrangement(s) for the other part.

Phoenix's point about the need for analytical concepts to be flexible enough to capture the full diversity of young mothers' family circumstances applies to young people more generally.

Wallace reports several instances of 'irregular couples' in Sheppey, including the case of Sarah and Martin which exemplifies the unworkability of the tidy 'single at home' versus 'married and left home' dichotomy. Wallace quotes Martin's account of the complex route by which he and Sarah had come to be cohabiting:

> we were staying round her mum's house, up her sister's, up her aunt's, we were just all over the place. So we thought we might as well live together. It was two days there, two days up her mum's, two days round her sister's. We were all planned out all week. Plus then of course we got Amy (their daughter) so obviously we had to be together' (Wallace, 1987, pp. 161–2).

Equally instructive for the analytical difficulties which it presents is the case of the young man reported on by Stanley from her research in Rochdale. Ostensibly this individual is unemployed, single and living at home, but in practice,

> during his parents' working day, he sets up a different household, one with his long-term girlfriend, who is also unemployed and at a formal level living with her full-time employed parents. This 'shadow household' is the household around which both of them organise their finances, their time, their commitment, their leisure activities *and* the work (but not formal employment) that both do (1992, p. 124, emphasis in original).

Such examples of 'semi-cohabitation', 'irregular couples' and 'shadow households' illustrate the need for analytical flexibility.

Theorising the transition to adulthood is made problematic by other factors besides the diversity of the social relationships in which young people are involved. First, becoming adult involves a number of different shifts for the individual involved. It is by no means a straightforward matter to identify the causal connections between these changes. Irwin (1995) has highlighted the difficulties of specifying the links between the transition from education to employment and life course events such as leaving the parental home, cohabitation and parenthood. Secondly, theories of the transition to adulthood are always open to revision because of the inevitable changes occurring in the wider social, economic and political environments in which individual transitions take place; for example, earlier models of the transition to adulthood have been made redundant by the growth of cohabitation either as an alternative or as a prelude to marriage. Equally fundamental rethinking has been necessitated by the return of mass unemployment and the growth of insecure and irregular employment, changes which have had disproportionately large effects on young people in the 16 to 25 age group (Land, 1996). Taken in combination with other recent developments, including altered welfare provision (Jones and Wallace, 1992), these changes represent a very different set of circumstances to those which prevailed when conventional ideas about the transition to adulthood were formulated. In this situation, the very idea of young people becoming progressively more independent has been brought into question.

## Dependence and independence in the home lives of young adults

The concepts of dependence and independence are central to the analysis of transitions to adulthood, but it would be too simple to equate life in the parental home with dependence, and leaving home with independence. As noted already, young people can achieve a significant extension of independence by entry into the labour market while still several years away from finally leaving home. In addition, it is unusual for dependence to cease completely as soon as a young person leaves the parental household. Many studies have now demonstrated how support continues to be given to adult children who have moved into homes of their own (Finch and Mason, 1993; Jones and Wallace, 1992). Indeed, as Leonard (1980) first argued, from the parents' perspective, providing material and emotional support for children at this time of *household* disruption is a means by which *family* solidarities can be sustained despite the changes occurring. Put simply, young people's dependence on and independence from their parents are matters of degree which will vary in each case according to a variety of influences. One of the most important of these influences will be the degree of dependence on others, such as partners and friends and (in different ways) employers and state bodies. It is as true of young people in the process of leaving home as it is for people in other situations (such as people with disabilities (Morris, 1993) and older people (Baltes, 1996)) that dependence is a multi-faceted phenomenon, not a simple 'problem' to which independence is the unproblematic solution.

One characteristic of dependent relationships is that the support provided to individuals is only rarely unconditional. In the case of a child's dependence upon her or his parents, conventional ideologies emphasise that the relationship is grounded in love not calculation, but it is acknowledged too that something of an exchange process is present. Jenks (1996, p. 14) describes the dominant perspective as one in which 'Adults, though primarily mothers, "sacrifice everything" for their children and they, in return, are expected to experience "the best time of their lives"'. Against the background of being given support, guidance and love by their parents, children are encouraged to make the most of their situation, while accepting and acknowledging their dependent status, and also striving towards independence as a long-term goal. This complex combination of elements makes for instability in parent–child relationships, partly because both parents and children can find it difficult to adjust to children's greater independence. As most individual biographies attest, conflict accompanies the renegotiation of children's spheres of autonomous action at various points along the transition to adulthood. The moment of leaving home comes at the end of long, drawn-out processes involving potential disagreement over the rights and obligations of family and household members. The issue of dependence is at the heart of these processes.

Access to money of their own earned through work allows many young people to achieve a greater degree of independence. Against this, rates of remuneration paid to young people are in general terms relatively low, and even those in full-time employment are likely to need these incomes to be augmented by contributions from parents, at least to some degree. According to Irwin (1995, p. 8), 'the "independence" enabled by a youth wage is partial, and contemporary household structures standardly enable dependent young adults to be net consumers where the costs of their day-to-day living are subsidised by their parents'. Another way of expressing this is to say that youth has become 'an extended period of semi-dependency' (Irwin, 1995, p. 99). Awareness of the limited nature of young people's financial independence is particularly acute in households where they are unemployed (Allatt and Yeandle, 1992; Hutson and Jenkins, 1989), but it is far from being restricted to such situations.

The systems of money management in households which include young adults and their parents can take many forms, but market principles rarely dominate the processes of give and take within these families. Families are not founded on or held together by purely economic considerations, and the question of who contributes what to the common purse of the household has a symbolic significance far beyond monetary calculations. It is usual for there to be some contribution to household budgets when young people start earning an income, but payments of what is variously referred to as 'keep', 'board money' or 'lodge money' tend to be set at levels well below those which would cover all costs (Allatt and Yeandle, 1992; Coffield, Borrill and Marshall, 1986; Hutson and Jenkins, 1989; Jones, 1995; Wallace, 1987). Such 'spoiling' of young people by their parents may be a means of maintaining a close relationship, as Leonard's (1980) pioneering analysis suggested, and in the process it can operate to reproduce or even strengthen the bonds of dependency which tie children to their parents. Wallace's (1987) study of young people on the Isle of Sheppey found that parents subsidised their children in other ways besides asking for only low levels of keep, including giving them money to go out or buying them clothes. In addition, Wallace and others have found that the management of young people's incomes is frequently taken over by their parents, who allocate it to savings accounts and certain items of regular expenditure. Financial responsibility and control may thus continue to rest with parents even after young people become independent earners.

As is the case with other households, those which include young dependent adults operate in the context of competing moralities in which rival judgements are made about members' rights and responsibilities. A sea change has occurred in these moralities relating to money since the earlier part of the twentieth century when young people were expected to contribute most of their earnings to the household budget (Jones and Wallace, 1992). In contrast to this arrangement, the prevailing norm has become one whereby parents 'spoil' their children who continue to live at home. However, there is considerable variation in precisely how parents operationalise this concept while at the same time being 'fair' to all their children despite differences in their individual circumstances. In some households more generous arrangements may be made for young people who are unemployed or who are in low-paid work, while proportionally greater contributions to household budgets are expected of those in better-paid jobs. By contrast, in other families, Allatt and Yeandle (1992) found that a 'flat-rate' system, with all children paying the same amount irrespective of income, was considered the most fair. Further variations have been reported according to whether parents judge their children to be individually responsible for their adverse economic situation (for example, by not taking up opportunities of employment available), and whether the young people are saving up to get married and to establish a home of their own (Wallace, 1987).

The discussion so far may suggest that young people's economic dependence dictates their acceptance of whatever domestic arrangements their parents choose to operate, but in reality a more subtle process of negotiation is involved. Coffield, Borrill and Marshall (1986) note that unemployed young people did not simply acquiesce to whatever support parents were prepared to give, since they frequently took issue with their parents over money matters. More generally, Jones and Wallace (1992, p. 88) have observed that adolescence is 'a phase of considerable ambiguity, involving some delicate negotiation between children and their parents'. Young people's dependence on their parents presents a challenge for both parties, as do changes in the relationship as it evolves. In broad terms, young people's assessments of the appropriate balance between autonomy and acceptance of parental guidance and control will tend to emphasise the importance of the former while their parents will be more likely to stress the latter. Similarly, issues over appropriate levels of contributions to household budgets and housework also generate conflicting judgements about the meanings which independence and responsibility have in practice. While both parents and children may be committed to the long-term objective of the latter becoming independent, the route which they follow to achieve independence and the time taken are almost inevitably matters of contention.

As we have argued, framing the relationship between young people and their parents in terms of the concepts of dependence and independence oversimplifies the situation in several important respects. First of all, for as long as parents have legal and moral responsibility for their children, parental objectives include the provision of care for as well as the exercise of control over their children. It follows that 'When young people make bids for independence, parents steer a course between care and control' (Brannen *et al.*, 1994, p. 204), mindful of the problems of withdrawing from decision-making processes too readily. Similarly, young people have various objectives, and these too may be in conflict with each other. Independence is not sought equally in every sphere of life, and many young people are reluctant to give up those aspects of dependence which can be equated with being looked after. If relationships of dependence are problematic, so too is the ideal of young people taking full responsibility for themselves, which Hutson and Jenkins (1989, p. 99) describe as a 'seductive myth'. They argue that the very notion of a totally independent individual, wholly responsible for his or her welfare, is unfeasible in a modern industrial society.

Becoming adult involves coming to terms with the diverse rights and responsibilities associated with independence, and parents usually play a crucial role in easing this transition. According to Hutson and Jenkins (1989, p. 99), 'mothers and fathers are caught between the attempt to encourage or teach financial and other independence, something which may necessitate the son or daughter experiencing a degree of hardship, and the understandable wish to ensure that not *too* much hardship is involved' (emphasis in original). They note that it generally falls to mothers to 'take the strain' of dealing with the competing demands and pressures which are present in households which include young people who are long-term unemployed, since it is mothers who are 'the managers, mediators and negotiators at the heart of the symbolic economy of family relationships' (Hutson and Jenkins, 1989, p. 153). This argument ties in with other research findings which identify the mother as the household member most likely to have day-to-day responsibility for operating what Brannen and Wilson refer to as 'strategies in the deployment of resources' (1987 p. 11). It also squares with Wallace's (1987) emphasis on the importance of the supportiveness of 'Mum' in the domestic world of young adults, and the centrality of mothers' capacity to communicate with their adolescent children which Brannen and her colleagues (1994) highlighted. At a more abstract level there is also consistency here with Finch and Mason's point that women's life experiences tend to make them more sensitive than men to what they call 'the delicate balance of dependence and independence' (1993, p. 72) which is at the heart of family relationships.

The mother–child relationship takes on even more significance in lone-mother households and in families where a stepfather is present. The gender of the young person also has an important bearing on her or his relationship with parents, there being markedly different sets of expectations about appropriate behaviour for young women and for young men, of which the expectation of greater contributions by young women to housework is merely one example (Wallace, 1987). Social class and ethnicity constitute further influences on precisely how young people and their parents renegotiate the former's dependence as they grow older. In the study by Brannen and her colleagues (1994), middle-class parents tended to operate covert strategies of control through talking and negotiation, while working-class and ethnic minority parents were more likely to operate with more fixed sets of rules about acceptable behaviour. Attention has also been drawn to the significance of situations where a member of the household has a disability (Keith and Morris, 1996; Parker, 1993).

The varying domestic contexts from which young people move towards independence indicate why it is more appropriate to speak of alternative transitions to adulthood rather than one uniform pattern. Closer examination of the diversity of young people's trajectories also serves to highlight the dangers of making unsupported assumptions about normal or typical behaviour. Keith and Morris's (1996) analysis of the care provided by children for parents who have a disability notes that discussions of this relationship in terms of the latter's unusual dependence overlook how common it is for children and young adults in all types of households to be expected to make contributions to household and family routines. Keith and Morris further suggest that a parallel can be drawn between the requirements made of children in households with a disabled parent and those made of children in lone-parent households. Both disability and lone-parenthood frequently entail dependence on the agencies of the welfare state, as do circumstances like unemployment and homelessness. All of these may be considered to be beyond the capacity of the individuals concerned to control. Just as it is not within the power of most young people to effect a successful transition to adulthood unaided, it is equally the case that parents do not have an unlimited capacity to assist their children's achievement of independence. It is for these reasons that attention needs to be paid to the broader housing market, labour market and other social policy contexts within which young people set out to leave home.

## Wider influences on young people's changing family and household ties

One of the most important obligations accompanying the dependence of young people is the commitment to strive to become independent adults and by doing so set some limits to their parents' responsibilities (Hockey and James, 1993). The social pressures on young people to achieve independence are modified to the extent that their parents want them to remain living at home. Hutson and Jenkins (1989) found that most parents strongly disapproved of their children leaving home until they considered them ready to do so. In addition to 'spoiling' their children, several mothers told Hutson and Jenkins that they deliberately avoided family arguments so as to encourage children to stay living at home. The researchers' subsequent observation that 'Local cultural norms do not expect that an unmarried child should leave home before marriage' (1989, p. 57) is pertinent here, since the South Wales context in which Hutson and Jenkins carried out their research appears distinct. In other studies, parents proffered more positive evaluations of children leaving home, for example through easing space shortages (Allatt and Yeandle, 1992) or making life easier more generally for parents to have the home, and more time, to themselves (Burgoyne and Clark, 1984; Mason, 1989). Interestingly, Brannen and her colleagues found parents of 16-year-olds divided roughly equally between 'those who are positive, non-committal, ambivalent and negative' (1994, p. 28) about their children leaving home. These proportions could be expected to change as the children became older, but parental expectations about children leaving home will always be tempered by prevailing circumstances both within the home and beyond it.

A good deal of comment has been passed on how labour market conditions affect young people's ability to achieve independence. The growth of unemployment and of part-time and/or insecure jobs among young people clearly presents serious obstacles to their ability to achieve economic self-sufficiency. In Coffield, Borrill and Marshall's (1986, p. 199) study of young people in north-east England, 'those unable to find a job could not win from family, friends and older adults the status and respect given automatically to a wage earner, and so could not even start to move along the path to adulthood'. In such a context, parents frequently respond by seeking to assist their children in their search for work in whatever ways they can. Allatt and Yeandle's (1992) research illustrates this point. They note that parents went through job advertisements for their children and took them to job interviews or career centres. Parents in more affluent households are more likely to seek to enhance their children's employment prospects through supporting further education (Jordan, Redley and James, 1994). While the form of parental assistance to young people may vary, there is a common thread in parents' recognition that the transition to work is harder now than it was during the three decades of full employment following 1945.

The provision of greater parental assistance to young people in their search for work does not necessarily facilitate their transition to adulthood in the broader sense, and may even serve to compromise it. Jones (1995, p. 58) reports that for some young people 'adult independence means emancipation from parental control as well as "standing on your own two feet" in economic terms'. Where such beliefs are held, even the most well-intentioned involvement by parents can be counter-productive. The same tension surrounds parental efforts to help children to secure good quality accommodation when the moment of leaving home arrives. Here too, as Jones (1995) observes, over-involvement can be experienced negatively. As a consequence, assistance may well be presented by parents as a loan rather than a gift, in order to reduce the inference of dependence and obligation on the part of the recipient. Still, Jones (1995) found that some young people were unwilling to accept such help because they had no means of repayment, a point which echoes Bell's (1968) earlier finding in his study of young couples in Swansea. The reluctance of young people to accept material assistance from their parents might be explained by reference to the conditional nature of this assistance, and their concern that parental help often comes with strings attached (Jones, 1995; Jones and Wallace, 1992). The conditional nature of parental support is likely to be only part of the explanation, however, since attention also needs to be paid to the symbolic significance in modern societies of adulthood and independence being individual achievements.

There are numerous references in the literature on adolescence to opposition to parental direction being undertaken as an expression of individual freedom. According to one 17-year-old female living in Belfast, 'Your parents tell you not to do things but you do it anyway ... the more you're not allowed to do, the more you do it' (Gillespie, Lovett and Garner, 1992, p. 101). In similar fashion, a respondent in Sharpe's study responded to her father's attempt to restrict her sexual activity by saying 'I felt that I was damned if my dad was going to stop me. It had exactly the opposite effect instead: defiance' (1994, p. 85). Of course, parental power does set some limits to what young people can do, but the sanctions available to parents seeking to discipline their children diminish over time. In any event, the strict imposition of discipline threatens to undermine the relations of closeness and trust between the generations which many parents seek to establish (Brannen *et al.*, 1994). Furthermore, it is now more problematic than it used to be for parents to point to the benefits of conforming to conventional patterns of becoming adult. Against the background of the disrupted transition from education to work and rising rates of divorce, it is difficult to present conformity to the work ethic and the institution of marriage as a norm, although parents' tolerance of the alternative arrangements developed by their children should not necessarily be taken to imply uncritical approval.

The assertion of the individual's right to determine her or his involvement in the labour market is a key source of friction between young people and their parents. Wallace (1987) reports that parents often found their children's rejection of job offers difficult to understand, and she notes that one response was to require unemployed young people to contribute more to household tasks. As other studies have also discovered (Coffield, Borrill and Marshall, 1986; Jones and Wallace, 1992), Wallace found that such parental pressure is exercised more frequently over daughters than sons, and she goes on to argue that 'for girls, living independently was seen as an ideal – which they could fulfil with the right job and enough money – whereas for boys it was mostly forced upon them by circumstances' (1987, p. 159). Young women's greater readiness to seek independence from their parents is reflected in their average age of leaving home being two years lower than the comparable figure for young men, but this pattern is the result of a number of other factors besides gender differences in expected household contributions. Becoming a parent also figures in explanations of the lower age of leaving home found among young women. While over half the young mothers in Phoenix's study continued to live with their parents, others 'subscribed to the social construction of motherhood as signalling adulthood and independence, and made definite decisions to push for independence by leaving their parental home' (1991, pp. 151–2). Such actions are, of course, constrained rather than free choices, but they do serve to illustrate that young people are not so dependent that they have no control over their lives.

## Conclusion

Thinking about transitions to adulthood has been thrown into a state of flux by shifting labour market circumstances, modification of welfare state arrangements, altered relationships with parents, and changing notions of individual autonomy and responsibility. The young mothers studied by Phoenix (1991) did not regard their situation as one which necessitated marriage. They followed traditional patterns of marriage and conception only if their partners were in secure employment. Further, only a minority of the sample had set up home with their partners 21 months after the birth of their child. It would, of course, be wrong to read too much into the findings of one study of the atypical group of young women under 20 who become parents, but the connection between changing patterns of employment, partnership and parenthood which it suggests is consistent with the other empirical evidence we have discussed in this chapter which also points towards young people's re-evaluation of relations of dependence on parents, partners, employers and the state (Beuret and Makings, 1987; Irwin, 1995; Jones, 1995; MacDonald and Coffield, 1991). Parents of young people going through the process of becoming independent have also had their ideas about appropriate behaviour affected by these broad patterns of social change, leaving a degree of normative ambiguity (Finch and Mason, 1993). In current circumstances, transitions to adulthood are necessarily negotiated according to individual circumstances rather than following a fixed pattern.

The particular course which any negotiation of becoming adult takes is difficult to anticipate with any precision, although the broad contours of the advantages and disadvantages attached to different positions in terms of social class, gender, ethnicity and other structural factors can be identified. In analysing the survival strategies developed by young adults who had been unemployed for a long period, Wallace (1987, p. 140) found it useful to distinguish between 'swimmers' and 'sinkers' according to whether they took advantage of opportunities for work in the informal economy; long-term unemployment did not necessarily entail a common trajectory. The diverse housing strategies of the young people studied by Pickvance and Pickvance (1994) also highlight the importance of avoiding over-deterministic models of the relationship between social structure and individual actions. People's choices, preferences and aspirations need to be taken into account alongside constraining factors such as the economic resources available to them as a household.

As Berrington and Murphy (1994) emphasise, the decisions that young people make which lead to their leaving home are generally not decisions about leaving home *per se*. Rather they are decisions about other events which result in their living away from their parents. For some, this will be to do with getting married or setting up other types of partnership, while for others it will be consequent on education, training or job opportunities. These decisions, of course, also have an influence on the future paths which their lives take, including their familial and domestic careers. It is a theme of this book that the patterns involved here have become more diverse and more complex in recent years. Yet there are also some systematic changes occurring which, while different from the past, are nonetheless built into contemporary understandings about family and domestic arrangements. In particular, cohabitation is now accepted by many as an appropriate pathway into a permanent partnership. Equally there are other aspects of family and domestic organisation that appear to have been slow to change, even though there are ideological currents which are suggestive of significant modifications. A good example of this is the continuation of gendered notions of economic and domestic contributions within many longer-term partnerships, especially where there are children in the household. The next chapter will explore these issues further, concentrating on contemporary partnership formation and the early phases of marital organisation.

# 4 Love, Cohabitation and Early Marriage

Having examined key aspects of adolescence and early adulthood in the last chapter, we now focus on patterns of household and family formation. As discussed in previous chapters, there have been major demographic shifts occurring in these areas, shifts which reflect broader underlying trends in how romantic and sexual relationships are understood within contemporary society. These changes are not uniform. Like all cultural change, their trajectory is never straightforward; there are ambiguities within them that make their interpretation complex. Most importantly, the cultural changes which are occurring affect different groups within society in different ways and at different speeds. Consequently while the demographic trends concerning the early phases of household and family formation are clear enough, the reasons for them, and their personal and social implications, need to be interpreted with caution.

## Love

This point applies especially to the first of the topics to be discussed in this chapter: love. Love is clearly of immense significance within contemporary society. As a key element within the cultural construction of familial relationships, it receives a great deal of attention in a wide range of popular, artistic and even (quasi-)scientific media. Accounts of the joys, tensions, dilemmas and satisfactions of love are the standard fare of magazines, television, novels, cinema and theatre. No other emotion receives the attention given to love in contemporary culture. Certainly no other emotion is given the same legitimacy as love for influencing and excusing people's actions. Romantic/sexual love in particular is used to justify behaviour which in other contexts – and in other eras – would have been unacceptable.

Part of the dominant cultural conception of romantic love is that it is inherently mysterious. It is extremely difficult to define and 'strikes' people in ways over which they are supposed to have little control (Jackson, 1993; Sarsby, 1983). It is usually portrayed as a genuinely personal and emergent emotion, not one which is socially constructed or developed to order. In other words, it represents a particular form of attraction between two people which is glorified culturally in being inexplicable. In a world which is often seen as increasingly rational, romantic love stands apart as one of the few areas of life in which apparently pure emotion is allowed to reign. The continuing popularity of 'real life' as well as fictional stories rooted in romantic love – and its loss – in the media reflect the special power which this form of love holds within our culture.

Curiously, sociologists have until recently shown rather little interest in 'love', leaving the topic to social psychology which has traditionally been more concerned with exploring patterns of sexual and other inter-personal attraction (for example, see Aron and Aron, 1996; Berscheid and Meyers, 1996; Dion and Dion, 1996). In part this reflects sociology's historical neglect of emotions in general, a neglect which has only recently begun to be reversed (Beck and Beck-Gernsheim, 1995; Cancian, 1987; Duncombe and Marsden, 1993; Giddens, 1992; Hochschild, 1983; Illouz, 1997; Jackson, 1993; James, 1989). Yet, many family sociologists recognised that the social and economic basis of marriage was fundamentally altered with industrialisation and the dominance of wage labour over other forms of production, though it was mainly historians who devoted critical attention to the claims about emotional solidarity that were being made (Anderson, 1980; Gillis, 1997; Luhmann, 1986; Medick, 1976; Shorter, 1975; Stone, 1979, 1988). In essence, it was held that as individualised wage labour became the norm, replacing household/family production as the main means of social reproduction, so the influence on marital choice by parents and other 'outsiders' was reduced.

More specifically, because the younger generation relied less for their means of livelihood on resources which parents controlled, they could more readily disregard the latter's wishes and interests. Within this perspective, associated strongly with both functionalist and Marxist theorising, the nuclear family became increasingly independent of wider kin. This in turn encouraged the development of personal attraction, and hence romantic love, as the major rationale for marital selection (Cancian, 1987; Gillis, 1997; Luhmann, 1986; Macfarlane, 1987; Medick, 1976; Stone, 1979). Interestingly, writers diverge widely over the period in which they see this as happening, reflecting in part the different socio-historical eras in which economic change first emerged. In Britain the roots of change are usually located in the late eighteenth century, while in the United States the key period was the early twentieth century with the rapid growth of major urban centres.

Yet whatever the period seen as most crucial, key among the changes described is the development of marital choice based on criteria of strong personal attraction and compatibility. This compatibility and attraction in turn became the normative standard of marriage itself, and not just of marital selection. Certainly in Britain, a sense of emotional commitment – love, for want of a better word – has long been seen as the only legitimate rationale for marriage (Jackson, 1993; Sarsby, 1983). Other factors were undoubtedly important – the need for economic security, the desire for sexual expression, or whatever – but the way marriage was explained was by reference to the feelings which existed between the couple (Illouz, 1997). Until recently, the decline of such love, or even its eventual replacement by emotions of indifference or dislike, was not seen legally or socially as grounds for separation or divorce even though marriages in which this happened occurred quite frequently. Nonetheless, love took pride of place as the most socially justifiable rationale for marrying.

Within contemporary societies, the appeal of love as the proper basis for marital selection, and increasingly for the continuation of a marriage, remains very powerful. Importantly, how such love is understood is not static. Indeed its conceptualisation remains somewhat vague and socially malleable. Such imprecision permits different expectations to be held among different social groups and for change to occur in social understandings over time, though the shifts which develop are gradual and often difficult to recognise. This becomes more complex with the interplay of different cultural representations and, in particular, because of the contrast between much-lived reality and the varied images portrayed in popular media. In addition, romantic love is itself gendered. The ways in which males and females experience and 'do' such love varies, along with other forms of emotional expressivity (Cancian, 1987; Duncombe and Marsden, 1993; Jackson, 1993).

Before examining contemporary conceptions of romantic and sexual love in more detail, it is worth discussing the belief that love is a superior basis for marriage. Within the dominant culture, other bases of marriage are seen not simply as different but generally as less moral and less worthy. Thus to marry for wealth without the commitment of love is seen as morally inappropriate. To marry for domestic convenience is also disparaged, except possibly for some older people where a straightforward companionship without a sexual/romantic element may be socially validated. Equally, arranged marriages in which parents (and possibly other kin) play a significant part in selecting a spouse are taken by the majority to be less fulfilling at a personal level and also contrary to individual rights of citizenship. In other words, part of the contemporary expression of full adulthood comprises control over the personal sphere, including matters governing sexual expression, household arrangements and marriage without others having the right to override the individual's desires and wishes (Giddens, 1992). Stacey's (1998, p. 262) reference to the process of 'democratising intimacy' captures this trend nicely.

Moreover, in line with the discussion of individualisation in Chapter 1, this development of personal autonomy within modern societies is seen as precisely that: a development, something which represents a better and higher state of evolution than that which existed previously or exists in other societies. In other words, the dominance of individual choice, and within that of love, is taken to be a culmination of previous arrangements, both in the sense of growing out of these and in the sense of being the most complete. Thus, from within the culture, it appears that love is the 'natural' basis for romantic/sexual partner selection. Love is not seen as a social construction, as a mode of selection rooted within a particular social formation, but instead as something which is inherent in human nature. It may not be allowed to bloom fully in other cultures, but where it is, it becomes the 'obvious' expression of personal commitment.

Yet there is nothing 'obvious' about romantic and sexual love as a basis for long-term relationships. It is no more natural than any other form of selection (Beall and Sternberg, 1995; Dion and Dion, 1996). Indeed there are arguments that it is a less satisfactory basis for long-term commitment because it is essentially unstable. Depending as it does on a mutual emotionality, the prospects of constancy over the life course are limited. If stability over time is the aim – though of course that itself can be brought into question as social conditions alter – then selection of partners on the basis of something more constraining than emotion alone seems preferable. Arranged marriages, for example, in which a wider kin group has a stake in the continuance of the union are likely to generate more stability, though the cost may (or may not) be lower levels of satisfaction or contentment (Shaw, 1994; Warrier, 1994). While research on it remains sparse, arranged marriage is a common form of marriage among some Asian ethnic groups in Britain. However, here too, 'westernised' notions of love and marital choice appear to be having an impact on more traditional patterns, with the individuals who are marrying being given more opportunities to influence partner selection than previously (Berrington, 1994; Bhopal, 1997; Gardner and Shukur, 1994; Shaw, 1994).

The argument here is not that passionate love is found only in modern (or late modern) societies. Rather it is that only in such societies is this form of love seen as having major legitimacy as a basis for selecting marital or other long-term partners. Undoubtedly, passionate love occurs elsewhere, as numerous art forms including especially poetry, drama and literature attest. But, as Goode (1959) has argued, the problem, so frequently reflected in these literary accounts, is how such passion is socially controlled. Far from being the basis of lifelong commitment between spouses, it is instead seen more often as an unreliable form of solidarity and thus cannot act as an appropriate mainstay for marriage (Stone, 1988). Those who fall in love may be left for their passion to dissipate. More frequently though, social sanctions of different forms and intensity are brought to bear, either by the respective kin sets or by the couple's peer groups.

In contrast, in contemporary societies, passionate heterosexual love is encouraged as a particularly authentic experience, sometimes leading to marriage, sometimes not. As noted, it is seen as normal, socially desirable and transformative. Far from being discouraged, it is welcomed, recognised as a sign of maturity, and perceived as one of the major ways in which the individual can find personal fulfilment. Those who do not experience such love, or whose love has not been fully realised, often have a sense of loss or of incompleteness, of an emotional void which can only partly be compensated for by other forms of relationship. As Giddens (1992) has argued, in late modernity the notion of expressing the self through exclusive, intimate relationships has attained far greater cultural prominence than it had even a generation ago. In this scenario, the absence of an intimate loving relationship can make life appear more 'empty' than it does in cultural formations where such ties are defined as less central to self-realisation. However, the dominance of western culture also means that such imagery is increasingly pertinent within other cultures too.

Given its social significance, it is no surprise that people receive a good deal of tutelage in contemporary discourses of love (Jackson, 1993). In particular, adolescents are heavily socialised into the ways of romantic and sexual love. This is evident in many aspects of 'youth culture', from music, magazines and soap operas to the topics of everyday conversation. However, it is not just through 'youth culture' that people learn about being in love. Families are also important in this, implicitly teaching some of the 'rules' of love relationships. Thus people do not fall in love haphazardly. They do so – or at least interpret the emotions they are feeling as 'real love' – at particular stages in their lives. Traditionally, for example, those who continue through higher education tend to be willing to experience this form of love at later ages than those who do not. As Mansfield and Collard (1988) argue, people have to be willing to accept that the time is right for 'settling down' before they define a relationship as the 'real thing'.

Equally impressive is the way in which people tend to fall for others who are rather like themselves. There is, in other words, a degree of homogeneity in the love market. People fall in love predominantly with individuals who are socially equivalent and who are thus likely to be acceptable to the others in their social net-works. Both family and friends have more or less subtle ways of helping to define the characteristics and qualities of eligibles. Of course, individuals do not always follow other people's ideas about eligibility – sexual attraction can indeed be more mysterious than this suggests – but by and large they do, particularly when love is converted into a long-term cohabitation or marriage. Direct parental influence on this process may have reduced with recent changes in partnership patterns, but there can be no doubt that love continues to be socially and economically structured, reflecting the status differences found elsewhere in social life. (Indeed, as Mullan (1984) interestingly pointed out, without such predictability, com-puter-based dating agencies could not operate as they do.)

As noted, love is inherently unstable. The particular emotional commitments we recognise as love may, for a whole range of reasons, alter, or through circumstance become unmanageable. In line with the limited attention sociologists have paid to emotional worlds, there is little information on the overall patterning of love, interesting though such studies would be (Gillis, 1997; Jamieson, 1998). Sometimes love results in longer-term partner-ship, whether marriage or less formal cohabitation; sometimes it does not. More pertinently, what starts off as passion is trans-muted over time into a more mundane, less exhilarating relation-ship (Noller, 1996). How this is perceived and interpreted itself varies across couples and over time. Sometimes it is expressed as a deepening of the love that there is between the pair, with the high emotionality of 'falling in love' being replaced by a more 'mature' commitment based on a fuller understanding of each other's needs, as well as a shared biography. Alternatively though, these changes in the emotionality of the tie can be experienced as indicative of its 'failure' and as grounds for terminating the rela-tionship. The changing patterns of commitment common in mar-riage will be discussed in the next chapter, with marital break-down and divorce being a major topic of Chapter 6.

## Cohabitation

As we saw in earlier chapters, the demography of family formation has altered quite dramatically over the last twenty years. A significant element within this has been changes in cohabitation patterns. Although the 1960s are commonly seen as the period in which sexual liberation flourished, at the end of that decade relatively few couples were living together outside of marriage. There is little reason to believe that most couples in self-defined 'serious' relationships were not sexually active. But in general, such sexual activity was not overtly acknowledged. Especially for those who had not previously been married, it tended to remain clandestine.

Certainly, few couples were recorded as cohabiting then. According to the figures collected for the *General Household Survey*, only some 5 per cent of those marrying for the first time in the second half of the 1960s acknowledge living together before their marriage. For marriages in which one or both spouses had been married before, the figure is much higher at 66 per cent (see Table 2.4, p. 29) but of course, the number of second marriages was much lower, approximately 70,000 out of a total of 400,000 marriages each year, compared to well over 100,000 second marriages out of fewer than 300,000 marriages in the mid-1990s (Marriage and Divorce Statistics, OPCS). Interestingly, data on cohabitation not resulting in marriage are unavailable, reflecting the stigma attached even then to cohabitation as well as its rarity. A generation on, cohabitation has not only become the dominant mode of premarital commitment – in effect a new form of engagement – but also occurs widely as an alternative to marriage (Haskey, 1995). Nearly 30 per cent of all 'non-married' women aged between 20 and 39 are currently cohabiting (G.H.S., 1997), although this includes few ethnic Indian, Bangladeshi or Pakistani women (Berrington, 1994).

Researchers have only recently examined the demography of cohabitation (Haskey, 1995). This is, of course, a more difficult task than understanding the demography of marriage. There are, for example, more complex definitional problems. Even knowing when cohabitation begins and ends is far from straightforward. Being a legal contract, marriage has a definite beginning: the marriage ceremony and registration. With cohabitation the process is often more piecemeal and subtle. For some, especially those who are already living away from the parental home, the 'decision' to cohabit may not even appear like a decision: for example, the couple may well keep their own homes, while actually spending more and more time together. Equally, the different potential elements of cohabitation, including a sexual relationship, a shared residence, and a common housekeeping, may develop over different time periods. In a sense, the 'household' and the 'family' elements of cohabitation do not coincide; each occurs to its own timetable and neither is necessarily marked by a clear beginning.

But if we know little about the demography of cohabitation and its dynamics, we know even less about its social organisation. There are few studies which have investigated the social patterning of these relationships directly. Most have done so from the perspective of marriage: that is, they have looked at the premarital patterns of those who are now married. Given that not all cohabitation results in marriage, the accounts gathered from these sources are bound to be partial. It would be particularly useful to have more studies that looked at such matters as people's different pathways into cohabitation; how the relationships develop over time; what people expect from these ties; the social and personal meanings which are attached to cohabitation; how decisions about marriage and childbearing are made; the division of work and responsibility in cohabitation and the processes by which cohabitation is terminated. The rest of this section will focus on some of these issues, though the arguments should be regarded as tentative because the information available is so limited. Moreover, given the rapid changes there are in the demography of cohabitation, it is quite likely that its social organisation is also altering. This is a topic in which studies may quickly become dated.

An obvious question to pose is why cohabitation has increased so rapidly. What is it that has led to this major change in patterns of household (and family) formation? A number of factors appear to have contributed to this, some directly to do with the individual, some more removed. On the surface, the most obvious reason concerns the liberalisation of sexual attitudes which has developed since the mid-1960s. While the social changes of the 1960s can easily be overemphasised, one area in which there was significant change in attitude was in sexual expression, notwithstanding religious and ethnic differences (Berrington and Diamond, 1999). The dominant message prior to this period was that virginity mattered, especially for women; they should 'save themselves' for the person with whom they wanted to share the rest of their lives. Boys/men may pressurise for sexual intercourse, but this should be resisted for fear of losing 'respect' as a consequence. This particular moral perspective received general support from all sources: schools, churches, media, families. At most, sexual congress was permitted, provided it was not flaunted, once a couple became engaged and had pledged their future together. The fear of illegitimacy, and the stigma attached to it, acted as a strong deterrent.

Although the reduction in family size since the first decade of the century indicated that people were able to control their fertility, it was only in the 1960s that contraception became recognisably reliable. Equally it was only around this period that public discussion of contraception appeared acceptable. In 1958 the Church of England first acknowledged that contraceptive use was fully compatible with Christian practice – a position the Catholic Church still refutes – and in the early 1960s the contraceptive pill became available. Aside from its reliability, this had a major impact because it gave control of contraception to women. It was, however, only as late as 1967, with the passing of the NHS (Family Planning) Act, that contraception become readily accessible to unmarried women in Britain. Prescribing practice before this mirrored cultural norms and asserted that unmarried women should not be sexually active. It was also in 1967 that abortion laws were made more liberal in Great Britain (though not in Northern Ireland) (Hawkes, 1996; Lewis, 1992; Macintyre, 1976).

So, strange as it now seems, it was not until the late 1960s that the majority of unmarried women had the option of effective control over fertility. This undoubtedly had a major impact on the way in which sexual behaviour was managed and understood. For unmarried females, full sexual relations could for the first time become both a part of the expression of self and a measure of love within relationships. This was certainly an element emphasised in media and other accounts celebrating the growth of youth culture in the late 1960s. Images of sexual freedom pervaded common understandings of the changes occurring. Yet to a large extent the moral basis to this change had still to be firmly established. Many of that generation were sexually active only within established relationships and, often through convenient fiction, little was revealed to parents (Schofield, 1968, 1971; Wilson, 1980).

Parental control is another factor influencing the rise in cohabitation. The issue here is not solely why cohabitation has become normalised since the 1980s, but also why it was so uncommon before that. In part, what has changed are the constraints which affect the options open to younger people: for example, parental control has changed, both in terms of expected behaviour and with regard to the resources they control (Berrington and Diamond, 2000; Kiernan and Lelièvre, 1995). There is also a normative generational influence, for many of the parents in question were themselves members of the 1960s generation which began to explore greater sexual freedom. Notwithstanding the issue of HIV/AIDS, they seem to have less concern than their own parents about limiting their children's sexual experience, and in any case have less power to do so. Again though, ethnic differences are important here, with South Asian parents (and family members) continuing to exert stronger control, particularly over their daughters' sexual behaviour (Berrington, 1994; Bhopal, 1997).

Importantly too, changes in higher education and housing have led to more young people, again especially females, leaving home at earlier ages for reasons other than marriage. As we saw in the last chapter, marriage and employment are no longer the predominant route into independence (Berrington and Murphy, 1994; Jones, 1995). More people are able to live in their own housing, even if only a room in a shared house, than previously. This of itself makes it easier for couples to start cohabiting. Moreover, the wider housing market has altered radically with the growth of owner-occupation. Until a generation ago, building societies sought to protect their investments, in large part through judgements about the respectability of those to whom they offered loans. Given the dominant views about 'living in sin' – and note again how redundant this term has become – they were extremely unlikely to lend money to couples who were unmarried. This issue no longer plays a part in decisions about whether to advance money. In the other sectors of the housing market too, the changing moral climate has largely made cohabitation an irrelevancy. Thus, housing has been opened up to cohabiting couples, removing one of the major constraints limiting people's options.

One further influence has been the change in divorce. As the figures given in Tables 2.4 and 2.5 (pp. 29 and 30) indicate, couples in which one or both individuals had previously separated or divorced were the most likely to cohabit. The social controls exercised over couples marrying for the first time were far less effective with couples who had previously been married, and established their independence. Moreover the symbolism of marriage as a union 'for life' no longer held quite the same power. Indeed, for those who had not yet obtained a divorce, cohabitation was the only option. As the number of separations and divorces increased, so the number of previously married people cohabiting also grew. This in turn meant that cohabitation ceased to be as much a moral issue as it had been. It stopped being stigmatised as sinful, and over the 1980s and 1990s became more common, especially amongst couples who were committing themselves to a longer-term relationship.

It is difficult to be clear about the personal significance of cohabitation because the information we have is so skewed towards those in long-term relationships. Some themes can be identified though. For the majority of people, cohabitation seems to represent something about commitment. The pathways into cohabitation may be varied, with different elements being brought in to play at different times – overnight stays slowly being transformed into cohabitation – but by the time people define themselves as cohabiting, they are making a statement to each other, and outsiders, about the greater permanence of their relationship. Equally though, for many people, living together retains important elements of independence. Its attraction is that it is not formal or legal; nor is it a promise that the tie will necessarily last for ever, even if this is the intention. It is a commitment, but one which has routes out as well as ways forward (Nock, 1995; Brown and Booth, 1996).

For many people cohabitation appears to be a stage rather than an end state. But the stage it is can vary, and importantly the way it is understood at the time may not be the way it is understood later (McRae, 1993a). Thus some people – perhaps the majority – begin to cohabit as a prelude to marriage. For them it represents engagement, a sign of their commitment. But at the same time it is also a trial marriage; a chance to see how compatible they are and whether they really do want to make their relationship more permanent. Here the ideology of independence is important. The couple have not yet made an irreversible decision; they do not have rights over one another; they are free to be more independent if they wish.

In fact, for many, the idea of independence may be largely illusory: that is, the commitment they have already made to each other is so evident that independence plays relatively little part in their lifestyles. Most of their free time is spent together; they do not explore other relationships; and often their lives are dominated by setting up home and planning their wedding. In reality, the cohabiting phase for these couples is probably very little different from the previous generation's very early phases of marriage. The emphasis is much more on commitment than independence. And while not having the same force as marriage, cohabitation still creates a web of expectations, obligations and possessions which become the more difficult to break away from as the cohabitation becomes more established (Kiernan and Estaugh, 1993). Currently 60 per cent of cohabitations result in marriage, though the percentage has been declining (Ermisch and Francesconi, 1996).

In turn, approximately 30 per cent of cohabitations are terminated (without marriage) within ten years. For some, living together can reveal traits and habits which are unacceptable and result in the relationship ending. Others recognise from the start that the cohabitation in which they are involved is not permanent. The relationship is an important one and living together meets their current needs. But it is not a relationship to which they are committing themselves long-term. In these relationships there is likely to be a greater emphasis on individual independence. The couple may do much together but frequently they also emphasise the importance of being involved in different activities and relationships so that each can sustain their separate identities. The relationship may end over some conflict. But equally it can end because one or both have decided that it is time for their lives to take different directions. They may decide they want a new job or to move elsewhere, that now is the right time to travel, or because they have become involved in a new sexual relationship.

Similarly, one of them may decide they want to 'settle down', establish a more committed relationship, and perhaps have children. This, for example, was a strong element in some of the accounts Mansfield and Collard (1988) collected in their study of early marriage. Their respondents had a clear idea that they were ready for a different phase of their life, ended a previous cohabitation and established the tie that eventually led to their marriage. Of course, for some what had started off as a temporary cohabitation developed into a longer-term one. The couple may never make the decisions necessary to end the relationship. They may continue to celebrate a joint lifestyle that affirms the value of independence; or they may transform it into a more settled version, either through a conscious reevaluation or via a less overt process of adjustment.

One important question is how similar cohabitation is to marriage. Is it a distinct kind of relationship, embodying different principles of organisation, or is it in key respects essentially the same, especially with regard to the early years of marriage? Interesting though this question is, the shortage of studies of cohabitation makes answering it somewhat speculative. However, it would seem that those involved define it differently and frequently consider that their relationship is a more egalitarian one than most marriages. In making any comparison, it is important to be precise about the dimensions which are being compared. Here we will consider just three aspects of the relationship: the degree of autonomy each partner has; the division of labour within the tie; and the character of their commitment. Of course, in all three of these there is much variation to be found, so generalising needs to be treated cautiously.

As noted above, the level of commitment which people have to cohabitation appears in the main to be relatively high. Some people in particular phases of their lives cohabit without an expectation that the relationship will continue in the long term. However, most cohabit only when they think there is a strong possibility of the relationship being sustained. Indeed many treat cohabitation as a prelude to marriage, as a form of engagement. For these people especially, the cohabitation is perceived as a form of trial marriage, or at least a preparation, without any real thoughts that the tie will not at some stage be formalised. Yet the idea that the relationship is an informal one is important. Not only is there still an escape route if the relationship becomes problematic, but equally the demands that each partner can make of the other, and the extent to which the relationship is embedded in external structures, are limited. Neither partner can take the other for granted in the way which many report as happening quite quickly within marriage (McRae, 1993a).

Similarly, the degree of autonomy which each person has within cohabitation is higher than within marriage. Roles are more flexible and less established; even more so than in marriage, the ideology of the relationship emphasises the notion of its being a personal construction of the couple. They 'build' their tie to reflect their own particular desires and ambitions. Here the language of 'construction' is particularly apt, as it indicates well the level of freedom and individual control exercised. Many couples value this, especially those who both have career ambitions and/or where the tie is not seen as necessarily being preliminary to marriage. Thus, following on from the discussion in Chapter 1, cohabitation is a form of partnership whose premise fits well with the development of 'projects of the self' (Giddens, 1991) and the individualisation which has been argued to be characteristic of late modernity. There are commonalities in the ways cohabitation is constructed by those involved, part of which is its distancing from marriage. Nonetheless, what the tie symbolises, whether or not perceived as a prelude to marriage, is individual choice, freedom of construction, and contingent commitment.

This in turn appears to be reflected in the division of labour found within cohabitation, especially where there are no children living with the couple. As Mansfield and Collard's (1988) research shows, couples take pride in the extent to which they are creating a domestic organisation which is different from marriage. Rather than the adoption of traditional roles, there is a far greater emphasis on fairness and equal sharing. While disagreements may arise about appropriate standards, issues about the distribution and balance of different activities are ones which are left more open to negotiation than in most marriages. Even though tasks may become routinely assigned, there is often a greater degree of vigilance in monitoring the demands made of each individual. When cohabiting couples marry, this concern, or even respect, for equality appears to receive a lower priority. In part, this results from the very formality, permanence and normative structuring of marriage. Equally, though, plans to have children in the near future are often given as a reason why the balance of shared activity within the tie is no longer sustainable. As discussed below, the presence of children is usually taken as necessitating a more differentiated division of labour than when there were no children.

Mansfield and Collard's (1988) research showed that plans to have children are often a major factor in cohabiting couples' decisions to marry. However, an increasing number of cohabiting couples are having children outside marriage – though less is known about whether these couples do decide to marry later. In the mid-1990s, there were some 200,000 births outside marriage, comprising a third of all births (compared to 126,000 in the mid-1980s, a fifth of all births), but approximately 60 per cent of these births were to women who were cohabiting with their child's father. There is little information on how the birth of children affects the cohabiting relationship, though from the copious research on motherhood and parenting (Boulton, 1983; Lewis and O'Brien, 1987; Phoenix, 1991; Phoenix, Woollett and Lloyd, 1991; Richardson, 1993) it appears highly likely that it does significantly change the relationship. (See the next section of this chapter.) In particular it is likely to reduce the degree of autonomy that mothers have within the union and foster a more conventional division of labour than existed previously.

With the increasing number of divorces and never-married mothers, the number of cohabiting couples living with children from previous unions has grown significantly. The general topic of stepfamilies will be discussed fully in Chapter 7. Many of the issues which impinge on this family form do so irrespective of whether marriage takes place or not, the composition of the household mattering more than the legal status of the adult couple. Nonetheless, the sense of permanence is likely to be important, not just in terms of the length of time the relationships have had to develop, but also with regard to the degree to which parenting roles are shared. This is nearly always a problematic issue but may be especially so in newly-formed and potentially short-lived cohabitations. Here again, there is a lack of sociological research into the dynamics of stepfamily cohabitation, though it can be readily recognised that the needs and interests of adults and children may diverge significantly. This is an issue to which we shall return in Chapter 7.

The final matter to consider in this section is the ending of cohabitation. Marriage itself is of course one way in which 'cohabitation' as a distinct phase ends. In 1995, 60 per cent of marrying couples were cohabiting – or at least they gave the same address – at the time of their wedding (Marriage and Divorce Statistics, OPCS). Other couples end their cohabitation through separation. Indeed as Buck and Ermisch (1995) show, cohabitation is far less stable than marriage: a significantly higher proportion of cohabitations are terminated in any given period. Again we know little about the processes involved, though they are likely to be influenced by a range of factors. The presence of children is an obvious one; so too is the length of time the couple have been sharing a home. The longer this is, the more complexities there will be about the division of property; though it may be that cohabiting couples tend to maintain a clearer sense of individual property than married couples do. Some couples define their relationship as temporary and recognise that they will be moving on. This may be at another point of change in their lives, for example, when they leave university or when they get a new job, or it may be when they find the relationship no longer satisfies them in the way it originally did.

Overall though, our lack of knowledge of the 'natural histories' of cohabitation means that we have little idea of the emotional impact of the ending of cohabitation. It seems likely that it is less traumatic than divorce, partly because cohabitation does not carry the same symbolic weight as marriage. Because the continuing voluntariness of the tie is manifest, particularly if there are no children, ending the relationship is likely to be less problematic socially and personally, (though it can be more so legally (Barnes, 1996; Kiernan and Estaugh, 1993)). The couple's lives are that much less intertwined. One interesting – and counter-intuitive – discovery of research in this country and elsewhere is that couples who cohabit prior to their marriage are more likely to divorce than couples who do not (Berrington and Diamond, 1999; DeMaris and Rao, 1992; Haskey, 1992; Lillard, Brien and Waite, 1995). The reasons for this appear complex. They may include aspects of religiosity, with couples not cohabiting having a different view of the sanctity of marriage from those who do. Alternatively it may be that marriage alters the character of their relationship in ways that cohabiting couples do not envisage. Ironically, this may reflect changes in the perceived permanence of the tie, leading to a decreased sense of autonomy, aspects of the other being taken for granted, and the emergence of a more rigid division of labour (Berrington and Diamond, 2000; Brown and Booth, 1996; Thomson and Colella, 1992).

## Partnerships, children and domestic organisation

Notwithstanding the changes there have been in partnership, household formation and childbearing patterns, there are also major continuities with the past. So, while women have been bearing children later, while more children are born outside of marriage and while a higher proportion of women are choosing not to have children at all (see Chapter 2), the great majority of women do still become mothers and the great majority of children are born to cohabiting couples, either married or unmarried. Thus even in the mid-1990s, when more than a third of all births were outside marriage, only around 15 per cent were born to women who appeared not to be living with the child's father (see Table 2.3, p. 28). And the birth of children continues to have a major impact on the organisation of domestic relationships. This section of the chapter will focus particularly on how children affect the division of responsibility within partnerships. Frequently it is asserted that fathers now participate far more in child-rearing activities than they did in the past. While this is so to some degree, there can be no doubt that in the large majority of cases, childcare continues to be a predominantly female responsibility, carrying significant consequences for mothers' economic and social activities inside and outside the home. One of the clearest ways of seeing this is by looking at the employment

**Table 4.1**  *Mother's employment status by age of youngest child 1995 % (Great Britain)*

| Youngest child, aged | Full-time | Part-time | Unemployed | Not employed |
|---|---|---|---|---|
| 0–4 | 17 | 34 | 5 | 44 |
| 5–9 | 22 | 44 | 6 | 28 |
| 10+ | 32 | 45 | 3 | 20 |

*Source*: General Household Survey, 1998.

**Table 4.2**    *Mother's employment status by age of youngest child 1985 % (Great Britain)*

| Youngest child, aged | Full-time | Part-time | Unemployed | Not employed |
|---|---|---|---|---|
| 0–4 | 8 | 22 | 6 | 64 |
| 5–9 | 14 | 46 | 3 | 37 |
| 10+ | 28 | 42 | 3 | 27 |

*Source*: General Household Survey, 1997.

patterns of mothers with young children. Table 4.1 provides details of this.

There is a very clear relationship between the age of the youngest child in the household and the participation of mothers in paid work. In 1995, only 17 per cent of mothers with pre-school children were employed full-time, with a further 34 per cent in part-time jobs. Thus some half of all these mothers were in effect caring for their children full-time. By the time their youngest child enters secondary school, only about a quarter of mothers have no employment, though the largest group (45 per cent) are employed part-time. Note, however, how much this has been changing in recent years. Table 4.2 provides the equivalent data for 1985, when only 30 per cent of mothers with children aged 0 to 4 were employed, with as few as 8 per cent employed full-time.

Yet, despite the changes, full-time housework is experienced for a period by the majority of women. Currently some 85 per cent of women have children (Birth Statistics, 1995), and, as Table 4.1 indicates, the largest proportion of these have a period out of employment while their children are young. This period is certainly far shorter than it was for their mothers' and grandmothers' generations, but it still represents a significant phase in their lives. Furthermore, a large proportion return to employment in a markedly different capacity, that is, on a part-time basis rather than a full-time one, after they have children. As Table 4.1 illustrates, nearly half are still in part-time employment when their youngest child is at secondary school.

Recent research has shown that occupational status has an impact on rates of employment return (Glover and Arber, 1995; McRae, 1993b). Using data from the Labour Force Survey, Glover and Arber (1995) report that around a quarter of mothers of pre-school age children in professional and other higher level occupations are employed full-time compared to some 10 per cent of mothers in routine non-manual or manual jobs. This is partly a result of greater job security, but also a consequence of higher pay rates allowing alternative childcare to be funded. However, as Glover and Arber (1995, p. 168) comment, 'low rates of full-time working, high rates of part-time working and of withdrawal from the labour force remain the characteristics of mothers' employment', a finding echoed by Jacobs (1997).

Moreover, the period of caring full-time for young children is highly symbolic. Generally occurring early within the partnership, it appears to set the pattern for the organisation of the relationship in the years that follow. Once a pattern is established within the marriage, it is frequently continued with only minor modifications being made as household circumstances alter. From the research that has been done, there is little evidence of any substantial renegotiation of responsibilities as wives re-enter the labour force, as children age, or even when husbands retire or are made redundant (Brannen and Moss, 1991; Mason, 1987; McKee and Bell, 1986; Morris, 1990a). This does not imply that no changes occur in the detailed management of the home or in how tasks are divided. Such change is inevitable as the demography of the family alters, along with its members' interests and commitments. Rather, what it refers to is the absence of any radical shift in the division of *responsibilities* between household members. In most cases, this remains heavily gendered.

Interestingly, in their study of newly-wed couples, Mansfield and Collard (1988) found that most couples were building a conventional domestic division of labour into their household organisation soon after their marriage. Equality in most spheres, including employment and domestic labour, was emphasised as an ideal by the couple, especially if they had previously been cohabiting. However, once the couple began to make plans for having children, the idea of broadly similar roles began to dissipate: for example, on marriage, and with thoughts of future childcare arrangements, couples often began to prioritise the husband's employment above the wife's, on the premise that after the birth of children her prime responsibility would, unlike her husband's, change. Whereas previously, domestic and paid work had been seen as the responsibility of both, once the possibility of children came to the fore, divisions in responsibilities became more marked. One powerful indication of this was that whereas fewer than a third of the men in the study had changed jobs at or near the time of the wedding, over two-thirds of the wives had. Moreover, the husbands' moves typically involved career progression and development whereas for the wives the job changes more commonly resulted in a loss in pay, conditions or status (Mansfield and Collard, 1988, Chapter 7).

All types of work structure the experiences of those involved. Full-time housework and childcare are no different in this respect. The conditions under which this work is done are quite distinct from those in most other work settings (Boulton, 1983; Hunt, 1978; Oakley, 1974; Phoenix, 1991; Richardson, 1993). The most obvious feature of domestic labour is that it is unpaid, making the full-time housewife economically dependent on the money her husband earns. This money does not comprise her wage or reward; rather it is money for which she has the major responsibility of transforming into as a high a standard of living as possible for all members of her household.

This has major implications for the way housework is understood socially. First, because there is no payment, it is implicitly defined as not equivalent to 'real' work. Indeed, it is generally not seen as 'productive work' warranting reward; rather, in Hunt's (1978, p. 561) words, it is experienced more as 'personal service'. Secondly, because they receive no payment, full-time housewives frequently perceive that they have little right to spend money on themselves. The money they have access to is for the welfare of the household overall rather than their own personal consumption. Moreover, at this phase of family life when the household has least money, managing the domestic economy well frequently entails a relative neglect of the housewife's own needs. In contrast, her husband, whose work is perceived to provide the money on which the household depends, is frequently seen as having a more legitimate claim on that income for personal consumption. He, after all, is the one who earns it, a view which effectively over-looks the work the housewife does in transforming the wage into a standard of living.

Thus the full-time housewife's work is not only unpaid, but also often perceived as being of lesser value than employment. And because her own contribution is not rewarded financially, or even perceived in financial terms, the full-time house-wife/mother comes to be defined as economically dependent on her partner, even if some aspects of marital ideology suggest otherwise. The actual outcome of this depends on the house-hold's overall level of income as well as the money manage-ment patterns which develop. Often in households where there is least money, wives appear to have greatest control over its expenditure. However, as research has shown, this is mislead-ing. What housewives have in reality is the responsibility to manage the household economy with limited, if not inade-quate, resources rather than the power to spend as they please (Burgoyne, 1990; Pahl, 1989; Vogler, 1994; Vogler and Pahl, 1994). Overall, in this phase of their marriage when they are without their own income, most full-time housewives feel eco-nomically dependent on their husbands.

A further feature of domestic labour that marks it off from other forms of work is its privatised character. With its increased division of labour, the dominance of factory produc-tion and the gradual removal of married women from employ-ment, nineteenth and early twentieth century industrialisation encouraged the development of the specialist housewife role. In doing so, it fostered a model of domestic servicing in which each household catered separately for its own needs (Barrett and McIntosh, 1982; Gilding, 1991; Smart, 1996). Nonetheless at that time there were still many communal elements to this work. In particular, for many working-class families over-crowded conditions meant that basic amenities, including water and cooking facilities, were shared. In addition, daily shopping, the use of facilities like public wash-houses, the presence of kin locally and the high proportion of married women in the full-time housewife role offered many housewives opportunities for social participation (Kerr, 1958; Roberts, 1984; Young and Willmott, 1957; see Allan, 1985).

Increasingly though, as the twentieth century developed, those features which fostered participation altered. Standards of domestic provision within the home improved, so that the use of communal amenities became less common. Most households possessed their own cooking, washing and cleaning appliances. New developments such as refrigeration, together with more effective transport for the majority of the population, also led to new patterns of shopping and consumption: the local shop was replaced by the out-of-town supermarket. Moreover, with owner-occupation and public housing replacing privately rented accommodation as the main form of tenure, different patterns of geographical mobility developed which resulted in people having less knowledge of those who lived nearby than they had had in the past. At the same time, with changes in employment patterns and in particular the 'feminisation' of the labour force, the numbers of full-time housewives decreased, leaving many localities relatively 'empty' during the working week (Devine, 1992; Richards, 1990).

These changes have had a significant impact on the experiences of full-time housewives. They have resulted in the role becoming structurally more isolated. In contrast to most forms of employment in which organisational conditions encourage social participation, housework as it is currently constructed offers few opportunities for sociability. The work is individualised; there are no set coffee or meal breaks; and there are no extra-organisational facilities (like trade unions, social clubs, professional meetings) for integrating with others. Without these forms of structural support, the full-time housewife has to make her own social contacts where she can. The result is that a proportion of women in this position can feel extremely isolated (Boulton, 1983; Oakley, 1974; Richardson, 1993).

Caring for young children is often experienced as being far more creative and expressive than most of the other tasks associated with domestic labour, though elements of it are also found to be highly constraining. The demands which young children make are time-consuming as well as repetitive and frustrating. The aspect of childcare which dominates most mothers' experiences is the degree of responsibility they have for their child(ren). In Boulton's (1983, p. 78) phase, it is 'a responsibility without bounds', both in terms of its impact on the mothers' activities and in the amount of time it involves. At an everyday level, childcare rules; whatever needs to be done is done in ways and to timescales which are heavily influenced by the needs of the child(ren) (Tivers, 1985).

However, childcare does offer some opportunities for meeting others sociably in a way which other aspects of housework do not. Contact with other mothers is highly important to most people in this situation (Bell and Ribbens, 1994). They provide relief from the monotony of the day, but as significantly also frequently act as a flexible resource that can be drawn on as needed. This may entail practical help, for instance, with 'emergency' or routine childcare, or advice and support on whatever matters are creating concern (Allan, 1989). Paradoxically, it is the structural isolation of full-time housewives that makes the need for informal relations with others so paramount. Yet while such informal contacts are key, somewhat ironically they can also cement the loss of separate identity that 'responsibility without bounds' frequently entails: that is, because interaction with these 'co-workers' is built around childcare and its associated practices, the relationships cannot provide a very full challenge to the underlying sense many mothers with dependent children have of their identity being constantly submerged within the mothering role. Their social dependence on other mothers, while providing many satisfactions and benefits, tends to reinforce their perception of themselves as, in that well-worn but deeply meaningful phrase, 'just a housewife'.

From this discussion, it is evident that the full-time housewife and mother is in a structural position quite different from that of most other workers. The resources that she typically has at her command are quite limited. Economically she is disadvantaged. Within a society dominated by wage labour, her lack of earnings leads to a devaluation of her work and a financial dependence on her husband to whose earnings she is rarely defined as contributing (despite doing so through her unpaid servicing work). In addition, she is disadvantaged socially. Her work does not bring her into contact with many others in a fashion that easily fosters a fuller social integration. While this may not make her dependent socially on her partner, it does frequently leave her with less opportunity than he has for participating socially. This imbalance is compounded by the potential he has to oversee her work and to criticise her for the way she distributes her time. Comments such as 'I wish I could sit around chatting with my mates' may be made half in jest, but they nonetheless have a force which stems from the unequal power husbands have over wives who work full-time in the home.

## Conclusion

This chapter has been concerned with the early years of partnership and marriage. In an ideological climate that emphasises the role of personal relationships as a principal route to self-fulfilment and happiness, there has been a marked move away from understandings of marriage which emphasise aspects of social commitment to a perspective which highlights the continuing quality of the relationship. As this happens, the belief that marriage is a life-long commitment is undermined, as is the once strong normative link between sexual expression and marriage. The result is an increasing emphasis on love as the basis for partnership and an acceptance of cohabitation as morally unproblematic, whether or not it leads to marriage.

Whether or not love is a basic human emotion, its expression and significance are culturally constructed rather than being uniform across place and time. What people take as love, the emotions that are experienced and the ways in which these are socially managed are all elements within a broader framework of understandings about the nature and character of personal relationships within social life. As we discussed in Chapter 1, several writers have argued that a process of individualisation has developed in modern society, in which the 'right' of individuals to seek personal happiness is prominent. An element within this is the emphasis placed on sexual/romantic love as a both basis for the development and, importantly, the continuation of partnerships. With some significant ethnic differences, love is now taken as the principal rationale for developing and sustaining relationships. Moreover the decline of love is now given far greater legitimacy as a justification for the ending of committed relationships than it was in the past. The idea of 'empty marriages' in which the spouses gain little fulfilment from one another is still current, but maintaining such unions for their own sake carries little force culturally. What matters increasingly is the continuing personal solidarity the couple feel towards one another rather than any previous promise of a lifelong commitment.

The rapid growth of cohabitation at the end of the twentieth century needs to be understood as an element within wider changes in the social construction of partnership. Originally involving those who were separated or divorced, and often invoking opprobrium and stigma, cohabitation has now become part of the normal route into marriage for the majority of couples. Moreover, growing numbers of couples are cohabiting as an expression of their commitment to one another without any assumption that this will eventually lead to marriage. Along with changes in divorce and the greater acceptance of gay partnerships, the normalisation of cohabitation expresses very clearly the changes there have been to the balance between social and personal commitment in the social ordering of personal life. Changing forms of contraception and, in particular, women's greater control of fertility, have played a significant part in liberalising sexual relations and making cohabitation acceptable, but this is just one element within a broader mosaic. These changes reflect altered perspectives of the purpose and meaning of marriage. Marriage and other forms of partnership are now perceived by the majority as being about individual fulfilment and personal happiness rather than social order and material welfare.

Despite the demographic changes there have been, the majority of people still marry, particularly when they decide they would like to have children. In turn, children usually entail significant modifications being made to the domestic division of labour. Childless cohabiting couples often emphasise a joint approach to paid and unpaid work, but once children are born, or indeed envisaged, the worlds of male and female work tend to diverge along traditional lines. In particular, responsibility for childcare remains predominantly a maternal one, with the provision of household income being seen as principally a male responsibility. It is a husband's career that is prioritised over a wife's; and it is wives who assume most responsibility for domestic servicing. Thus for many couples, the birth of children encourages a more rigid division of labour and increases women's social and economic dependence, albeit somewhat less than it did for previous generations.

The next chapter develops these themes by focusing on later phases of marriage. In particular it will examine the domestic division of labour more fully and assess the differential freedoms and responsibilities which husbands and wives typically have. This will entail analysing how financial resources are divided within marriage, as well as looking at other aspects of control and power, including domestic violence.

# 5  Marriage: The Structure of Domestic Relationships

We saw in the previous chapter that marriage is usually perceived as a highly personal relationship, one actively constructed by the two people involved in ways which reflect their own personalities and interests. At the same time, marriage is also frequently portrayed as one of the central social institutions in society, with change in its patterning being seen as threatening to social order. The reality is undoubtedly more complex. From a sociological viewpoint, the key to understanding the organisation and dynamics of marriage lies in recognising that as a significant social institution it will inevitably change as the social and economic formation of which it is part evolves. Obvious though this point is, it is often overlooked. To be incorporated as a central facet of social life requires adaptation in response to changes occurring elsewhere. In this sense, to be unchanging is to be structurally insignificant.

Thus marriage is never static. Individual marriages change over time, but, more importantly, the patterning of marriage also changes historically. One generation's marriages are not the same as those of the generation which follows nor of the previous one. This raises the issue of what 'marriage' actually is and, in particular, what aspects of marriage concern us here. This is especially relevant in a period characterised by historically high cohabitation rates, diverse household patterns, and greater freedom of sexual expression. Many of the traditional elements previously inherent in social understandings of marriage now also occur outside of formal marriage. At its simplest, marriage comprises the set of relationships constructed by couples who are legally recognised as being married. From this angle, the task of the sociologist is to specify how the diverse and common ways in which different aspects of these relationships are organised and structured. While this is clearly important, a different response is also pertinent, especially at a time when the social conventions governing traditional marriage are being questioned.

As people increasingly construct 'marriage-like' relationships outside of marriage, legally defined, then instead of looking at marriage as such, it becomes appropriate to ask how different aspects of 'marital' matters are organised generally. Questions can be posed about dominant patterns and trends in, say, household formation, the division of labour within households, the management of sexual relations, and the resources available to different household members, independent of the legal ties between those involved. In this, the emphasis is on the patterning of domestic and sexual 'partnership' rather than on marriage as embodied through a civil, religious or other publicly recognised ceremony.

If the organisation of marriage is more than personal, it remains important to ask in what respects it is influenced by structural characteristics within the wider society. This is a question that has long been of concern to sociologists. A part of the answer was provided in the previous chapter in which arguments about the heightened importance of love and personal compatibility in marriage and cohabitation were discussed. Closely tied to these ideas are notions about changes in the distribution of power within marriage. There is a widespread consensus that in the past marriage was structurally unequal, with husbands being highly advantaged. In this, marriage reflected the patriarchal nature of most social and economic activity. There are debates about the genesis of these inequalities but in general there is agreement that a significant move towards greater equality has subsequently been evolving.

What is far less clear from the various accounts which have been produced is exactly when these changes occurred, how far they have gone, what aspects of marriage have been altered, and who has been most affected by them. As discussed in Chapter 4, since the 1950s there have been strong arguments that marriage has become more companionate (Burgess and Locke, 1953; Fletcher, 1973). While expectations of emotional compatibility, common interests and shared time do not of themselves generate equality, there is a presumption in these largely functionalist approaches that, in practice, a more equal participation and sharing is entailed. At the same time though, these accounts of the growth of companionate marriage are built upon ideas of 'partnership' characterised by a high division of labour, a point which Parsons (1955) in his famous analysis of family interaction emphasised. In this, the responsibilities of husbands and wives inside and outside the home were seen as markedly differentiated, but because they were interpreted as complementary this was not taken as an impediment to the creation of more equitable relationships.

By the early 1970s, the functionalist domination of family sociology was being challenged. Far more critical accounts of family life emerged, incorporating a more sophisticated understanding of the nature of structured inequality within marriage (Barker and Allen, 1976; Bernard, 1976; Oakley, 1974, 1976). Nonetheless, the idea that the character of marriage was shifting remained powerful. In particular, the changes which had occurred in the labour market since the 1950s lent weight to arguments that wives were no longer as dependent on their husbands as they had been in previous generations (Finch and Summerfield, 1991; Summerfield, 1994). The greater participation of married women in employment was taken as providing wives with greater freedom and, together with other changes in women's social position, seen as empowering. While this was so, there was a tendency to extrapolate the changes occurring further than was actually warranted. Within British sociology, the publication of Young and Willmott's *The Symmetrical Family* in 1973, with its vision of husbands and wives having interchangeable roles in and outside the home, represented the apogee of such thinking.

Ideologies of marriage were also seen to be altering, with different satisfactions now being sought from the partnership. As discussed in Chapter 4, love was increasingly interpreted in ways which emphasised the rewards that emotionally close relationships could provide, with marriage being seen as far more than just a convenient domestic, sexual and familial arrangement. With significant social class and gender differences in its manifestations, the notion of the marital ideal now fully embraced emotional compatibility, 'togetherness' and the joint construction of a shared life (Crow, 1989a; Mansfield and Collard, 1988). In turn, with the increased acceptance of divorce, there was reduced tolerance of marriages which failed to provided intrinsic emotional fulfilment. Thus, marriage emerged as a relationship in which self-realisation and expressivity became increasingly central (Finch and Morgan, 1991).

## Equality and difference

Perceiving marriage as a relationship built upon mutual emotional interdependence fosters a sense of its being a relationship between equals. Yet, as feminist and other writers have demonstrated, it is highly debatable whether marriage has really become a structurally equal tie. Leaving aside issues of the gendered character of emotional expressivity (Duncombe and Marsden, 1993, 1995; Wood, 1993), other aspects of marital organisation continue to be highly differentiated. In particular, while aspects of wives' overall work patterns have been altering, there is less evidence that husbands' work patterns are also changing in a manner which impacts significantly on the organisation of domestic life: that is, while wives are now far more likely to be employed, research repeatedly shows that this has relatively little effect on the distribution of domestic responsibilities. As suggested in the previous chapter, wives still carry the major responsibility for domestic servicing, childcare and the management of familial relationships. Of course, this *may* not be important as a dimension of inequality; theoretically it is possible to have separate but equal spheres of responsibility within marriage. Usually, however, differentiated relationships have inequalities of power and resource distribution associated with them.

Determining whether this is so in marriage is not straightforward, given the dominant images of marriage outlined above. In particular, power, be it marital or political, is a notoriously difficult concept to define and operationalise (Lukes, 1974; Wrong, 1979). Different models make different assumptions about its character, and as a consequence seek different types of evidence to demonstrate its workings. Often, what proponents of one model regard as convincing evidence is considered by others adopting a different stance as anything but persuasive, disguising as much as revealing the real relationships of power. Similarly, mapping the distribution of activities and resources within households and understanding their significance is complex, partly because of the role that 'fairness' and 'sharing' play in the imagery that families have of their domestic allocation practices (Allatt and Yeandle, 1986; Doucet, 1996).

The standard approach to analysing power in marriage is the 'decision-making' model. With a history dating back to Blood and Wolfe's (1960) pioneering study of over 900 marriages in Buffalo, New York, the approach involves asking wives or husbands, occasionally both, who is more influential in making the important decisions which affect family life. While this seems simple enough, there are numerous problems associated with it, some more obvious than others (Allan, 1985; Cromwell and Olsen, 1975; Dempsey, 1997; Edgell, 1980; Safilios-Rothschild, 1969): for example, one issue for any decision-making study concerns the areas of decision-making which should be included. Presumably most would agree the decisions in question should be about significant rather than trivial matters, though there may be disagreement about what counts as significant. If a range of decisions is included, how should these different issues be weighted in calculating differential 'power'? Should questions be asked only about contentious issues, ones where husbands and wives have had a disagreement or at least an active debate? And how are these areas to be known in advance? Can areas in which frequent decisions need to be made be treated the same as ones made infrequently? Can people remember who was most influential in deciding infrequently-made decisions? Do frequently-made ones become routinised so that in effect no decision is made?

However, more fundamental questions than these methodological ones can be posed. To ask people about who made a decision assumes both that a decision was actually made in a purposeful fashion, and that the process by which that decision was reached is recognised by the respondents. Yet, as Lukes (1974) and others have argued, the exercise of power is not so simple. Many decisions are made in a routine and uncritical fashion. These may be decisions made frequently, where habit or 'standard practice' prevails: for example, in many households, decisions over routine childcare matters may normally be made by mothers without much consultation. Does this indicate power, or does it signify that this area of life has been delegated to her and in effect indicate the power of her husband in not having to address such matters? Or they may be decisions which are infrequently made. Let us stay with the example of childcare. Early in their marriages, many couples 'decide' that if they have children, responsibility for routine childcare will fall on the wife. Husbands' careers will consequently be privileged with wives' employment being given a lower priority (Mansfield and Collard, 1988). Yet how frequently is this key decision seriously debated? Is this really a 'decision' made by most couples or is it a largely unquestioned assumption shared by both parties? And if the latter, what does it say about the exercise of power?

Furthermore, people are not always conscious of the processes by which decisions do get made. In many marital decisions, especially those which involve radical change, high expenditure, and/or an element of contention, a good deal of debate and negotiation can occur before a decision is finally reached. This, of course, could signify a quite equal partnership with each side contributing to the final decision. Yet consultation and negotiation may also be a way in which decision-making is managed, rather than (or as much as) a genuine element of the decision reached (Edgell, 1980). In other words, those who are most powerful may use this form of 'open' approach to foster compliance without ever really having the outcome they favour put at risk. In Dempsey's (1997) terms, the negotiation takes a 'token' form. A false sense of participation and sharing is promoted which effectively disguises the real basis of power within the relationship. But if this is possible, it is, of course, equally possible that other strategies are being used by husband and wife to obtain their required outcomes without their spouse being fully aware of the games which are being played. Whatever the reality here, the important point is that the decision-making process itself is rarely as straightforward as the decision-making perspective presumes. Simply asking one or even both spouses who makes particular decisions, however important the issues referred to are, cannot reveal the full exercise of power. The processes are more complex than this (Jordan, Redley and James, 1994).

An alternative view of power is one which recognises that decisions are important in indicating where power lies but questions the necessary significance of the decision-taker. People who appear to be making decisions are not always the ones exercising most control. Indeed, one indicator of real power is being able to delegate decisions knowing that the 'right' choices will be made without the need for supervision, persuasion or coercion. What 'right' means here are decisions which further, rather than counter, the interests of those who are doing the delegating. Thus the key research question does not focus on who makes decisions but on whose interests are best served by the decisions which are reached.

In marriage, it is quite conceivable that one spouse makes most of the decisions but does so in ways which benefit or favour other family members more. In particular, a wife may make many of the important decisions within the household in ways which routinely prioritise the needs of her husband and children over her own. For instance, she may organise family activities in ways she knows will please them, shop for food which they prefer, and spend more on their clothes and entertainments than on her own (Charles, 1990). Does this make her powerful? She is, after all, responsible for these decisions; they are her acts. Or does it make her powerless, with everyone else's interests being put before hers? Because 'family' involves ideas of love and personal commitment, decisions one spouse makes which protect or further the interests of the other cannot be read simply as an indicator of lesser power. Within the relationship, the act of giving, of sacrificing one's own interests in favour of those of one's spouse can as easily be interpreted as an act of love as it can submission to domination. Perhaps it is the intrinsic benefits which matter most to her; satisfaction comes from seeing those she loves gain pleasure. In this sense, her interests are being served by the steady confirmation of her identity as a good mother and wife.

While there is a real problem in determining who benefits from decisions that are made, there are also clear difficulties in accepting at face value accounts which emphasise the intrinsic satisfactions of actions when those actions appear not to have extrinsic benefit. So in the example above, it may be that the wife does gain a vicarious satisfaction from the pleasures accruing to her husband and children. But equally, it is in the interests of those who are more powerful to persuade the less powerful that the intrinsic satisfactions they (the less powerful) are getting compensate for the explicit gains the more powerful are receiving. The more that power differentials are legitimised and seen as morally appropriate, the more secure that power is. By disguising the true disparities in a relationship, a contented (or grateful) sub-ordination can itself be a demonstration of power inequalities. However, assessing whether this is in fact happening is complex: for example, in the case above, husbands may be seen as exercising their power in this way, but it would be more difficult to argue that the children involved were also doing so.

A different approach to the analysis of power and inequality in marriage focuses explicitly on the distribution and allocation of resources within the relationship. Rather than asking who makes decisions or whose interests are best served by them, it concentrates more directly on who gets what. Clearly, some of the problematic issues raised above apply with similar force to this approach. In particular, even if inequalities in the distribution of resources can be demonstrated, problems remain if the apparently disadvantaged party in the relationship claims to be supportive of that distribution. This problem, common in all studies of power, is compounded in marriage because of the nature of the personal commitment on which the tie is based. However, a focus on resource distribution within marriage makes these issues overt and allows questions to be posed about why the resource inequalities which exist are so routinely tied to gender. In particular, it enables the connections between what has been called 'the black box' of the household (Brannen and Wilson, 1987) and the wider social formation to be appreciated. The key argument here – and one made throughout this book – is that what goes on within households, families and marriages can be understood only by placing these social units within their broader context. Specifically, the inequalities which exist within marriage, and the changes which are occurring in these, need to be located within the patterning of inequalities which exists outside the home. We can then begin to see how the decisions which couples take, contested or otherwise, and the interests which these decisions serve, are not independently constructed but are elements within a much larger structural framework.

## Households and work

To see this, let us consider the work done within households. In his influential study *Divisions of Labour*, Pahl (1984) developed the concept of 'household work strategy'. His concern was the range of work that contributed to the overall well-being of the household, including formal and informal paid work, work done for other households in exchange for work they do for you, self-provisioning (that is, goods produced for the household's own consumption), and routine housework. Pahl drew on the notion of 'strategy' to indicate that households came collectively to decisions about how to deploy their efforts within the constraints of the economic opportunities open to them. Questions have been raised about just how 'strategic' these decisions (or non-decisions) are (Anderson, Bechhofer and Kendrick, 1994; Warde, 1990). Strategy does after all imply a relatively high level of planning as well as some control over outcomes (Crow, 1989b). In some households there may be a great deal of negotiation about how work is best distributed; also, some have a good deal of control over just how much time is devoted to different forms of work. However, in households with fewer resources, the notion of strategic planning might be an unaffordable luxury or quite unfeasible (McCrone, 1994). In these circumstances, whatever work opportunities that present themselves have to be accepted, irrespective of any notion of planning.

Household work strategies will be discussed further in Chapter 9, but the term is employed here because it encourages questions to be posed about the distribution of different forms of work within the household. In the context of marriage, a key question concerns the priority given to different forms of work for husbands and wives. To what extent is the division of work within different households strategically decided? To what degree are these matters largely taken for granted, representing 'non-decisions' rather than purposeful decision-taking? In the first half of the twentieth century, there was hardly an issue here. The great majority of wives gave up employment and took on the major, if not sole, responsibility for domestic labour. As we saw in Chapter 4, most women also currently experience a period of full-time childcare and domestic work, usually early in their marriages. However, for many this phase is now relatively short. As Table 4.1 (p. 73) indicates, by the time their youngest child goes to secondary school, some three quarters of mothers are in employment. An important question is whether this employment leads to a renegotiation of responsibilities in the home, altering the structural dependence of wives/mothers. In order to examine this, it is necessary to consider how the labour market is structured and, in particular, the types of employment typically available for women.

Despite the claims made about the promotion of equal oppor-tunities since the mid-1970s, the employment structure has remained highly gendered. Women and men routinely work in different types of jobs, in different types of industry, and receive different rewards for doing so (Beechey, 1986; Crompton and Sanderson, 1990; Sly, Price and Risdon, 1997). Illustrating this is not at all difficult. To begin with, there is a very high concentra-tion of female employees in particular forms of work: for example, three-quarters of all clerical and secretarial workers are female, as are two-thirds of all personal service workers (cooks, cleaners, nursing/care assistants, hair-dressers) and sales staff. Just as importantly, these three broad areas of employment – clerical, personal service and sales – account for more than half of all female employees (Sly, Price and Risdon, 1997). By any standards, this is a remarkable level of concentration in a small number of occupational spheres.

Tied in with this level of concentration are two other key fea-tures of the occupational structure: levels of pay and participation. Over the last twenty years there has been remarkable consistency in the relationship between male and female pay. Broadly speak-ing, whatever skill level they occupy, women in full-time employment receive around two-thirds of the pay of men in equivalent types of jobs. Table 5.1. shows the hourly rates of pay which, on average, full-time manual and non-manual male and female employees received in 1999. Comparable figures of rela-tive earnings are given for previous years in Table 5.2 to illustrate how little change has occurred. Importantly these figures exclude any overtime pay, which in general increases these differentials further. Broadly similar differences occur even when skill level is broken down further: that is, males in the higher professions sys-tematically earn more than women in this work; unskilled manual women routinely get paid less than unskilled manual men. These differences do not arise from women being paid less than men for the same work. Equal pay legislation in Britain and Europe has reduced levels of such basic discrimination. Rather they arise primarily because of segregation in the types of jobs which men and women typically have.

**Table 5.1** *Average hourly rates of pay, April 1999 £s (Great Britain)*

|  | Men | Women |
| --- | --- | --- |
| Manual | 7.54 | 5.56 |
| Non-manual | 13.49 | 9.37 |

*Source*: New Earnings Survey, 1999.

These pay rates are for full-time workers. However, as can be seen in Table 5.3, there have been major increases in the proportion (and number) of women who are employed part-time. Currently some half of all women in employment are employed part-time (Sly, Price and Risdon, 1997). Officially, part-time work can be anything up to 30 hours per week, though the average part-time worker is employed for approximately half the hours of a full-time worker. Importantly, part-time workers are usually less well-paid than full-time workers in the same type of job (Beechey and Perkins, 1987; New Earnings Survey, 1999). Part-time work has other disadvantages as well, often having limited promotion prospects, less generous fringe and sickness benefits and reduced pension rights. Overall, part-time work tends to be seen not simply as lesser participation in employment but as representing a lesser commitment to it as well.

Of course, not all wives are employed in lower-level posts, and not all part-time work is low-paid or disadvantaging. There are increased opportunities for married women with appropriate

**Table 5.2** *Women's average hourly rate of pay as % of men's average hourly rate of pay Full-time (Great Britain)*

|  | Manual | Non-manual |
| --- | --- | --- |
| 1975 | 68 | 61 |
| 1985 | 71 | 62 |
| 1999 | 74 | 69 |

*Source*: New Earnings Survey.

**Table 5.3**   *Percentage of women employees employed part-time (Great Britain)*

|      | % of all women employed | % of all women employed part-time |
|------|------|------|
| 1951 | 33 | 12 |
| 1961 | 37 | 22 |
| 1971 | 43 | 34 |
| 1981 | 45 | 39 |
| 1991 | 50 | 51 |

*Source*: Beechey and Perkins, 1987; Census, 1991.

qualifications and experience to develop more high-powered careers. As we have seen, more wives (including those with school-age children) are employed full-time than a generation ago, and more are involved in 'careers' rather than routine 'jobs'. The women's movement in general, together with employers' awareness of prospective labour shortages due to demographic change, has resulted in companies adopting more 'women-friendly' recruitment, retention and promotional policies, as symbolised by Project 2000 to which a number of large companies aligned themselves in the early 1990s.

Yet overall, wives tend to occupy a secondary position within the labour force. They do so in a double sense. First, as argued above, the labour market remains highly gendered, with women's typical occupations having a lower status, lower prospects and lower rewards than men's. And secondly, although a minority of wives earn more than their husbands (McRae, 1986), most do not. Thus within the household, husbands' employment is routinely given priority over wives'. Typically, though with some variation, wives fit their employment around the perceived needs of other household and family members much more than husbands do (Brannen and Moss, 1991; Mansfield and Collard, 1988; Sharpe, 1984).

This happens at a range of levels. Chapter 4 illustrated how childbearing has an impact on employment, but equally how the growth of part-time employment is a direct consequence of the need, or desire, to be available for children and to manage the household. Amongst most couples with children, it is mothers far more than fathers who are responsible for organising childcare. Moreover when contingencies arise, such as children's illness or days when schools are closed, it is usually mothers who take time off, though this obviously depends on the details of work schedules and the other 'back-up' support available inside and outside the household (Brannen and Moss, 1991; Warrier, 1994). Further, husbands are typically freer to participate in work-related activities outside standard hours, be these formal or informal work meetings, trade union or professional activities. This is a relative matter, affecting some workers more than others. The issue, though, is not whether wives are able to engage in extra-curricular work activities when they wish, but the ease with which they can do so, and how such participation comes to be seen by all (including the women involved) as reflecting on their commitment to employment and consequently on their social identity.

The tensions between career and family development are most apparent in professional-type occupations which require high levels of commitment during their early phases, the very time when childbearing and child-rearing are also likely to be most demanding (Spencer and Podmore, 1987). If career momentum is lost in these years, it can become difficult to compensate. However, the processes involved in this apply to all levels of jobs. For many couples, there is a degree of incompatibility between the demands of employment and the demands and opportunities of family formation and household management, an incompatibility that becomes the greater when both individuals are employed in demanding jobs (Hochschild, 1996). How these are handled will vary from one couple to another. There can be a good deal of negotiation, certainly more than there was a generation or so ago, especially over specific, individual events, such as who stays home to cope with idiosyncratic or episodic contingencies. Typically, however, the general resolution of this tension comes through one of the spouses accepting (or being assigned) the major responsibility for family and domestic organisation, while for the other employment is more central. And in most households, though again not all, it is – for a range of reasons connected with socialisation, labour market segmentation, differential abilities and skills, and gender identities and relationships – wives who take on responsibility for childcare and household management.

The usual consequence of these processes is that the basic division of responsibilities arising early in the marriage are not
significantly renegotiated in later phases. Most husbands continue
to be defined (by themselves and their wives) as having the fuller
commitment to employment and the major responsibility for
financial provision. In contrast, wives' main commitment and
responsibility is defined (by themselves and their husbands) as
more that of organising and managing domestic life. These
definitions of their respective roles are supported by others
outside the household, seen as 'normal' (sometimes even
'natural'), and given strength through their congruence with
dominant gender ideologies. In turn, they frequently become
important elements within each individual's sense of self,
reflecting and sustaining their personal and social identities as
masculine and feminine.

Of course, some renegotiation of domestic contributions
occurs. Changes in this, as in other spheres of family life, are
routine. It would be curious if the division of specific tasks and
activities was never reconsidered, as the material and social circumstances of the household altered. The very fact of ageing,
especially of infants becoming school–age children and thence
adolescents and young adults, together with changing patterns of
employment, is bound to have some impact on the household's
mode of organisation. However, because husbands' employment
continues to be prioritised over wives' and because in general,
childcare tasks become less demanding as children mature, the
changes which arise are rarely ones which significantly undermine
the understandings of gendered domestic roles which emerged in
the early phases of a marriage. Husbands may make a larger
domestic contribution when their wives stop being full-time
housewives, but this rarely leads to their redefining their primary
responsibilities.

Indeed, as Gershuny, Godwin and Jones (1994) argue, the time
distribution of paid and unpaid work done by husbands and wives
becomes more unequal the more fully wives are employed. To
draw on Hochschild's (1990) evocative term, employed wives
frequently undertake a 'double shift', combining paid work with
domestic work disproportionately, compared to their husbands.
On the basis of 'time budget' studies, in which couples record the
time they spend on their various work and leisure activities, it is

clear that the relative (paid and unpaid) workloads of husbands and wives are most equal when wives are full-time domestic workers in the home. When wives return to employment, whether part-time or full-time, the distribution of work becomes more unequal precisely because domestic work continues to be their responsibility. Bittman and Pixley (1997) report similar findings for Australia, again based on detailed data on partners' time use. Gershuny, Godwin and Jones (1994) recognise a degree of change, with the inequalities between husbands and wives in total work performed reducing over time. However, they argue that because different forms of work are so gendered within the culture, such change is slow, occurring through gradual shifts in patterns of socialisation rather than as a simple consequence of direct negotiation between couples.

The division of work responsibilities also patterns how husbands' and wives' financial contributions to the household are perceived. Husbands' earnings are usually taken to be primary and, in a sense, more essential: that is, without the income he earns, the household would struggle to survive. Because this income is seen as critical, his employment is accepted as his major commitment. Even if personal satisfaction comes from familial and domestic life, his job is typically the element of his life which is prioritised. In contrast, a wife's employment, however significant for her well-being and for the welfare of the household generally, tends not to be held in the same light (Ward, Dale and Joshi, 1996). The income her employment generates is usually recognised as important if the household is to maintain the lifestyle it has developed, but in most instances it is nonetheless taken as secondary to her husband's earnings. Normally contributing a smaller amount, it is perceived as providing 'extras' or even 'luxuries' which the household could manage without if necessary. But to the degree that her employment is perceived as 'secondary' and thus 'voluntary' in a way her husband's is not, it does not substantially alter her primary responsibility of domestic organisation and household management. In contrast, husbands are much more likely to be regarded by themselves and others as 'breadwinners' (Potuchek, 1997).

This orientation to spouses' differential work commitments may have been modified somewhat in recent years as more households come to rely on two incomes to sustain their desired lifestyle, but the fundamental categorisation of male and female responsibilities has not been changed radically in most households. Negotiations over the division of activities within the household may now be more varied and complex than in the past, with more domestic activities undertaken jointly (Sullivan, 1996), but the division of primary responsibilities has not been substantially recast. Interestingly too, Mason's (1987) research on the division of responsibilities in retirement suggests that people often perceive little point in changing established divisions of labour later in a marriage. Those patterns upon which the marriage has been based for thirty or more years have stood the couple in good stead. Why alter a working relationship now, even if there are some perceived inequalities within it, particularly if wives consider the domestic sphere to be an area in which they are powerful?

## Money management

We can understand some of these issues more fully by examining the control and management of money within households. Until recently, this was a topic which received little attention from sociologists. There was an assumption, perhaps especially within more functionalist approaches to family sociology, that money was distributed evenly within families. What mattered were the overall financial resources available to the household, and the differentials there were between households, rather than the distribution of money between different household members. Recent research, however, has shown that it is important to consider how money is controlled and managed within the household if the realities of contemporary domestic life are to be understood (Burgoyne, 1990; Pahl, 1980; 1983; 1989; Vogler, 1994; Vogler and Pahl, 1994; Wilson, G., 1987). Although much of it has been quite small-scale, it has revealed the sometimes subtle ways in which the resources available to husbands and wives can differ.

Pahl's work has been particularly influential. She distinguished four broad patterns of money management within couple-based households (Pahl, 1983, p. 245–9; see also Pahl, 1989; and Vogler and Pahl, 1994).

(i)  *The whole wage system*: where typically the husband will hand over his whole wage to his wife, apart from a set amount for his own personal spending. She pools it with any income she has and is responsible for managing all household budgeting and expenditure. In fewer households, a whole wage system operates with husbands having sole responsibility for managing finances. With this latter arrangement, husbands have a great deal of control, often allowing their wives no personal spending money at all. It is a system which has been found to be common in studies of abused women (Binney, Harkell and Nixon, 1985; Homer, Leonard and Taylor, 1985; Pahl, 1985).

(ii)  *The allowance system*: where normally a husband gives his wife a set amount of money for specific areas of household expenditure. He retains the rest of his income and pays for agreed items from it. Thus both spouses have their own areas of responsibility. Where a wife is not employed and has no other income, she may feel she has little claim on money for her own use as the money she gets is for housekeeping rather than personal expenditure.

(iii)  *The pool (or shared management) system*: where both partners have equal access to all the money that comes into the household, and both are seen as having responsibility for managing household budgeting and expenditure. Both have access to personal spending money.

(iv)  *The independent management system*: where both partners have their own incomes which are kept separate rather than being pooled. Each partner will have responsibility for specific items of expenditure, though what these are varies. The essence of this system is that each person remains in control of their own money.

A problem with such typologies is that while many cases fit well into one or another category, there are inevitably some which are hard to place unambiguously. This is particularly so with issues like the management of household finance as so many variations are possible in practice. Moreover, as Burgoyne (1990) has pointed out, how money is organised and managed in a household is not static. Patterns are likely to alter as the earnings of husband and wife vary, as they will across different phases of family life: for example, the patterns established when a wife is at home caring for young children may well be different from those developed when the children are at school and she is employed part-time, and different again from those when she is employed full-time. Similarly, if the husband becomes unemployed, new ways of handling money may be negotiated between the couple.

However, Pahl's model does allow us to examine the relationship between the management of money within a household and the allocation of personal resources. A key question is whether different forms of household management result in husbands and wives receiving different benefits. In particular, do some forms represent a greater degree of equality? Do others signify female control or male dominance? On the surface, it would seem that the shared management system indicates a good degree of equality, while the whole wage system gives power to whoever it is who keeps the wage. However, the issue is not quite this simple. Conceptually, the problems are similar to those raised earlier in the discussion of decision-making. Just because someone is given responsibility for managing a budget does not necessarily mean that they are free to spend money as they wish. They may, in effect, be managing it in a way that benefits others more than themselves. In this, there is a difference between the day-to-day management of household money, the strategic control that is exercised and the access they have to money for their own ends.

This can be seen well in Vogler and Pahl's (1994) research, notable for being the first large-scale British study to examine patterns of household money management. The data they analyse were collected through interviews with over 1200 couples from six localities in Britain. Using self-report techniques, 26 per cent of Vogler and Pahl's sample classified themselves as using the *female whole wage* system; 10 per cent as using the *male whole wage* system; and 12 per cent as using the *housekeeping allowance* system. A negligible number of couples (2 per cent) said they operated the *independent management* system, but half of the couples claimed to organise their finances on the basis of the *pool* system (Vogler and Pahl, 1994, p. 270). This is perhaps not surprising, given the emphasis on equality within contemporary ideologies of marriage. In addition to asking which of the categories best fitted their system of financial management, the couples in the sample were also asked which of them had ultimate responsibility for organising household money. Two fifths of couples who placed themselves in the pool system both claimed that ultimate responsibility was shared jointly; but the remaining cases were divided equally between those in which at least one of the partners recognised that either the husband or the wife had ultimate responsibility. Thus in effect, in this research a six-fold classification applied, as detailed in Table 5.4 (which ignores those few couples reporting an *independent management* system).

Vogler and Pahl use this classification scheme to answer two questions: first, do husbands and wives experience financial hardship to the same degree; and secondly, do they have similar access to personal spending money? To explore the first issue, respondents were asked about the economies they had made over the previous two years to make ends meet, focusing on fourteen different items ranging from food and heating to social activities (1994, p. 278). The most noticeable difference was that wives were more likely than husbands to have cut back on meals and clothing, supporting the idea raised earlier that wives often 'make do' in order to protect the welfare of other household members. They also found that experiences of financial deprivation were linked to the system of financial allocation used in the household. Wives were much more likely to have experienced financial deprivation in households characterised by the housekeeping allowance, the female whole wage or the female pool systems. This was true irrespective of overall level of household income. The result is that wives in low income households using these systems of allocation were doubly disadvantaged, managing limited resources by cutting back on their own needs.

**Table 5.4**   *Household allocation systems*

| | |
|---|---|
| Female whole wage | 27 % |
| Male whole wage | 10 % |
| Housekeeping allowance | 13 % |
| Male managed pool | 15 % |
| Female managed pool | 15 % |
| Joint pool | 20 % |

*Source*: Vogler and Pahl, 1994, p. 272.

The same broad patterns were found with regard to personal spending money. Each of the couple was asked who normally had more money to spend on themselves. In the majority of cases (58 per cent) both spouses claimed there was no difference between them, a finding which may be influenced by the emphasis on equality in contemporary marriage. In 27 per cent of cases one or both spouses recognised the husband had more personal spending money, while in the remaining 15 per cent one or both thought it was the wife who had more. Importantly though, the three systems of financial allocation which were most associated with greater male spending were again the housekeeping allowance system, the female whole wage system and the female managed pool system. Thus in terms of both financial deprivation and personal spending money, these three systems of household allocation were clearly associated with wives being relatively disadvantaged.

Moreover, households in which these three allocation systems were used tended to be less well off than households in which the other systems of allocation were used: for example, the mean monthly income for households using the female whole wage system was approximately 80 per cent of that for households in which the male whole wage system was used. Thus, while at higher income levels there was greater equality, when families have fewer resources, the wife is the one most likely to bear the brunt. As Vogler and Pahl (1994, p. 285) conclude: 'In low income households the wife's responsibility for household finances served to protect the husband from the level of deprivation which she was experiencing and to guarantee his access to some personal spending money'. This finding is consistent with other studies which have also emphasised how, especially in poorer families, female 'control' of household budgets does not so much indicate power as responsibility for stretching inadequate resources, in part by prioritising others' welfare ahead of their own (Pahl, 1989; Wilson, G., 1987).

## Unemployment

One area of recent social change which might have led to a significant modification of domestic organisation is unemployment. The 1980s in particular saw levels of unemployment which would have been considered unacceptable in the preceding decades. With increases in married women's employment since the 1960s, this led to some speculation that the traditional division of household responsibilities might be modified, if not actually reversed, in households where husbands were made redundant. In reality the research evidence shows very clearly that such a modification did not usually happen. To understand the reasons for this, it is necessary to consider the impact which male unemployment has on the household. Of course, patterns of unemployment are highly varied. Some people experience unemployment for only a short period, managing to find new employment soon after being made redundant. Others have months and sometimes years without obtaining any secure employment. They may find short-term jobs for days or weeks, but in general are confronted with unemployment long-term. Each pattern creates its own tensions and responses within households so that treating the impact of unemployment as uniform is foolhardy.

However, from the research evidence collected since the early 1980s, it is possible to make some general arguments (Gallie, Marsh and Vogler, 1994; Harris, 1987; McKee and Bell, 1986; Morris, 1985, 1990a). Most importantly, unemployment typically leads to poverty. While some people receive quite generous redundancy packages, this is unusual. Most people do not receive significant compensation for redundancy and so quickly find themselves living at the economic margins. With male unemployment, one response to this might be for the couple to modify their roles with the wife becoming 'the breadwinner' and the husband taking on domestic responsibilities. In reality, this rarely happens (Gallie, Gershuny and Vogler, 1994). If anything, as McKee and Bell (1986) have argued convincingly, the poverty generated by unemployment makes the traditional division of labour more marked.

There are numerous reasons for this. A key factor is the interplay of the gendered character of employment and the state benefits system. As we saw earlier, women's full-time employment is normally paid significantly less well than men's, so that a household relying solely on a female wage is likely to be financially poorer. Moreover, where a wife is employed part-time, it is rare that the household can survive on this alone. Once the impact of the benefits system is considered, it becomes even less likely that a household will rely long-term on female-earned income. Because Income Support is means-tested rather than based on insurance contributions, income from any source reduces the benefit available for the household. In terms of net gain, the effect of this is that female employment often generates very little extra; earnings are deducted from the benefit paid, so that when costs associated with employment, like travel and meals, are also considered, the financial benefits of female employment for the household overall are often negligible. Furthermore, in Liebow's memorable phrase, unemployment does not fall like rain equally on everyone (cited in Sinfield, 1981, p. 19). It characterises some local labour markets more than others, and affects people without qualifications more than those with them. But in turn, households and families live in specific localities and often, though not always, share similar educational and other social attributes. In consequence, declining labour markets may well affect more than one household member. Certainly opportunities for wives to earn high incomes in areas where there is high male unemployment tend to be limited.

Consequently, employment levels for wives of unemployed men are significantly lower than the national average. Whereas nearly two-thirds of wives of employed men are themselves in full- or part-time employment, only about one-third of wives whose husbands are unemployed are in employment (Davies, Elias and Penn, 1994). Thus rather than signifying any radical renegotiation of domestic roles, male unemployment is more likely to be associated with wives not having employment. This minimises rather than encourages the likelihood of change in the domestic division of labour. The result is that wives feel 'doubly isolated', with little freedom to organise their lives independently of their husbands (McKee and Bell,1986). While much of his time is spent in the house, he is at least able to come and go quite freely within the constraints imposed by having little money, whether looking for work or engaging in other activities.

Moreover, various studies have shown that male unemployment often generates extra burdens for those women responsible for running the household (McKee, 1987; Morris, 1990a; Waddington, Wykes and Critcher, 1991). Thus, managing budgets is clearly more problematic when there are minimal resources coming into the household. Given the structural pressure for housewives to prioritise the needs of other household members ahead of their own, those attempting to manage at the poverty line are highly likely to forfeit their own needs in the interests of others. Furthermore, the experience of unemployment tends to undermine men's sense of self-worth. Because of the significance for many men of earning a living and providing financially for their families, unemployment can strike at the heart of their perception of masculinity. As a result, many wives appear loath to ask husbands to commit themselves more fully to domestic labour. Asking them to take on traditionally 'feminine' roles is seen as akin to hitting them when they are down. Wives more typically define their task as one of boosting self-esteem rather than undermining it further (Harris, 1987; Morris, 1985).

Thus it is in only a minority of cases, usually where a wife remains employed full-time (Gallie, Gershuny and Vogler, 1994), that men's unemployment ever leads to significant rearrangement of domestic roles. More frequently, the financial and social consequences of male unemployment reinforce the traditional division of domestic labour. It may be that non-traditional patterns are developed in households where neither partner has experienced significant episodes of employment since leaving school, though actually there is little evidence of new ideologies of masculinity and femininity incorporating gender equality emerging among this group (Wallace, 1987). And of course, if male unemployment within households tends to reinforce a conventional distribution of responsibilities and tasks, so too does female unemployment (Coyle, 1984). If wives are not in employment, it goes virtually without saying, and in most households without critical debate, that they are thereby available to assume their conventional role of managing everyday domestic affairs.

## Gay households

So far we have been considering heterosexual couples and arguing that their relationships are structured in ways which generate a marked division of labour and foster an unequal distribution of resources. But what happens with other couples?

In gay relationships, does a division of labour develop in equivalent ways and with equivalent results? The little research there
has been on this suggests that gay couples differ from heterosexual couples, and in particular married ones, both in their
desire to construct more equal relationships and in their
achievement of this; for example, Peplau, Venigas and Miller
Campbell (1996) refer to the ways in which many gay couples
prioritise an 'egalitarian ideal' and are far more vigilant in monitoring their success in achieving this than most heterosexual
couples.

Indeed many gay couples, whether male or female, actively
strive for relationships which are marked by *difference* from
dominant heterosexual patterns. Importantly for these relationships, they are nowhere near as grounded in an established and
socially validated division of labour, being less tied to an exter-
nally established gender order (Weeks, Heaphy and Donovan,
1999a). As Dunne (1997) suggests in her study of lesbian
couples, there are two elements in play here which make same-
sex partnerships different from heterosexual ones. First, structural inequalities are less institutionalised. In particular, labour
market inequalities do not shape these relationships as routinely
as they do heterosexual ones. Of course, some individuals may
have better-paid or more demanding jobs than their partners;
some may be employed only part-time or not at all. Where
such differences occur, they are likely to encourage different
roles within the household and possibly differential resource
distribution. But the extent to which they do so is far less
embedded within the cultural formation than is the case with
heterosexual partnerships (Heaphy, Donovan and Weeks,
1999).

Secondly, and largely for this reason, the sets of gendered
assumptions upon which heterosexual couples construct their
relationships are self-evidently of lesser consequence within gay
couples. Lesbian partners in particular tend to emphasise the
absence in their relationships of social conventions governing the
distribution of domestic and other responsibilities. Rather than
being constrained by the power of the dominant gender order,
they feel much freer to construct their relationships in ways they
choose, and in ways which are not experienced as unfair or
unequal. While men in gay relationships are less likely to focus on

issues of domestic inequality, they frequently emphasise the extent to which being in a gay partnership allows them to escape the constraints of dominant gender roles and to express alternative forms of masculinity (Oerton, 1997; Peace, 1993; Weeks, Heaphy and Donovan, 1999b).

But while gendered ideologies and differential access to material resources do not play the same role in fostering inequality for gay couples as they do in heterosexual partnerships, nonetheless many gay couples emphasise the need to be diligent in ensuring their relationships do not slip into routines which unintentionally become marked by inequality. Thus, whereas relatively few heterosexual couples emphasise the need to monitor and renegotiate their relationship (though see, for example, Risman and Johnson-Sumerford, 1998), this is an issue of continuing consequence in many gay relationships; for example, in Weeks, Heaphy and Donovan's research into gay partnerships and 'families of choice', their respondents stressed the importance of being reflexive and actively renegotiating their relationship's basis to ensure it remained balanced (Heaphy, Donovan and Weeks, 1999; Weeks, Heaphy and Donovan, 1999b). Such conscious monitoring of emergent patterns within these relationships, and the readiness of couples to alter their behaviour, contributed as much to the degree of equality achieved in the ties as the absence of structured gender differentials.

The fuller reflexivity characteristic of gay relationships is linked to a further feature that distinguishes them from most marriages. Despite high levels of divorce, marriage continues to be seen, ideally at least, as a lifelong relationship. This is built into conventional understandings of what 'marriage' means. In gay partnerships, that sense of permanence is muted. It may reflect the couple's current hopes, but there is frequently a greater sense of 'contingency' about these relationships, a recognition that circumstances or desires may alter in a fashion that would lead to the relationship's ending. These ties are, in this sense, much closer than marriage normally is to Giddens's (1992) 'confluent love' (see Chapter 4). This is a form of love in which commitment is premised solely on the satisfactions and pleasures which the relationship bestows; it is not built upon vows about the future, nor structurally embedded within a broader institutional framework. Once the relationship no longer meets the needs of those in it, that of itself is justification for its discontinuation. Many gay relationships seem to reflect this form of commitment; they self-consciously remain contingent upon continuing satisfaction. As a result of this, reflexivity and negotiation play a larger part in these relationships than they do in many (though not all) heterosexual relationships. Within this relational climate, equality has a much firmer footing and a higher priority (Weeks, Heaphy and Donovan, 1999a).

## Domestic violence

So far in this chapter, no mention has been made of violence as a form of control in marriage, though there is now plenty of evidence that physical coercion does play a significant part in a sizeable minority of marriages. Straus, Gelles and Steinmetz (1980) estimated that domestic violence occurred in one in eight marriages in the United States. And in an early analysis of domestic violence in Britain, Marsden (1978) calculated that serious violence occurred in some 5 per cent of marriages. Conversely, on the basis of recent research in north London, Mooney (1996) suggested that between a quarter and a third of women suffer domestic violence at some stage in their lives. However, domestic violence often remains hidden from public view, with those suffering it being too frightened or embarrassed to make it known, so such estimates are always open to question (Elliot, 1996; Hanmer and Maynard (eds), 1987; Nazroo, 1995). While attitudes have altered since the early 1970s when the first refuges for battered women were opened (Dobash and Dobash, 1987; Pahl (ed.), 1985), marital violence is still frequently perceived as essentially a private issue which couples need to resolve between themselves (Foreman and Dallos, 1993).

Some American research, specifically that associated with Straus's Conflict Tactics Scale (Straus, Gelles and Steinmetz, 1980; see also Straus *et al.*, 1996), concludes that both husbands and wives at times use violence against their spouses. Based on large-scale questionnaire surveys in which couples are asked to report violent incidents, this research views domestic violence as a component of dysfunctional relationships to which some spouses resort in periods of conflict. Contentiously, it is not seen as a means by which one spouse (or partner) attempts systematically to control the other. (For critical reviews, see Dobash and Dobash, 1992; Dobash *et al.*, 1992; Johnson, 1995.) Most British research into domestic violence adopts a quite different perspective. Predominantly based on interviews with relatively small samples of abused women, it concludes that domestic violence is frequently a means by which particular husbands do exercise a high degree of control over their wives. Such violence is neither isolated nor haphazard, but threatened or used systematically by husbands as a means of enforcing their will.

In a recent attempt to evaluate these two different perspectives, Nazroo (1995) conducted a study of 96 couples drawn from General Practitioners' lists of patients. The couples were selected from patients who had recently consulted their doctors over a stressful event. Some two-thirds of those that Nazroo approached agreed to participate in the study. The crucial point about this sample is that it was not based on respondents known to have experienced marital violence. Violence may have been a factor in their initially consulting their GPs about stress, but this played no direct part in the selection of respondents. While the sample cannot be treated as representative of the population overall, it does offer a solid basis for understanding the context of domestic violence. Both partners were interviewed separately and asked in detail about all non-playful episodes of physical aggression that had occurred within the marriage.

Like Straus and his colleagues, Nazroo found that violent acts were not only perpetrated by husbands but also by wives. He reports that 38 per cent of the men in the study and 55 per cent of the women had been violent at some time in their current relationship and this involved over three-fifths of all the couples. In this regard, the study seems to support those interpretations which see violence as a non-gender specific issue of relationship dynamics. However, there were very significant differences in the nature of the violence used by some of the male respondents which undermine this conclusion. To see this, it is necessary to focus on what most would recognise as the more serious episodes of violence. This entails violence which is injurious (defined as violence which has a definite possibility of causing physical injury) or intimidating (defined as violence that is deliberately used to frighten or intimidate the partner) (Nazroo, 1995, p. 492). When only these more significant forms of violence are considered, the balance between husbands and wives changes markedly. Nineteen of the 96 men in the sample had been this violent, compared to only six of the women. Moreover if this is further narrowed to violence which is threatening, rather than violence used in self-defence, the number of women included is reduced to four.

The contexts and consequences of this level of violence were also quite different for men and women. Of the four women, one had punched and kicked her husband during psychotic breakdowns; two had once thrown a heavy object; and one had punched her partner, but came off worse when he retaliated. In none of these violent episodes did the male partner suffer serious harm or feel threatened. They all felt able to control the violence. In contrast, the violence committed by men was far more damaging. Eight of the nineteen repeatedly beat up their partners in a severe fashion, with a further two doing so on one or two occasions. One wife was less severely beaten up physically, but she was also assaulted sexually. Six were assaulted in a less severe fashion, and the remaining two were slapped and pushed coercively (Nazroo, 1995, p. 486). Most importantly, these attacks were experienced as highly threatening. The women were unable to protect themselves as the men did, and did not know when the next assault might come. Thus not only was the violence far more severe and more frequent, but it also left them in a state of fear. It thus represented a quite different, and more threatening, experience to that of the violated men.

As can be recognised, the serious male violence reported in this study, as in other research (see, for example, the studies reported in Hanmer and Maynard, 1987), was directly concerned with issues of control. It involved husbands using aggression, and importantly the fear of aggression, as a means of dominating their wives and ensuring their subjugation. Women's violence towards their partners, and some of the male violence, was not of this form. This raises the issue of whether it is appropriate to conceive of all instances of domestic violence as equivalent. In an analysis which reconciles some of the disputes between those who view domestic violence as a component of dysfunctional relationships and those who perceive such violence as about coercion and control, Johnson (1995) suggests that the different schools fail to recognise two distinct patterns of domestic violence. Johnson terms the first of these 'common couple violence': principally this comprises occasional outbursts of violence within relationships at times of high stress. Such violence, Johnson argues, is not systematic and does not function as a means of subjugation; nor is it gender-specific. It is a form of physical response to contingent relationship tensions resorted to at times, typically infrequently, by some individuals (both male and female) in some couples. It is, according to Johnson, this pattern of domestic violence which research using measures like Straus's Conflict Tactic Scale uncovers.

The second pattern of domestic violence which Johnson analyses is radically different from 'common couple violence'. He terms this second pattern 'patriarchal terrorism', a graphic term which accurately describes the serious violence reported by Nazroo as well as those researchers adopting a more feminist perspective. This violence is neither occasional, contingent nor gender-neutral. Instead it represents a systematic, repeated and quite deliberate means by which some men exercise control and domination over their partners. As with Nazroo's sample, fear is a major element within this pattern of control. Johnson's terminology rightly emphasises that it is a form of terrorism in which the victim lives in constant fear, never knowing when the next attack will occur. Indeed, often there is no need for further violence: a raised arm or even a certain glance may be sufficient to assert control and produce the desired compliance. While all domestic violence may be censured, it is this pattern, highlighted most effectively in research based on samples of abused women who have sought refuge in shelters, which is most damaging individually, and significant politically and socially.

One consequence of Johnson's second pattern of domestic violence (patriarchal terrorism), is that the women involved are frequently left feeling personally inadequate and socially isolated. Despite the increased awareness there is of domestic violence, research has shown that each victim tends to individualise the problem and to see it as, in some sense, her own fault. Partly, this is due to a loss of confidence as a result of the physical abuse and the systematic verbal undermining that usually accompanies it. But it is also a result of women being socially assigned the prime responsibility for domestic and familial relationships. When these relationships go seriously awry, it is easy for the woman to blame herself for not managing them properly. She must be doing something wrong – emotionally, sexually, domestically – if this is happening to her marriage. In turn, feelings of shame arise because the state of her marriage is so far removed from contemporary ideals of what partnerships should be like.

As a result, these emotions frequently contribute to the women involved being socially isolated (Dobash and Dobash, 1980). Not wanting to be stigmatised, they often try to hide the violence from people they know. In addition, though, they generally fear their husband's reactions if they do tell other people of their experiences. Detailed accounts of such domestic violence regularly reveal that husbands threaten their wives with further violence if ever they report what has happened. Frequently too, women who have escaped to refuges describe how their husbands policed their activities, opening their letters and leaving them with little or no money (Homer, Leonard and Taylor, 1985). At times, it seems remarkable that the men involved are able to dominate their wives to the extent they do. However, as in Nazroo's research, the key is the fear which they are able to generate through the threat of violence, as well as its execution (Dobash and Dobash, 1992; Pahl, 1985).

Importantly, when abused women do confide in others, the support they receive is often muted. At a formal level, the relevant agencies by no means always provide appropriate or supportive services (Hague and Malos, 1993; Lupton and Gillespie, 1994; Malos and Hague, 1997; Mullender, 1996). In particular, despite policy initiatives, the police are often still regarded as treating domestic violence as different from other forms of violence, as just a domestic dispute (Radford and Stanko, 1996). Equally, informal support is often less effective than might be assumed. There is a pervasive sense that others who have not experienced domestic violence cannot possibly understand it. Moreover, practically, friends and even kin can rarely be of much help. There are no ready solutions to systematic abuse besides leaving the home. And often, friends and others do not want to become embroiled in a conflict over which they have little control. Indeed in some cases, particularly in communities where 'traditional' family values are firmly held, the dominant response may be one of trying to 'save' the marriage (Bhatti-Sinclair, 1994).

This is why refuges for abused and battered women have become so important, even though the number of places in them remains below official recommendations made in the 1970s. When women do leave violent relationships for a refuge, they typically experience a high degree of support from others who know what it is like to be the victim of real and threatened violence, who have knowledge about the relevant support services available, and who have successfully come through the experience and begun to rebuild their lives (Binney, Harkell and Nixon, 1985; Pahl, 1985). In Dobash and Dobash's (1992, p. 90) words, refuges provide battered women with 'safety, an end to isolation, companionship, solidarity, independence and mutual assistance'. Importantly too, through the refuge, the women can access a network of other resources, including routes to finding more permanent housing. As Hague and Malos (1993) argue, empowering and personally transformative though refuges are, they are designed to meet the immediate needs of women escaping from violent relationships. In the longer run, what these women need is access to adequate material resources, not least safe, permanent housing, which will allow them the opportunity to reconstruct their lives without the fear of further violence (Dobash and Dobash, 1992).

## Conclusion: Marriage and structural dependence

As discussed in Chapter 4, structural inequality is often apparent in the early phase of marriage when there are young children in the family. In particular, wives who take a break from employment in order to care for infants and young children frequently come to feel highly dependent on their husbands for their way of life. This clearly alters when they return to employment, as their economic contribution to the household becomes more evident and their social participation more varied. Yet for many such women, especially those who return to paid work on a part-time rather than full-time basis, the patterns established in their marriages do not alter that noticeably. They remain in a disadvantaged position with regard to the overall distribution of resources within the household (Brannen and Moss, 1991; Delphy and Leonard, 1992; Dempsey, 1997).

In the great majority of marriages, the overall division of responsibilities continues in a relatively traditional form. Social class, generational and ethnic identities also influence the detailed ways in which households organise their activities, but gender is, without question, the dominant factor (Brannen and Wilson, 1987; Gershuny, Godwin and Jones, 1994; Warrier, 1994). Some men may now do more within the domestic sphere than their predecessors did. In this regard there has been a process of 'privatisation' occurring, though its timing and significance remains a matter of some debate (Allan and Crow, 1991; Pahl and Wallace, 1988; Procter, 1990). Particularly when there are children in the family, men's lives have become more 'home-centred'; increasingly they expect this area to provide them with emotional as well as material satisfactions. Many fathers are now more actively involved with their children than they were in preceding generations. Changes in domestic technology have also meant that opportunities to construct the home, both materially and symbolically, have developed in ways which have gradually altered men's perception of, and commitment to, the domestic sphere (Allan and Crow, 1989; Bowlby, Gregory and McKie, 1997).

Yet, despite this historic tendency towards 'home-centredness', along with wives' increased participation in employment, the division of responsibilities and resources within marriage has not been altering as much as is popularly imagined. Certainly, women's earnings give them a degree of financial independence which is highly valued, but, as noted, these earnings are typically less than their husbands', especially when children are still of school age. In turn, the demands made on their time continue to be different from those made of their husbands'. Men's timetables, shaped largely by their employment patterns, tends to be more 'blocked' than women's, thereby allowing 'space' for leisure. While the immediacy of children's demands reduce as they get older, the daily routine of domestic life, including the 'tyranny of meals' (Land, 1978), imposes a far more 'bitty' timetable on most wives. Indeed the combination of paid work and domestic responsibilities, including where appropriate contributing to care for infirm elderly parents, can leave wives with relatively little time for personal leisure pursuits (Green, Hebron and Woodward, 1990).

Thus in terms of control of the key resources of time and money, even in later phases of marriage, wives continue to be relatively disadvantaged. Such disadvantage grows in significance in the context of continued male dominance of 'public life'. Again it would be wrong to suggest that the public sphere is as closed to women as it has been in the past. Nonetheless, the character of male and female non-familial leisure activities continues to be quite distinct. Whereas men have easy access to a wide range of organisations and facilities, women's access tends to be more restricted and on occasion still dependent on male 'sponsorship', informally if not formally. The sometimes subtle, sometimes overt, control which men can informally exert in such settings makes many women wary of using them unless accompanied by others. (For a classic account of some of these processes, see Whitehead, 1976; Hey, 1986 and Hunt and Satterlee, 1987 are also relevant.) The fear of violence in public spaces is also an important factor in constraining women's leisure activities. The frequency with which physical and sexual attacks are reported in the media attests to the dangers which exist (Hanmer and Maynard, 1987; Hanmer and Saunders, 1993; Hester, Kelly and Radford, 1996).

Thus marriage in all its phases continues to be structurally unequal. The inequalities may not be as marked as they once were, but they continue, despite the rhetoric of equality which informs contemporary marital ideologies. In this regard, individual marriages are constructed within a wider social and economic environment patterned by gender socialisation and gender identities. The gendered inequalities of the public sphere are mirrored in the private negotiations through which marriages evolve. Ironically, this can be seen most clearly when marriages end, as Delphy (1976) has argued. These issues will be discussed more fully in the next chapter. It is sufficient here to note that poverty is common among single mothers, whether separated, divorced or never married. In Cheal's (1996) phrase, the 'income pools' to which they have access are shallower than those of married couples. This, in turn, can lead to relatively restricted social lives. In this, the experiences of no longer being married serve to highlight that husbands and wives have unequal access to resources, with wives as a consequence being structurally dependent.

# 6  Lone-Parent Families: Divorce and Single Parenthood

As we have seen, major demographic shifts have been occurring over the last three decades. Nowhere is this more evident than in the growth of lone-parent families. Since 1970, the number of family units in which there is only one parent has increased from under 600,000 to over one and a half million by the mid-1990s. Such rapid change is remarkable. Behind it lie two significant demographic trends, both of which are related to broader changes in familial and sexual relationships. They each reflect an acceptance of diversity and individual choice which was far less pronounced in previous eras. The first of these trends is the increased incidence of marital breakdown, or, perhaps more accurately, the increased tendency for unhappy marriages to be legally and socially terminated. The second trend is the rise in births to unmarried mothers. Not all of these births lead directly to lone-parent families, as a significant proportion of these mothers are cohabiting at the time of the birth. However, increasing numbers are not, and of course those who are will experience lone parenthood if their cohabiting relationship ends.

This clearly indicates that the routes into lone parenthood are varied, as indeed are the routes out. However, before discussing these issues in depth, it is worthwhile considering terminology. We have so far been referring to 'lone-parent families' in an unproblematic way. In reality the issues are more complex: for example, does it matter whether we use the term 'single parent' or 'lone-parent'? Is there a difference between these two? And should we here be referring to 'families' or 'households'? With what type of organisation/unit are we principally concerned?

In many respects, the distinction between 'lone' and 'single' parent is an arbitrary one. However, given that 'single' at times also carries the meaning of 'unmarried' (that is, never married), it is perhaps more appropriate to use the term 'lone-parent' when referring to the broader category of all lone-parent families. However, it must be remembered that neither of these terms is fully appropriate, at least not for all the families involved. Parents do not necessarily stop being involved as parents simply because they do not live together as a couple. Their parenting role can, and many would say should, continue, albeit often in an attenuated form. The ending of a marriage or cohabitation does not mean that all contact with any children involved also ends, even if in practice this happens more often than many policy-makers and researchers deem desirable. In referring to families/households (in which there are dependent children but only one parent normally present) as lone-parent families, we must not assume that the other parent has no continuing social relationship, and no economic or legal responsibilities.

A further issue raised here is whether we are talking about 'lone-parent families' or 'lone-parent households'. The term 'lone-parent family' is more common in everyday discourse, but 'lone-parent household' is generally the more accurate. In other words, what marks off lone parenthood from dual parenthood is not the absence of the other parent in a kinship sense, though this may sometimes be the case, but rather the absence of the other parent from the day-to-day organisation of parenting and household routines. Thus, normally when the topic of lone parenthood is raised, the issues being addressed concern the practical management of a domestic unit in which there are dependent children but only one adult. Of course, this 'practical management' embraces matters to do with child development, control and socialisation, issues which are within the cultural realm of 'family' more than 'household', as well as with the running of the home and the coordination of the domestic economy.

Moreover, the term 'lone-parent household' carries its own difficulties (Rowlingson and McKay, 1998). In particular, when a lone-parent forms a household with one or more other adults, this does not always entail the end of lone parenting. Aside from questions about when a cohabiting partner becomes a step-parent, what happens when a lone parent moves back in with her (or his) parents, or shares a household with another lone parent? In these cases, the term 'lone-parent household' raises as many issues as it resolves. Essentially, both 'lone-parent family' and 'lone-parent household' are problematic terms, reflecting the general difficulty of defining criteria which clearly distinguish 'family' from 'household'. In this chapter we are going to follow common usage and generally allow the term 'lone-parent family' to signify the lone-parent family/household complex, despite the terminological concerns which arise.

## Divorce

As we have seen, the divorce rate has increased very significantly in the last thirty years. Table 2.1 (p. 25) provided details of this increase, in terms of both the numbers and rates of divorces occurring. The divorce rate has risen from 4 per 1000 marriages in the late 1960s to over 13 per 1000 marriages by the mid-1990s. Increases in the divorce rate have been relatively low since the early 1980s when it stood at approximately 12 per 1000 marriages, but nonetheless, if the situation remains as it is now (with no further increase), 40 per cent of couples currently marrying will divorce (Haskey, 1996a). In other words, from being a comparatively rare event prior to the 1970s, it is now almost a 'normal' occurrence. Like some of the other demographic changes occurring since the 1970s, including cohabitation and births outside marriage, this represents an enormous shift in patterns of family organisation. It needs to be remembered too that these figures represent legal marriages which have been legally terminated. In addition there is a large, though imprecisely known, number of cohabitations which also end. While probably the majority of these are not perceived by those in them as 'marriages', some are closely akin to marriage in their social, economic and domestic consequences. When these cohabitations end, the distinction between this and divorce is likely to be quite small. Similar emotions are likely to be experienced and equivalent issues have to be resolved.

As the numbers of divorces have increased, the tendency has been for divorce to occur earlier in a marriage, though, as

**Table 6.1**  *Percentage of divorces by length of marriage in years (England and Wales)*

| Length of marriage | 1974 | 1984 | 1997 |
| --- | --- | --- | --- |
| 0–4 | 16.3 | 21.1 | 21.7 |
| 5–9 | 29.6 | 28.3 | 28.1 |
| 10–14 | 18.6 | 18.9 | 17.9 |
| 15–19 | 13.0 | 13.2 | 12.3 |
| 20+ | 22.4 | 18.5 | 20.0 |

*Source*: Marriage, Divorce and Adoption Statistics.

Table 6.1 shows, this has been quite a gradual change. Over a fifth of all divorces currently occur within the first four years of a marriage, compared to only 16 per cent in the mid-1970s. Conversely, a fifth of divorces occur in marriages which have lasted for twenty or more years, a proportion which is comparable to that for the mid-1970s and the mid-1980s. Yet while the proportion of divorces arising after twenty years of marriage has remained relatively stable, the absolute numbers of couples divorcing after this length of marriage has increased. In 1974, there were approximately 25,000 divorces of couples who had been married for at least 20 years; the equivalent figure for 1995 was over 30,000.

As the number of divorces has increased, so too has the number of children who experience a parental divorce. It is important to recognise that divorce does not affect only the couple: it also impacts very heavily on children in the family. The ways children experience divorce will be discussed more fully later in this chapter. Here the focus is on the number of children of different ages whose parents divorce each year. Details are provided in Table 6.2 for divorces occurring in 1997. As can be seen from this, over half of these divorces involved couples who had children under the age of 16. Broadly speaking, there are as many such children experiencing their parents' divorce each year as there are divorces. Haskey (1997) has estimated that currently 7.5 per cent of children experience parental divorce by their fifth birthday, 19 per cent by their tenth birthday and 28 per cent by the time they are sixteen.

These tables, together with Table 2.1, all detailing some of the official statistics routinely generated through divorce procedures,

**Table 6.2** *Number of children whose parents divorced 1997 (England and Wales)*

| Age of child | Number of children |
| --- | --- |
| 0–4 | 41,524 |
| 5–10 | 67,085 |
| 11–15 | 41,700 |
| All children | 150,309 |
| Total number of divorces | 146,689 |
| Total number of divorces with children under 16 | 80,670 |

*Source*: Marriage, Divorce and Adoption Statistics.

provide an overview of the demography of divorce. Very extensive changes have clearly occurred since the 1960s. In coming to understand these changes though, it is important to recognise what these figures represent. They are statistics generated through the legal procedures of divorce. They represent the formal, legal ending of a marriage. In this they are very accurate. However, from a sociological viewpoint, divorce as a legal act is only one element, albeit an important one, of the social reality of divorce. As sociologists, we need to focus not just on the legal outcome, but on the social processes resulting in that legal occurrence and with its consequent social and economic ramifications.

In particular, it is important from a sociological perspective to focus on the ending of a marriage rather than on the divorce itself. Currently, there is a high correlation between these two. The great majority of marriages which have ended in emotional, sexual, social and economic terms are also legally terminated by divorce. This though has not always been the case: for example, until 1857, divorces could be obtained only through an individual Act of Parliament. This made divorce an impossibility for all but the wealthiest couples. Indeed, until 1949, when Legal Aid was made available for divorce, relatively few couples could afford the high legal costs of divorcing (Gibson, 1994; McGregor, 1957). Many couples lived in moribund, 'empty-shell' marriages – sometimes unhappily in the same household, sometimes in different households – without seeking divorces. In Britain it is really only since the 1969 Divorce Reform Act that divorce has become easily available to the majority of people.

This Act has been central in shaping contemporary notions of divorce in Britain. Prior to 1969, the law treated marriage as a contract between two people who agreed to abide by certain 'rules'. The breaking of those 'rules' through adultery, desertion and cruelty could result in the injured ('innocent') party obtaining a divorce by suing for breach of contract. However, unless a spouse could be proven to have broken the marital contract, the other spouse could not secure a divorce. Thus, even if a husband or wife had left the spouse and was living with another partner, he or she could not divorce unless they could prove that the spouse had also committed adultery or otherwise broken the marital contract. The social ending of the marriage was not of itself relevant for divorce unless the 'innocent' spouse decided to sue for divorce.

The 1969 Act changed this fundamentally, being premised on a very different view of marriage (Farber, 1973). Instead of seeing marriage as a contract, under this legislation, marriage was perceived much more as a relationship. When that relationship broke down, that in itself justified its ending. Thus the key issue under the 1969 Divorce Reform Act was whether there had been an 'irretrievable breakdown' of the marriage. If there had been, then divorce was appropriate and was sanctioned by the courts. This still left the issue of how an 'irretrievable breakdown' was to be defined. The 1969 law continued to define adultery, desertion and unreasonable behaviour as serious breaches of the marital tie and so took them to represent irretrievable breakdown, though over time what came to be defined as 'unreasonable' altered significantly (Gibson, 1994). Symbolically though, the other ways in which the Act defined 'irretrievable breakdown' were most significant. It allowed divorce when the couple had been living apart for a period of two years, provided both agreed to the divorce, or when they had been living apart for five years if only one of the spouses consented to the divorce. In theory the Act also removed issues of 'innocence' or 'guilt' from the legal proceedings, relying solely on whether the marriage was judged to have broken down irretrievably; though, as Smart (1984) argues, issues of

**Table 6.3**   *Grounds for divorce 1997 % (England and Wales)*

|  | Women | Men |
|---|---|---|
| Adultery | 15.7 | 10.1 |
| Unreasonable behaviour | 36.9 | 7.7 |
| Desertion | 0.4 | 0.3 |
| 2-year separation | 13.5 | 8.9 |
| 5-year separation | 3.5 | 3.1 |

*Source*: Marriage, Divorce and Adoption Statistics.

culpability continued to play a part in decisions over custody and property disputes.

Because of the inclusion of the 'five year' provision, for the first time a divorce could be obtained by either party, irrespective of the other's wishes and their own behaviour. It was not the same as divorce on demand, but it did mean that, given time, individuals were no longer tied into a marriage against their wishes. This legal change emphasising marriage as a 'relationship' rather than a 'contract' was clearly consonant with changing perceptions of marriage and partnership. The increased emphasis on love and personal satisfaction within cultural understandings of marriage led to the social acceptance that a marriage should be terminated when the personal relationship between the spouses had deteriorated to a degree that was irretrievable. As Kiernan, Land and Lewis (1997) show, modifications to divorce laws since 1969 have been premised on, and thereby helped consolidate, 'relational' understandings of contemporary marriage.

Interestingly though, living apart for either two or five years is used only in a minority of cases as grounds for divorce. As Table 6.3 shows, adultery and unreasonable behaviour are the two commonest grounds for obtaining a divorce. However, it would be wrong to assume from this that the 1969 Divorce Reform Act actually made relatively little difference. What it symbolised was the importance of the quality of the marital relationship and the acceptance of divorce as a solution to marital difficulties. It would seem that once couples decide they want to separate, they proceed to divorce using whatever legal grounds are most expedient. This may involve citing adultery or unreasonable behaviour, but whether the adultery or behaviour really was the reason for the breakdown of their relationship is a secondary consideration.

Note from Table 6.3 that some 70 per cent of divorce petitions were brought by women, and only 30 per cent by men, which is a common feature of recent divorce statistics. This does not necessarily reflect a greater dissatisfaction with marriage among women. Rather it reflects their greater need to formalise the legal, financial and domestic arrangements following marital separation. Given especially that wives are more likely to be caring for any dependent children involved, regularising post-separation provision, including securing a degree of financial stability and protecting housing rights, is likely to be a higher priority for them than for their husbands. Because of their greater access to material resources, men have less immediate interest in instigating divorce proceedings and formalising the ending of the marriage.

While we can be precise about the legal grounds used in obtaining a divorce as these are formally recorded in court, we know far less about the causes or reasons for divorce. The distinction between 'grounds' and 'reasons' is an important one. Although the grounds, especially adultery and unreasonable behaviour, *may* be strongly linked to the breakdown of a marriage, they are not necessarily the prime or only factors involved. Moreover, by themselves they hardly count as a good explanation for divorce: for example, if a spouse leaves home to live with a new partner, that is highly likely to signify the end of the marriage. In seeking a divorce, the grounds of adultery may well be cited. However, in understanding why that marriage broke down, we would want to know far more about why the spouse became involved with a new partner and why that led to their leaving home – after all, many marital affairs do not result in separation or divorce (Lawson, 1988). In other words, we would need to know a good deal more about the processes which led to the marital breakdown before we could explain it. In Richards's (1982) helpful term, we would need to understand the way that the 'natural history' of the divorce developed.

Yet obtaining valid data on the processes of divorce is far from simple. Ideally the path a marriage takes would need to be tracked over a significant period of time prior to the separation, as well as for some period afterwards. Such data would need to be collected quite frequently in order to understand the issues that arose and the 'negotiations', of whatever form, the couple had about them. It would also need to be quite detailed. Even if a couple agreed in principle to take part in such a study, one or both might no longer wish to participate if their marriage was in difficulties. Revealing their thoughts and feelings to an interviewer at a time of high marital stress is unlikely to be a priority. Moreover, for the study to succeed, a large cohort of marriages would need to be tracked in this way.

Not surprisingly, few detailed longitudinal studies of marriage and divorce have been undertaken (Amato and Booth, 1996; Kiernan and Mueller, 1999). Instead, information about divorce has mainly come from two other types of study: post-divorce studies and correlational studies. In the former, individuals (or divorced couples) are asked to recount their experience of divorce and their understandings of why their marriage ended. Clearly this can produce insightful accounts of the processes involved (Vaughan, 1987). Those most closely involved are the 'experts' on what actually happened in their marriage. Nonetheless, there are major difficulties with such data. In particular, people's understandings of what happened in their marriage are *post hoc* reconstructions rather than 'factual' accounts and will vary over time. What seems most pertinent at one time may not be at another. They are seeking to understand the (usually painful) processes leading to the end of their marriage, perhaps justifying their own behaviour and seeking to reinterpret the past in a fashion that makes sense to them. In this, they are not necessarily falsifying their accounts, but the accounts are constructed with hindsight and cannot simply be taken as accurate portrayals of the issues which led to the demise of the marriage. Moreover, the accounts given by husbands and wives of the reasons for their marriage ending frequently conflict. A key factor in one partner's portrayal may be understood as subsidiary by the other partner. Their having these different understandings is not a problem in itself, but it does make using these accounts as an accurate description of what occurred problematic.

The most common way of seeking to explain why couples divorce relies on correlational data. In this, researchers attempt to specify differences in the circumstances of couples who divorce and those who remain married. By taking a relatively large sample, it is possible to highlight those factors which discriminate between the two groups and thereby identify which couples are most likely to divorce. What emerges is that couples who differ from one another on one or more of a range of socio-economic variables (social class, education, religion, age, ethnicity, for example), are more prone to divorce than couples who are similar. Recent research has also emphasised the consequences of social and material disadvantage, as well as reduced psychological well-being, in marital and other partnership breakdown (Kiernan and Mueller, 1999).

The one factor that has proved unquestionably important in accounting for divorce is age at marriage. In particular, people marrying as teenagers are particularly likely to divorce (Rowlingson and McKay, 1998). As Table 6.4 indicates, marriages occurring between 1985 and 1989 in which the bride was aged between 16 and 19 were nearly twice as likely to have ended in separation after five years as ones in which the bride was aged 20–24. Furthermore, this is almost three times as likely to have happened to teenage brides than to brides aged between 25 and 29. The reasons for this are not difficult to uncover. Typically, young couples have less experience of romantic and sexual relationships (as well as of other aspects of adult living); have known each other for shorter periods; have fewer educational qualifications; are likely to have low-paid jobs or be unemployed; have fewer material resources (including poorer housing); and are likely to have children early in their relationship. Given this 'vortex of disadvantage' (Ineichen,

**Table 6.4**  *Percentage of first marriages ending in separation within a given period (Great Britain)*

| | Year of marriage | | | | |
| --- | --- | --- | --- | --- | --- |
| | 1980–84 | | | 1985–9 | |
| Bride's age at marriage | 3 years | 5 years | 10 years | 3 years | 5 years |
| 16–19 | 20 | 27 | 38 | 19 | 32 |
| 20–24 | 5 | 9 | 21 | 12 | 18 |
| 25–29 | 1 | 4 | 10 | 8 | 11 |

*Source*: General Household Survey, 1998.

1977), it is not surprising that couples who marry young have a high propensity for divorce.

Yet in an important sense, these data are out of date. Table 6.4 concerns the experiences of people marrying in the 1980s, not of those marrying now. However, the numbers of teenage brides have declined significantly over the last twenty years. Only around 5 per cent of brides were aged under 20 in the mid-1990s compared to 30 per cent in the mid-1970s. One reason is that teenage mothers are now far less likely to be married than to be lone-parents (see Table 2.3, p. 28); the social pressure to 'legit-imise' the birth is now nowhere near as powerful as it was (Kiernan, 1997). Thus while young age at marriage has been a key factor in divorce, its relevance is now less than it was.

In addition to looking at reasons why individuals divorce, there is another, more structural question which can be asked: why is it that in Britain, along with other countries in the Western world, the divorce rate has increased so much? What factors have encouraged such a change? As with explaining why individual couples divorce, the reasons for this change are complex. However, a number of factors can be identified. To begin with, as we argued earlier, the trend in late modernity is for marriage to be understood as a relationship rather than a contract. Love, personal commitment and intrinsic satisfaction are now seen as the cornerstones of marriage. The absence of these emotions and feelings is itself justification for ending the relationship (Smart, 1997). Indeed, Furstenberg (1990, p. 380) has argued that in America current ideals 'virtually demanded divorce' if the couple are no longer in love.

This indicates how social responses to divorce have altered, with divorce attracting far less stigma than it did even in the recent past (Rowlingson and McKay, 1998). In turn, as divorce is 'normalised', so the emergent definition of marriage as being centrally concerned with personal happiness and fulfilment is bolstered further. Conflict which was previously seen as acceptable within a marriage is increasingly defined as unacceptable; incompatibilities which were tolerated are now seen as intolerable; and the absence of love, once seen as unfortunate but bearable, is now taken as indicative of the irretrievable breakdown of the marriage. And so higher levels of divorce themselves foster even higher levels in a self-supporting fashion.

But just as social conditions are important in promoting high levels of divorce, so too material conditions matter. Divorce rates will increase only to the extent that women in particular have access to alternative means of economic support outside of marriage (Cherlin, 1992; Kurz, 1995). In other words, where wives are highly dependent on the wages or property of their husbands for their own and their children's welfare, they are more effectively 'trapped' in their marriages than when they have other means of support (Delphy and Leonard, 1992). Thus, a key factor facilitating divorce has been the changed economic position of married women, both through shifts in employment practices and through the development of welfare services that ensure some minimum level of income for all citizens. Without a means of economic independence, the option of divorce as a way out of marital conflict is restricted.

Somewhat similarly, divorce is more difficult where others outside the couple have a strong interest in sustaining the marriage. The most obvious example of this is when family property is important for the economic well-being of a wider kin group. In peasant societies, for example, one can expect low levels of divorce as divorce potentially threatens the well-being of other family members. In an economy dominated by wage labour, on the other hand, in which payment is typically made to individuals as individuals, the ending of a marriage has less bearing on the material interests of any wider kin. In these circumstances, marriage is less 'embedded' within the economic system so that divorce has less social (as distinct from personal) impact. Similarly where a wider family's social standing is affected by divorce, as is indeed the case among some ethnic minority and religious groupings, there will be far more social pressure on couples to remain together.

## The impact of divorce: adults and children

The impact that divorce has on people's lives varies. The path the separation took will be important in shaping the way the post-divorce period is experienced (Kurz, 1995). In this regard, the 'natural history' of the divorce does not cease once a separation occurs or the divorce is granted, but carries on until the individuals become accommodated to their new circumstances. This process itself may take a longer or shorter time. For couples without children who agree they want their marriage to end, the repercussions of the divorce may be quite minimal, especially if disputes over property division are resolved. Both may quickly establish a new lifestyle which suits their purposes. However, when one spouse has unilaterally left to form a new relationship, when the marriage is long-standing, and/or when there are dependent children involved, the situation is usually much more emotionally, financially and socially complex.

Although it is sometimes argued that marriage is no longer treated as solemnly as it was, there is little evidence that people treat divorce casually. For most people, it is not a decision which is taken lightly (Rowlingson and McKay, 1998). It is a highly emotional and generally painful process, generating feelings of failure, anger, loss, blame, guilt, rejection, loneliness and self-doubt in different portions at different times (Walker, 1993). When there are dependent children, these feelings are usually compounded by worries over how the separation will affect them. When there has been domestic violence or child abuse, the separation may be seen positively, but for the majority a desire to protect the children's well-being, both short-term and long-term, generates additional tensions to an already stressful situation (Kurz, 1995). Furthermore, coming to agreement about each individual's future rights and responsibilities during this period of recrimination and charged feelings is rarely straightforward. Issues of financial provision frequently lead to high levels of conflict as standards of living are inevitably compromised when a household divides into two. Rarely are there sufficient resources to meet both spouses' aspirations.

As will become evident later in this chapter, lone mothers in general are materially disadvantaged. While some divorced mothers, particularly those with older children and/or professional qualifications may be better off, the majority are in poverty and dependent primarily on state benefits. Marsh, Ford and Finlayson, (1997, p. 71) found that only 45 per cent received any maintenance, averaging only slightly more than £40 per week. Until the early 1990s, there was wide variation in the income which courts ordered men to pay their ex-wives and children. Moreover, these orders were rarely policed effectively, so that many divorced mothers actually received very little. The courts also encouraged 'clean break', lump-sum settlements which at least resulted in less conflict over continued payments. With the creation of the Child Support Agency in 1993, and the specification of uniform principles about the financial obligations of non-residential fathers, there is more clarity over the amounts of support to be paid, even if some ex-husbands think these principles unfair. Nonetheless, even with these principles established, many ex-wives are actually no better off than they were. The main difference is that a lower proportion of their still minimal income comes from the state.

While there has been rather less research on the social consequences of divorce than on its financial repercussions, for many women divorce, like widowhood, has a significant impact on their informal social activities and relationships. At the beginning, the emotional costs of the separation may make them feel less like socialising than previously. Moreover, participation in activities that were previously affordable may now be too expensive. Some people restrict their interactions so as not to 'burden' their friends with their problems; indeed their friends may tire of hearing about the saga of difficulties faced. Others may feel stigmatised by their friends' well-meaning concern/pity. Many also find that the issues that are now important in their lives are not ones their friends share (Feld and Carter, 1998; Leslie and Grady, 1985; Milardo, 1987; O'Brien, 1987). Through such factors, existing friendships can become problematic in a way that undermines their continuation. Some tend to fade completely; others become less central. Typically, they are replaced, albeit gradually, by ties with people with comparable experiences and resources. In turn, as their networks are modified, the new relationships serve to establish their identity as separated/divorced people (Allan, 1989; Rands, 1988).

The increase of marital breakdown has led to concern over the impact of divorce on children, in particular the emotional damage parental separation causes children and the consequences for them of the absence of a male role model. There is now a substantial body of research on these matters, much of it North American (Amato, 1993; Cherlin, 1992; Demo, 1992; 1993; Demo and Acock, 1988; Furstenberg and Teitler, 1994; Hines, 1997; Richards, 1999). Great care needs to be taken in 'translating' this to a British (or European) context, as the legal and financial frameworks of lone parenthood are so different. This is an important point. There is a tendency to conceive of the effects of parental separation on children, solely in terms of their emotional response to parental conflict and loss, and to see this as 'fixed' rather than as socially and economically patterned. Yet just as age, gender and social class may well mediate those experiences, so too post-divorce responses will be influenced by the legal, financial and social standards which govern divorce in different societies.

In understanding children's responses to their parents' divorce, divorce needs to be viewed as a social process as well as a legal act. Children's reactions are influenced not just by the ending of the marriage, but also by *how* it is ended. Here the 'natural history' of the divorce is again crucial. And importantly, this involves not just the behaviour and responses of the parents around the time of the divorce, but also their behaviour towards one another and to the child(ren) in the phases leading to the decision to separate and in the period following the divorce. Evidence now suggests that a key element for children is how the divorce affects their parents' behaviour at these times (Amato, 1993; Burghes, 1994, 1996; Hines, 1997; Richards, 1999). As the 1989 Children Act recognises, divorce signifies the ending of a marriage not the ending of parenting.

Virtually all children find their parents' separation extremely upsetting. Often they have been 'protected' in some sense from the decision, and frequently feel they have been ill-prepared for the possibility of separation. Even when their parents' relationship is one of conflict and anger, children often normalise this in their own minds, and find it a shock when they are confronted with the reality of separation (Mitchell, 1985). The period following separation is one in which various negative emotions are experienced. Depending on age, these include anger, grief, uncertainty, sadness, despair, helplessness and guilt (Richards, 1999). Lacking any real knowledge of why the separation occurred, children often look back at their own behaviour in the period prior to separation and blame themselves. If they had behaved differently, their reasoning goes, perhaps the separation could have been avoided.

Equally, most children have concerns about the future. Parents may try to be reassuring, but given the anxieties and fears the children have, there is often no effective reassurance that can be given. Moreover, the parents themselves frequently do not know what will happen and how the marital disputes will be resolved. For them too, separation is a period of emotional upheaval and social disruption. In coming to their own understandings of what has happened, they are likely to experience similar emotions to their children's, as well as a sense of inadequacy as parents. They too need time to readjust and their emotional reactions are likely to feed back into the children's responses, adding to their fears and leaving them uncertain about how they (the children) can be supportive of their parent(s). Grandparents and others to whom the children might turn will also often have little idea how the future will unfold.

For many children, the period following separation is not only one of emotional turmoil but also one in which other changes are taking place (Burghes, 1994). In nearly all cases, for example, the household will have less money available than previously, with many being in poverty (Everett, 1991; Maclean, 1991). It is now well recognised that material disadvantage is linked to disadvantages for children in other important areas, including health and education (Alcock, 1997; Graham, 1993; Walker and Walker (eds), 1997). Additionally, a high proportion of families move house following a divorce, either for economic reasons, to be nearer to kin or in order to make a fresh start. This can be quite disruptive for the child(ren), especially if it means going to a new school and having to make new friends. Even if they do not move, the parent who has left may move away for similar reasons, making regular contact problematic. Although accurate figures are difficult to obtain, it is known that a high proportion of fathers effectively lose contact with their children in the years following divorce. In the United States, it is estimated that up to half of children have no real contact with their fathers after divorce, particularly if the father forms a new partnership (Furstenberg and Nord, 1985; Stephens, 1996; see also Simpson, McCarthy and Walker, 1995). If contact with a parent is reduced, contact with that parent's kin also frequently suffers (Ambert, 1988; Johnson, 1988; Simpson, 1994; 1998).

Thus a child's world can be altered quite radically by the relational and material consequences of their parents' divorce. At a time when they are likely to need stability in their lives to help them understand the divorce and adjust emotionally, they are often confronted with a set of further disruptions which make such adjustment all the more difficult. The longer-term consequences of divorce are difficult to discern. In both Britain and America, researchers have used longitudinal studies to understand how divorce influences later-life events, though generally the outcomes are hard to unravel as many different personal, economic and social factors are involved. The most reliable research has been concerned with life transitions. It indicates that children whose parents divorce are a little more likely to leave home at earlier ages, to cohabit, and to have a child outside marriage; though they are no more likely to marry or have a child within marriage (Cherlin, Kiernan and Chaselansdale, 1995; Elliott and Richards, 1991). The differences though are relatively small. We have little systematic knowledge about how other aspects of people's adulthood are influenced by the processes of parental separation and divorce.

There is little doubt that children cope best with separation and divorce if their relationships with their parents are positive and relatively stable (Buchanan, Maccoby and Dornbusch, 1996; Hetherington, 1979; Lund, 1987; Richards, 1999). Divorce is more difficult for children if conflict between the parents continues, and especially if they feel pressurised into taking sides. However, managing a divorce in a way that does protect children's interests is extremely difficult. As well as managing their emotional responses, parents need to resolve genuine conflicts of interest. Under these circumstances, providing children with a consolidated and supportive response in which a continuing positive relationship with both parents is fostered requires much of the parents (Simpson, McCarthy and Walker, 1995). It calls for trust, commitment and respect at a time when these are liable to be undermined with the break-up of their own relationship.

Thus, what is needed for the children's sake is a 'civilised' divorce, in which conflict is handled constructively; but being civilised in the immediate aftermath of separation is no easy matter emotionally. In the longer run there are also tensions for those seeking to achieve more active forms of consensual 'co-parenting' after divorce, in the manner that the Children Act and other policy initiatives envisage. Neale and Smart (1997) make the important point that active joint parenting, in the sense of a common involvement in different facets of a child's life, involves behaviour which effectively sustains not just 'parenting' but also aspects of 'family' and 'marriage'. (See also Smart, 1997). Because such parenting entails high levels of consultation and cooperation, the couple remain active in each other's lives in ways which 'mirror' significant elements of their couple and family identity. For the couple, the divorce represents a separation and a drawing apart; yet active co-parenting continues to bind them together in what remains a familial context. In this regard, it is far easier to 'manage' the more common post-divorce arrangement whereby one parent (usually the mother) has responsibility for day-to-day childcare, with the other maintaining limited contact and some degree of involvement over major decisions. Proposed changes to divorce legislation in the late 1990s will, if enacted, make mediation services more readily available to parents; nonetheless, the constructive resolution of the tensions inherent in active co-parenting will remain a complex and difficult process to manage (Walker, 1993).

## Lone-parents: diversity

As has already been indicated, there is a great deal of diversity as well as many commonalities in the circumstances and experiences of lone-parent families, (Rowlingson and McKay, 1998). To begin with, there are various routes into lone parenthood. As shown in Table 2.2 (p. 27), some lone-parent families result from marital separation and divorce, others from death, while an increasing number are formed through births to unattached women (Kiernan, Land and Lewis, 1997). As Figure 6.1 highlights, the routes out of lone parenthood also vary, though there is rather less reliable information about the trajectories out of these families than there is about their formation. Some cease because the children reach an age when they are no longer dependent. Other lone-parents marry or cohabit with a new partner. And a few will be reconciled with the children's other parent and re-form the original two-parent family. Thus lone parenthood is a transitory rather than a permanent status; recent estimates are that the mean length of time spent as a lone-parent is a little over 5

**Figure 6.1**    *Routes in and out of lone parenthood*

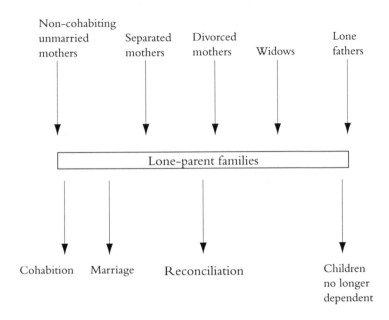

ROUTES INTO LONE PARENTHOOD

Non-cohabiting
unmarried              Separated      Divorced                              Lone
mothers                mothers        mothers        Widows                 fathers

Lone-parent families

Cohabition    Marriage       Reconciliation                    Children
                                                                no longer
                                                                dependent

ROUTES OUT OF LONE PARENTHOOD

Derived from Crow and Hardey,1992, p.148

years (Marsh, Ford and Finlayson, 1997; Rowlingson and McKay, 1998).

The pathways into and out of lone parenthood are only one aspect of the diversity found within lone-parent families. Many other factors also differentiate their experiences, including, the age of children in the family; the previous and current relationships the non-residential parent maintains with those in the lone-parent household; the financial resources the family has available; the employment patterns of the lone-parent; the type of housing in which the family lives; the level of geographical (and social) mobility there has been; and the ties and support offered by both parents' kin groups. These are all factors which are likely to impinge on the lone-parent 'experience' for both the adult and the children involved (Simpson, 1994).

For example, a lone-parent household with teenage children, headed by a divorced mother with good qualifications and a developed career, living in high-quality owner-occupied housing in a suburban area will have a quite different lifestyle to one formed by a young unmarried mother with pre-school children, dependent on state benefits and living in high-rise rented housing on a run-down estate. And both are likely to have markedly different experiences from a lone-parent household headed by, say, a skilled working-class widower, with children about to leave school, buying his own house on a 'respectable' council estate. The range of personal, material and social factors which collectively shape the experiences which different lone-parent families have is immense; each family has its own history, its own satisfactions and tensions. Moreover, these will change over time as children mature and as adjustment is made within the household to the different opportunities, contingencies and constraints which present themselves.

But while diversity within lone-parent families should not be underplayed, there are also numerous important commonalities which shape the experiences of many. In particular, the majority of lone-mother households live in poverty, a tendency which has been increasing (Bradshaw and Millar, 1991; Ermisch, 1989; Kiernan, Land and Lewis, 1997; Millar, 1992). This can readily be seen by looking at the main sources of income of lone parent families, details of which are given in Table 6.5. Despite benefit policies which permit lone-parents to receive increased levels of alternative income, four-fifths of lone-parents qualify for income-tested benefits, including half of the minority who have some form of paid employment (Marsh, Ford and Finlayson, 1997, p. 44). They are, in other words, funded at the level considered minimal for maintaining households. By state definition, they are on the poverty line. Given that governments throughout the 1980s and 1990s have been concerned with reducing benefit expenditure, it is not surprising that many lone-parent families have severe difficulty meeting their material needs (Bradshaw and Millar, 1991; Marsh, Ford and Finlayson, 1997; Millar, 1994; Popay and Jones, 1991; Rowlingson and McKay, 1998). Details of the incomes that lone-parent families received in 1996 are

**Table 6.5**   *Mean proportion of lone-parents' income from different sources\* % 1994*

| Income support | Family credit | Child benefit | Net earnings | Maintenance | All five sources |
|---|---|---|---|---|---|
| 45 | 5 | 17 | 20 | 8 | 95 |

\* excluding widows.
*Source*: Marsh, Ford and Finlayson, 1997.

provided in Table 6.6 together with a comparison of weekly income for two-parent families. It is notable that a third of lone mothers received less than £100 a week in 1996, compared to only one in thirty two-parent households; conversely, over three-quarters of two-parent households had an income in excess of £300 per week, compared to only one in seven lone-mother households.

The low income levels of female-headed lone-parent families are a consequence of a number of interacting factors (Burghes, 1993; Millar, 1989). Arguably the most important is the gendered inequality of the labour market which was discussed in the previous chapter. The low levels of pay characteristic of much female employment, combined with the indirect costs associated with employment, often mean that lone mothers are unable to have net earnings as high as the income available from the state even though this is set at minimal levels. While the relaxation of rules

**Table 6.6**   *Usual gross weekly household income in £s 1996 % (Great Britain)*

|  | 0–99 | 100–199 | 200–299 | 300+ |
|---|---|---|---|---|
| Single mothers | 47 | 31 | 7 | 15 |
| Widowed mothers\* | 4 | 12 | 42 | 41 |
| Divorced mothers | 28 | 42 | 19 | 11 |
| Separated mothers | 25 | 40 | 8 | 17 |
| All lone mothers | 33 | 39 | 13 | 15 |
| Lone fathers\* | 27 | 21 | 14 | 39 |
| Married couples | 3 | 9 | 11 | 78 |

\* small numbers in survey.
*Source*: General Household Survey, 1998.

governing Family Credit and the disregard of some childcare costs in benefit calculations have improved the situation, for many lone mothers, employment, especially part-time employment, carries few economic advantages even where it is available (Millar, 1994). Many lone mothers, especially those who become mothers at young ages, leave school with few qualifications and have limited employment prospects. Such women are doubly disadvantaged, typically being restricted to poorly paid employment, by their gender and by their low skill base.

The need to organise childcare can also act as a disincentive, especially for mothers of very young children, though recent policy initiatives to promote more flexible childcare policies should prove beneficial (Duncan and Edwards, 1997b). However, beliefs about children's needs also affect lone mothers' willingness to become employed. As Edwards and Duncan (1996) argue, the decisions lone mothers make are not based solely on economic advantage. Different ideologies about what 'good mothering' entails are also important. What Edwards and Duncan (1996) term 'gendered moral responsibilities' interact with ideas of economic advantage in shaping the way different mothers approach issues of employment. As can be seen from Table 6.7, the result of these various factors is that lone mothers are far less likely than those in two-parent households to be in any form of employment.

According to Marsh, Ford and Finlayson (1997), a little over 40 per cent of lone mothers have agreements to receive maintenance from their child(ren)'s father(s). In fact, only some 30 per cent

**Table 6.7**    *Employment of mothers with dependent children 1994–6 % (Great Britain)*

|  | Lone mothers | | Married mothers | |
|---|---|---|---|---|
|  | *All* | *Youngest child under 5* | *All* | *Youngest child under 5* |
| Full-time employment | 16 | 9 | 24 | 18 |
| Part-time employment | 25 | 17 | 42 | 36 |
| No employment | 59 | 74 | 34 | 46 |

*Source*: General Household Survey, 1998.

actually do receive any payment, and very few indeed rely on maintenance for their primary support. The proportion receiving maintenance payments is influenced by the history of the parenting relationships. As noted above, 45 per cent of divorced mothers receive some maintenance, while only 15 per cent of single, never-partnered mothers receive any (Marsh, Ford and Finlayson, 1997, p. 67). Moreover, the amounts involved are generally small. In Marsh, Ford and Finlayson's (1997) study, the average maintenance received by the 30 per cent of respondents who received any at all was £39 per week, ranging from token amounts to £230 a week; only a quarter of these mothers received more than £40 per week.

In 1993, the Child Support Agency was created with the remit of ensuring that non-residential parents accepted a greater degree of financial responsibility for their children's welfare. This was intended to have the advantage of improving the material welfare of lone-parent families as well as reducing public expenditure. Leaving aside the much criticised strategies adopted by this Agency, (mainly concerning its efforts to maximise its short-term 'success' by pursuing fathers who are already paying some maintenance rather than those who contribute nothing), it is questionable whether the first of these objectives has been achieved. In their study conducted eighteen months after its introduction, Marsh, Ford and Finlayson (1997) found there had been no change in the proportion of non-residential parents paying maintenance. This remained at 30 per cent, broadly the same as it had been since the late 1980s. Overall, few lone-parent families have benefited financially through the intercession of the Child Support Agency.

Reasons for this are not hard to find. The current policy is that non-residential parents are liable for a maximum of 30 per cent of their net income. (For details of the maintenance principles, see C.S.A., 1997.) While fathers' groups have argued that such a level of payment is punitive, reducing many to poverty and giving them little incentive to be employed, the reality is that even this level of financial support is rarely sufficient to match Income Support levels. Consequently, the lone-parent family may be no better off, often simply having the same income, though derived from a mixture of sources. If all non-residential fathers were to pay this level of contribution, the state's payment of benefit would be reduced quite significantly, but there may be no immediate financial gain for the lone-parent families involved. However, on the basis of their survey, Marsh, Ford and Finlayson (1997, p. 91) argue that a lone mother whose entitlement to Income Support is replaced by maintenance has her position 'transformed', in particular, through being more able to exercise future choices over employment. Unlike Income Support, maintenance is not affected by the recipient's earnings. With Family Credit entitlements for those employed for 16 or more hours per week, the consequence is that even those with few qualifications are able to improve their financial circumstances if they can obtain employment in addition. Thus the impact of maintenance payments does not lie in the amount actually received, but in the options for additional sources of income it facilitates.

There have been concerns about the impact on parenting relationships of the Child Support Agency's policy of enforced maintenance payments. Although there is little reliable evidence available, conflict caused between the parents over financial payments may militate against the other needs which these families (especially the children) have. In particular, tension over financial contributions may compromise efforts at reaching the level of agreement over parenting which family policies including the Children Act, 1989, recognise as in the best interests of children. Underlying this are the greater costs of running two households. A couple cannot separate and each continue to have the same standard of living as before. One or both will have fewer resources than they had previously. Working out what is 'fair' in such circumstances is problematic, especially if the non-residential parent has children with a new partner. The typical outcome is that mother-headed lone-parent families live at, or close to, the poverty line. However, the Child Support Agency has at least generated an official level of non-residential parental support which will inform future expectations, a matter which was ill-defined previously (Maclean, 1987). Whether the level set is regarded as too high or too low, it removes some of the ambiguity which previously existed and will help frame future settlements.

As well as being disadvantaged financially, lone-parent families, especially female-headed ones, tend to be disadvantaged in their housing (Bradshaw and Millar, 1991; Kiernan, Land and Lewis, 1997). This can be seen as a corollary of poverty more generally,

**Table 6.8** *Housing tenure and family type: families with dependent children 1995–6 % (Great Britain)*

|  | Owner-occupied | Socially rented | Privately rented |
|---|---|---|---|
| Lone-parent household | 35 | 53 | 11 |
| Other families | 77 | 16 | 7 |

*Source*: General Household Survey, 1998.

but it warrants consideration in its own right. Mother–headed lone-parent families are far less likely to be in owner-occupation than other families with dependent children. As Table 6.8 indicates, two-thirds of lone-parent families are in rented accommodation, with over half renting from local authorities or housing associations. This is perhaps not surprising for never-married mothers, many of whom are unlikely to be eligible for mortgages because of their age, lack of qualifications and current domestic circumstances (Burghes with Brown, 1995). However, the pattern is also apparent for other lone-parents. Whereas three-quarters of two-parent households are in owner-occupation, only a third of lone-parent households are.

Owner-occupation is not necessarily superior to other forms of housing. However, other measures indicate that many lone mothers are in unsatisfactory housing (Marsh, Ford and Finlayson, 1997): for example, one in five lone-parent families live in flats, compared to one in sixteen two-parent families (Table 6.9). As is now widely recognised, the absence of a private garden,

**Table 6.9** *Type of housing of families with dependent children 1995–6 % (Great Britain)*

|  | Detached | Semi-detached | Terraced | Flat |
|---|---|---|---|---|
| Lone-parent household | 7 | 31 | 39 | 23 |
| Other families | 28 | 37 | 29 | 6 |

*Source*: General Household Survey, 1998.

difficulties of access and the unreliability of lifts can create additional childcare problems. Similarly, lone-parent families frequently have less space and fewer household amenities than do two-parent families (G.H.S., 1997). Lone-parent families also form a high proportion of those recognised as 'unintentionally homeless'. Often the accommodation in which they are housed, as a result, is temporary: much of it being 'bed and breakfast' accommodation, unsatisfactory though this is for children. Furthermore, a comparatively high proportion of lone-mother households share accommodation, either with parents or with other lone-parent families. In some cases, this is entirely satisfactory, providing the lone mother with both adult company and informal resources for childcare. However, it can also result in overcrowding and a degree of tension in the ensuing domestic relationships. Returning to the parental home may have many short-term benefits, but it is rarely perceived to be a viable longer-term solution to lone-parent housing problems.

While lone mothers often live in relatively poor-quality housing, many still value the autonomy and security that their own 'home' provides. As Crow and Hardey (1991) discuss, subjective feelings about housing are not necessarily correlated with its quality. Some people long to escape the constraints of their present housing; others in similar housing situations are highly satisfied and feel it offers them a level of stability and control which they prize. How housing is experienced, and the aspirations people have for their future housing, depend on their previous housing and relationship histories and the extent to which current housing satisfies their material and emotional needs. In this context, being responsible for your own home can both be a constraint, especially where the housing is inadequate, and, yet at the same time, provide a high degree of satisfaction. The sense of having your own home over which no one else has rights, is culturally important and can be emotionally satisfying. Similarly, Graham (1987b) has argued that even though they are in poverty, many lone-parents *feel* better off because now, unlike when they were part of a couple, they have control over how their money is spent. They are, in Graham's words, 'better off poorer' (1987b, p. 59) because they now have far greater autonomy over their budgeting. Even though most of the limited money they have is taken up with paying bills, they are more secure in its management.

This same dialectic operates in other areas of social experience; for example, the circumstances of many lone mothers – not being employed, having little money, being responsible for childcare – can lead to a high level of social isolation. However, the experiences of lone mothers vary in this as in most other matters. Some are extremely isolated and feel very alone. They have few friends and relatively little support from family. For them, the home can become a prison. Others, though, are happy to be relatively inactive socially and do not experience this as oppressive. For whatever reason, they do not feel lonely but derive satisfaction from their apparently limited domestic and familial environment. Still others, while being in a similar material position, are able to use their resources to construct a much more active social life with friends and wider family (Rowlingson and McKay, 1998). And importantly, people may experience the same conditions differently at different times. What starts out as a sense of autonomy may later transform into feelings of loneliness; what at one time offers fulfilment may at a later phase create dissatisfaction. In this, of course, lone parenthood is no different from other aspects of family and domestic life. As emphasised in the introduction, change within families is routine and normal, as true with regard the emotions which family life generates as it is with family demography and family process.

Moreover, different family members experience the 'realities' of family life differently: that is, the experiences children have of living in a lone-parent family do not necessarily match those of their mother or father. Aside from issues to do with the absent parent, children will experience poverty differently and also have different responses to the ways in which household responsibilities are divided (Bradshaw, 1990; Hill and Tisdall, 1997). For example, however hard lone mothers strive to limit its impact, the development of adolescent markets in fashion and style result in some teenagers in lone-parent families being unable to participate fully in what have become mainstream activities. However much adults may deride the values of such adolescent markets, the power of consumerism in sustaining identities and defining boundaries within teenage culture is evident. These processes are precisely why Townsend (1979) and others emphasise the centrality of relative rather than absolute deprivation in understanding the real impact of poverty.

Conversely, some children in lone-parent families are given greater levels of responsibility than children in two-parent families. With only one parent in the household, the older child in particular may be treated as more competent, more 'adult' than other children. They may need to care for themselves or younger siblings for longer periods and they may be given more domestic tasks and responsibilities. At times this is seen as harmful, as indeed it may be. Obviously children can be left alone at too young an age and without sufficient supervision to ensure their welfare. Yet equally changes in childhood over the twentieth century have resulted in children being 'protected' and shielded from tasks which actually are not beyond their competence and which carry no risk. Rather than being harmful, the responsibilities some children in lone-parent families are given may be a positive aspect of their socialisation. However, it would be as wrong to generalise that such experience is always constructive as it would be to assert that it is always harmful.

## Single mothers and the underclass

Lone-parent poverty has attracted much attention well beyond academic circles. According to Cheal (1996, p. 29) 'Rapid growth in the number of sole-parent families, together with their high level of welfare dependence, has been a lightning rod for the politics of the family in recent years'. Some commentators have viewed the growth in lone-parent families, and especially the rapid increase in single (never married) mother families, along with rising long-term unemployment and the decline of traditional industrial communities, as part of a wider transformation within society. In particular, the 1990s saw a popularisation of the idea that an underclass is developing which consists of marginalised families, living materially disadvantaged lives, having little stake in the dominant social order and inculcating in their children values at odds with the majority. Whether housed in the inner-city or in run-down council estates, such families are stereotypically taken as contented to be dependent on the state, uninterested in stable employment and dismissive of conventional family behaviour. One populariser of this view is Charles Murray. Building on his beliefs about American ghetto life, Murray (1994) has argued that the rise in the numbers of single mothers is a consequence of over-generous welfare allowances which encourage the development of irresponsible family values, and generate welfare dependency. From this perspective, changes in patterns of single motherhood signify a dangerous tendency with inadequate socialisation of children, leading to a spiral of unemployment, delinquency and crime – the hall-marks of an underclass.

As we have seen, many lone-parent families are in poverty, and those formed by young, never-married women are particularly likely to have limited resources. Many are living in inadequate housing in impoverished areas. Yet it is far from clear that these families are part of an underclass in the sense Murray and other followers of the New Right assert (Morris, 1994). The concept of an underclass is a complex one, involving a range of different elements which are not always made explicit. In the United States, for example, the term is highly racialised, being used essentially to refer to the socio-economic circumstances of inner-city blacks. At times, this racial element is also evident in British usage, especially when framed in the context of the higher proportions of Afro-Carribean births occurring outside marriage (Song and Edwards, 1997) and of Afro-Caribbean children living in lone-parent families (Berrington, 1994). However, generally in Britain the idea of an underclass is not restricted to particular ethnic groups (Duncan and Edwards, 1997b).

We can identify three main themes within claims that single mothers constitute an increasing component of the underclass: values; marginalisation; and socialisation. In terms of values, there is little evidence that lone-parent families, or more specifically single-mother families, hold different values from others, whether this be about family life or about employment. Undoubtedly there are more diverse views in late modernity about the appropriate ordering of domestic and sexual relationships than in the past, but there is little indication that single mothers actively wish to raise their children alone. Most are committed to the material and other benefits of coupledom; and few view single parenthood as a preferred mode of living (though see Roseneil and Mann, 1996). Only a small minority of single mothers report that they became pregnant intentionally, and most knew that the housing and benefit levels to which they would be entitled would be low.

Even though for this period of their lives they are dependent on state benefits, few see this as desirable or wish to remain at this level of income in the long run (Bradshaw and Millar, 1991; Rowlingson and McKay, 1998).

The notion of an underclass entails a significant division between the majority of the population who participate fully in the social and economic mainstream and members of the underclass who are marginalised and excluded. Many single mothers are certainly marginalised economically, socially and geographically. Caring for young children and without employment, their opportunities for social participation are restricted. Their social worlds are predominantly built around ties of kinship, especially to parents (Rowlingson and McKay, 1998), and friendship, and often, through lack of resources, constrained by locality. Given the geographical distribution of unemployment and the tendency of housing policies to foster social homogeneity, many others living in the same localities will also be economically disadvantaged and socially marginalised. To this degree the notion of 'underclass' may be thought appropriate (Wilson, W., 1987), but it is important to recognise that these patterns are a consequence of social and economic structure and not the operation of choice in the way Murray (1994) suggests.

Fears are frequently voiced that children in single-mother families are not being socialised adequately for either employment or stable family life in adulthood. Dennis and Erdos (1993), for example, have argued that the growth in juvenile crime can be linked to the difficulty mothers in lone-parent families have in controlling their adolescent sons properly. There seem to be several elements behind these fears. First, there is an implicit sense that only men, with their greater physical strength, are able to discipline male adolescents appropriately. While strength may at times be an advantage, the role of coercion in adolescent socialisation can easily be overstated. Socialisation involves internalising values rather than submission to force, and the presence of a father in the home is not of itself essential for the latter. Indeed, typically it is mothers who are seen as responsible for instilling appropriate values. Secondly, there is a prevalent idea that boys need a father figure within the home if they are to grow up appreciating and accepting male responsibilities. Such a claim is questionable.

Being in a mother-headed household might alter the dynamics of the home, but it does not negate the power of dominant gender ideologies. Knowledge of masculine modes of behaviour does not come from fathers alone; it is immanent in the culture and enacted through, *inter alia,* schooling, media and informal relationships.

And thirdly, and perhaps most importantly, there is the view that young males need to be well integrated into acceptable social and economic roles if they are not to become delinquent. Without the constraints generated by commitment to the social order through employment and more traditional family life, including marriage and fatherhood, working-class male youths especially are seen as liable to adopt marginalised and anomic lifestyles (Dennis and Erdos, 1993; see Duncan and Edwards, 1997b; Kiernan, Land and Lewis, 1997). Yet, as W. J. Wilson (1987) argues, what matters here is that opportunities are available for the young men in question to enact their traditional gendered responsibilities. In particular, in areas of high unemployment, the possibility of embracing the traditional masculine role of wage earner and breadwinner are limited, especially for those who do not achieve well educationally, a characteristic feature of being brought up in poverty. Without reasonable prospects of secure employment, they have little to contribute economically to a family. Often the mothers of their children are financially better off controlling their own social security money than claiming as a couple. Thus, the absence of employment now and into the foreseeable future does little to encourage stable partnerships or full participation in family life (Rowlingson and McKay, 1998).

Overall, the idea that the growth in lone-mother households is associated with the development of an underclass in Britain is dubious. Certainly the economic transformations occurring in the late twentieth century have resulted in many communities becoming dislocated, many families experiencing long episodes of unemployment, and many individuals being marginalised. These processes have affected all types of family, including lone-parent ones. However, it is a mistake to assert that lone-parent families, including single-mother ones, are promulgating radically different values to those held by more prosperous families. Of course, different experiences generate different social and political understandings, but in the main lone-parent families do not reject

or denigrate a two-parent model. If their children are also disadvantaged in adulthood, it is a consequence of social and
economic structuring far more than a specific lifestyle choice, as
W. J. Wilson's (1987) research in America indicates. (See also
Morris, 1994.) Similar conclusions can be drawn from Duncan
and Edwards' (1997a) overview of the contrasting contexts
which different welfare-state arrangements provide for lone-
parent families. It is also worth remembering the conclusions of a
study undertaken in a previous moral panic about the generational transmission of poverty. From research into the existence
of 'cycles of poverty' which were claimed to trap the children of
the poor into a lifetime of poverty, Rutter and Madge (1976, p.
304) concluded that 'even where continuity is strongest many
individuals break out of the cycle and ... many people become disadvantaged without having been reared by disadvantaged parents'.

## Conclusion

The demographic shifts analysed in this chapter are profound. The
social, economic and moral constraints which shaped people's
reproductive behaviour in the first three-quarters of the twentieth
century no longer have the force they did. Although most people
still aspire to finding personal fulfilment through a lifelong union,
most also now recognise that this may not be the reality. Similarly,
while most people continue to believe that a (non-conflictual)
two-parent natal household constitutes the most appropriate setting
in which to raise children, they also acknowledge that other
arrangements are at times inevitable. No longer is marriage as insti-
tutionally powerful as it was, and no longer is childbirth linked to
marriage in the ways it used to be. Norms about the organisation
of reproduction have altered, with these matters increasingly seen
as issues of volition rather than moral imperative. Similarly, the
state's focus on the ordering of domestic life has changed. As
Kiernan, Land and Lewis (1997, p. 93) argue, in the late twentieth
century, the state increasingly withdrew from 'the business of regulating marriage' and 'gave more attention to ways of regulating
what had been the duties of marriage, particularly in respect of the
parental obligation to maintain and care for children'.

Changes in family life do not develop in isolation. The greater diversity now arising in marital and child-rearing patterns reflects broader changes in the ideological, social and economic environments within which people construct their domestic and sexual identities. In particular, this diversity can be linked to the emphasis on individual freedoms characteristic of the late twentieth century. Individual fulfilment is now seen as central to the accomplishment of successful family life to a degree that would have appeared incongruous to earlier generations (Halsey, 1993). More broadly, the increased incidence of births outside marriage, of divorce and of lone parenthood can be understood as one element within the wider mosaic of change which theories of post-modernity are attempting to capture. The trajectories of family life are no longer as entrenched and predictable as they were; diversity, and with it a greater degree of fragmentation and uncertainty, is now more readily accepted as inherent in contemporary family and household experience. In Stacey's (1998, p. x) words, there is a greater acceptance of 'the irreversibility of family diversity'.

The growth of lone-parent families and in particular, the large proportion of such female-headed families financially dependent on state benefits, has led to increasing public discussion and concern about their circumstances. Much popular debate around lone parenthood is framed in terms of the values held by lone mothers, especially young never-married ones, and the impact these have on their children's sense of social and economic responsibility. There are, though, other discourses used to explain contemporary developments in lone parenthood, as Duncan and Edwards (1997b) demonstrate. Politically, one of the most important tensions in recent debates around lone parenthood concerns the degree to which lone mothers are defined primarily as 'mothers' or primarily as 'workers' (Duncan and Edwards (1997a). To what extent, in other words, should women in this position be encouraged to provide economically for themselves and their children through employment and to what extent should their mothering activities be accepted as having priority over this?

The balance struck between these two positions is in part dependent on current understandings of what 'proper' mothering entails, and in turn on what children's 'needs' are. Whereas there was no expectation in the mid-twentieth century that mothers of dependent children should be anything other than full-time mothers, now, as we saw in Chapter 4, it is seen as appropriate that mothers of even very young children should be free to exercise choice over whether to stay at home full-time or be in some form of employment. Current policy initiatives with respect to lone mothers aim to facilitate such choice for them through generating more extensive and affordable childcare options as well as more flexible benefit policies. In the process, as well as increasing maintenance from non-residential parents, the state is attempting to restrain the escalating costs of the benefits it currently pays to lone-parent families. What impact, if any, such changes will have on the welfare of children in lone-parent households is rarely debated. However, if the policy initiatives being implemented reduce the extent to which children in lone-mother families experience poverty, that of itself is likely to prove beneficial to the well-being of the children in them.

One of the main routes out of lone parenthood, and one of the key 'solutions' to the problems of economic hardship which lone mothers face, is 'remarriage', be this an actual marriage or informal cohabitation. Yet while some of the financial disadvantages of lone parenthood may be resolved in this way, the creation of stepfamilies often generates other dilemmas and tensions. In the next chapter, we examine these issues. As with lone parenthood, there has been a remarkable growth in the numbers of stepfamilies, either directly or indirectly. This has certainly contributed to the increased diversity of contemporary family life, though not in a uniform fashion. There is much variation in the circumstances of stepfamilies, in the range of relationships they incorporate, and, consequently, in the issues which they need to resolve. In contrast to lone-parent families, there is hardly any public discussion of stepfamilies. In policy terms they are treated as equivalent to natal families, even though the network of relationships they entail is more complex and their successful management more demanding.

# 7 Stepfamilies: Reconfiguring Family and Household Boundaries

In general, stepfamilies are treated as if they were little different from families comprised of biological parents and their children. Indeed, as Burgoyne and Clark (1984) showed in their influential study, many of the adults in stepfamily households try hard to portray themselves as, in essence, no different from 'natural' families, that is, families comprising parents and their biological children. (In this chapter we shall use the term 'natural' rather than 'biological' to describe these parent–child ties. Neither term is entirely satisfactory but the meaning here is clear.) What they seek is to 'normalise' their familial arrangements and construct a domestic environment in which relationships are seen as no more problematic than those found in any other household (Ribbens, Edwards and Gillies, 1996). However, while this can sometimes be achieved, typically, stepfamilies are more complex organisations than natural families. While managing family relationships always involves tensions as well as satisfactions, the dynamics of stepfamilies have the potential to become particularly complicated. Because these complications have not received much widespread recognition, many of those who find themselves in stepfamilies, whether as adults or children, are relatively ill-prepared for the experience (Coleman and Ganong, 1995).

A further complexity about contemporary stepfamilies, or 'reconfigured families', as Coleman and Ganong (1995) term them, stems not from their relational dynamics but from their demographic character. While the number of stepfamilies has increased dramatically in recent years, the numbers in previous eras when death rates were high were also large. Arguably, the routes into stepfamilies then were more straightforward and caused fewer relationship difficulties than now, notwithstanding the negative imagery portrayed about them in traditional fairy tales (Hughes, 1994; Smith, 1990). Put simply, when a stepfamily stems from a parental death, the consequent network of relationships is likely to be less entwined than when the non-resident natural parent is still alive. In contemporary society, stepfamilies are only rarely a consequence of death. Much more frequently they follow the breakdown of the natural parents' relationship, with the result that the step-parent often 'replaces' the natural parent in a quite different fashion.

The increased demographic complexity is not only the result of the other natural parent still being alive and potentially having involvement with children in the stepfamily: it is also consequent on the different ways in which new partnerships are now being formed. Couples often cohabit for some period prior to marriage and, more importantly here, many individuals cohabit without formalising their relationship at all. They are formed and dissolved without any official recognition, so that we know little about their stability (Berrington and Diamond, 2000). This tendency clearly has consequences for stepfamilies, especially given the higher likelihood of those who have already been in established relationships to cohabit prior to any new marriage. The key point here is that stepfamilies are formed through cohabitation as well as through marriage, with cohabitations not always being long-lasting.

These processes of family and household formation make it difficult to obtain reliable data on stepfamily characteristics. Analytically as well as socially, the question is one of 'When is a stepfamily a stepfamily?'. Entailed in this are issues about both 'family' and 'household'. There is little problem in defining a household in which a natural parent lives with a new spouse and children from a previous relationship as a stepfamily. Indeed the same applies to relatively established cohabiting relationships, irrespective of whether the couple are married. However, just how established the cohabitation has to be is a moot point, and may generate different answers from the different people involved. Equally though, a form of step-parent relationship can develop when a separated natural parent establishes something other than a short-term relationship with a new partner without cohabiting permanently with that person. How the details of the consequent relationships evolve is likely to be quite variable, depending on many factors, including the parent's recent relational history and the extent to which the child has experience of (and continuing contact with) previous step-parents.

Similar issues arise with regard to the non-residential parent. If this parent forms a new relationship, when does that person become recognised by the children, by others and by themselves, as a step-parent? To what extent does the amount of time spent with that parent and their partner influence this? To complicate matters further, stepfamilies can be formed through parental remarriage or cohabitation after children have become adult. While much of this chapter will focus on stepfamily households in which there are dependent children, it can be recognised that other forms of family and household arrangements generate a range of differently patterned stepfamily relationships. In these matters, the contours of stepfamily ties are both varied and complex, a reality captured nicely by Simpson's (1994; 1998) use of the term 'unclear' (as distinct from *nu*clear) family in describing the diverse family and household patterns constructed following divorce.

Because of these issues, it is difficult to determine accurately how many people are involved in stepfamilies. Often indeed, people do not recognise that they are members of stepfamilies (Burgoyne and Clark, 1984; Ribbens, Edwards and Gillies, 1996). One could hazard a guess that most people's kinship now involves a number of stepfamily relationships. Even if someone has never lived in a stepfamily, it is highly likely that at least one of their children, siblings, grandchildren or other relatives will have done so, at least for some period (Allan, 1996). It becomes evident too that the simple question of how many stepfamilies there are becomes impossible to answer, at least in this generalised form. An estimate can be provided only if some parameters are placed around what counts as a stepfamily. The most usual focus is on stepfamily households in which dependent children are normally resident. Haskey's (1994a) analysis of stepfamilies and stepchildren provides the most comprehensive data on this for Britain, though the figures relate to 1991 and so are now a little dated. Using the above definition, he suggests there were nearly 500,000 stepfamilies in Great Britain at this time. Some 800,000 stepchildren lived in these families, approximately one in sixteen of all dependent children. Four out of five of these children lived with their natural mother and a stepfather; correspondingly, only about 20 per cent lived with their father and his new partner.

## Stepfamily tensions

As we have stressed, stepfamilies are more diverse than other family types. Even if step-relationships between people who do not live in the same household are ignored, there is still a great deal of variation. The age of the children, the length of time they have lived apart from their other natural parent, how long they have known the step-parent, the sort of role s/he plays within the household, whether the step-parent has other children, whether these step-siblings are living in the same household or elsewhere, whether there are any half-siblings born, and so on, are all going to play some part in the way in which these stepfamilies develop (Coleman and Ganong, 1990; Cherlin and Furstenberg, 1994). Equally though, there are other 'external' influences on the relationships which have a variable impact: for example, the part played in the children's lives by the non-residential parent; any continuing conflict between the natural parents over finances or contact; and how the different sets of kin, including the three sets of grandparents, respond to the members of the stepfamily.

But there are also important similarities which colour the collective experiences of stepfamily households. Certain structural characteristics of stepfamilies systematically pattern their development and mark them off from other families. However much members of stepfamilies may try to be a 'normal family', it is difficult for them to be just that. Of course, people's notions of what counts as a 'normal family' are in any event quite variable. Each family develops in its own ways, responding to the diverse history, personalities and interests of its members. In addition, different people coming together as a stepfamily have different ideals, images and goals about family life, so that any attempt by them to define a 'normal' family is bound to be problematic. Nonetheless, there are certain areas of family life which can often be taken for granted in natural families that create elements of tension in many stepfamilies.

## Family unity

One of the most powerful symbolisms of family in contemporary society is that of 'unity'. Indeed, whenever people refer to 'my' or 'your' or 'our family', they are making claims about the commonality there is between those who are considered as belonging and their distinctiveness from those who do not belong (Morgan, 1996). Thus the notion of 'family' implies ideas about solidarity and affinity, and, in consequence, about difference. This is not to deny that families are often the site of tension, argument and conflict. Culturally, everyone accepts that disagreements and rows occur within families. However, within this conception, such conflict as arises does not undermine the solidarity at the core of family life. If it is to remain a family rather than be dissolved through divorce or other irredeemable breakdown, each family needs to develop ways of handling episodes of conflict which allow for the symbolic reassertion of their collective commitment. While this sense of family solidarity and cohesion, of a group that includes and therefore excludes, may not always be the reality of everyday family life, it remains a powerful element within dominant conceptions of what 'family' means.

Thus, families have 'boundaries' around them which represent who is included and who is excluded, who is a member and who is not. Different boundaries are drawn around different sets of kin depending on the meaning 'family' has in the context in which it is being used. Like the boundaries of inclusion and exclusion constructed around different communities, these boundaries around families are not watertight or unchanging, although some formulations are more 'solidly' constructed than others (Bornat *et al.*, 1999; Cohen, 1985; Crow and Allan, 1994; Crow and Hardey, 1992). In particular, the boundaries around family in the sense of partners and children are usually strong, a point reflected in the portrayal of couples who are in the process of 'building' a home and 'starting' their own family. As research like Mansfield and Collard's (1988) shows, a dominant concern for most of these couples is establishing a shared identity that demonstrates the strong boundaries around this new grouping and demarcates them from their natal families in particular. Establishing a home of their own becomes an important project precisely because it expresses that shared identity, in a sense thereby establishing a physical representation of these symbolic boundaries (Allan and Crow, 1989). Similarly, the birth of children serves to cement this notion of a well-defined family. Within the culture, the possessiveness of expressions like 'our children' does not indicate property rights so much as signify the children's inclusion in a well-bounded family group.

With stepfamilies, the sense of unity and solidarity generated is more complex, even if we consider only those stepfamilies in which there are resident children. While the couple may be keen to create a shared identity, using the common cultural devices for expressing their commitment, their success in this will be coloured by the distinct histories they bring to their relationship. They are not starting with a *tabula rasa*; the presence of children in the home from the beginning is likely to have a significant impact on how they, as a couple, are able to symbolise their commitment. All couples, of course, carry a history with them which impacts on the development of their relationship, but this is more marked for couples in stepfamilies than for other couples: for example, children, no matter what their age, often make the expression of 'togetherness' and intimacy in courtship difficult. Not only may they intrude on 'private' moments but their needs are also likely to impinge on much of the routine time the couple spend together. Equally, if the step-parent moves into the existing family home, there are likely to be numerous reminders of previous family times. While decorations and furnishings can be replaced, photographs, mementoes and other minor legacies of the past are likely to remain. Just as the home can symbolise unity, so the existence of these artefacts, however mundane in themselves, can represent the diverse loyalties of the stepfamily's members and be significant for both the adults and child(ren) precisely because of this.

But the most important way in which the sense of family unity is attenuated in stepfamilies is through the involvement of the non-residential parent/previous partner in the new family's life. As we saw in the last chapter, it is now widely advocated that the

best interests of children are served by maintaining their relationships with both their parents after the latter's separation, despite
the difficulties there are with this (Richards, 1999). But a continuing, active relationship between a child and his/her non-
residential parent reflects the greater complexity of the boundaries
which can be drawn around the stepfamily. In Walker and
Messenger's (1979) terms, these boundaries are more 'permeable'
in stepfamilies than in natural families which have no equivalent
'outsiders' intervening. At the same time, it can be recognised
that maintaining a relationship with the non-residential parent is
good for the child but potentially undermining for the family
'project' of the new couple. Moreover, the new partner/
step-parent is likely to be drawn into any continuing tension and
conflict between the ex-partners, making acceptance of the relationship between child and non-residential parent more difficult.
However such matters are managed, the involvement of
the non-residential parent results in the symbolic boundaries
constructed around the family being less secure.

It may not just be the relationship with the non-residential
parent which militates against the unity of the family. Children
from this previous partnership also have wider kin relationships
not shared by others in the household. We know very little about
the patterning of these ties after divorce, and even less about the
degree to which they are attenuated by remarriage. Given the
limited involvement of many non-residential parents in their children's lives, it seems probable that many of these kin ties also
become inactive. However, changes in maintenance procedures
with the creation of the Child Support Agency and in the legal
position of grandparents with the 1989 Children Act may
encourage (and indeed can be seen as representing) a shift in cultural assumptions about the appropriate involvement of children
with non-residential parents and their closer kin. If, with increasing levels of divorce, policy initiatives to encourage fuller parental
involvement by the non-residential parent are at all successful, it
is conceivable that the latter's parents and siblings – the children's
grandparents, aunts and uncles – may also come to play a fuller
part in the children's lives.

As we have indicated in earlier chapters, talking about 'the
family' as a single entity is, at best, partial. The different members
of a family have different experiences, interests and solidarities.

With stepfamilies, this issue becomes more apparent, and the ambiguities, or even contradictions, of ideological stances which emphasise family unity become clearer (Robinson and Smith, 1993; Smith, 1990). Within the stepfamily, different individuals are likely to have different loyalties, and different notions of what 'their' family is. Some of the implications of this for aspects of the internal dynamics of these families will be discussed below. Here the issue to recognise is the extent to which the existence of these different loyalties (which themselves can vary) impinge on the understandings that the stepfamily collectively can develop about the unity which cements them together. As much as anything, it is the reality of these different loyalties that renders the shared identity of stepfamilies more problematic and increases the 'perviousness' of their boundaries.

## Diversity

While these issues apply generally, every stepfamily is also different, its own specific history shaping the experiences of its members. And, of course, that experience itself will change over time in different ways for the different individuals in the family. Consequently, generalising about stepfamilies as though they were all equivalent is problematic. Similarly, producing a typology of stepfamilies which adequately reflects their major variations and divisions is also complex.

One useful attempt at doing this was developed by Burgoyne and Clark (1984, pp. 191–5) from their study of stepfamilies in Sheffield. They constructed a five-fold typology based upon the family's own understanding of their circumstances and what the future held. Although it was not always easy to assign the families in their sample to particular categories, sometimes because the couple themselves could not agree, their classification is useful in highlighting some of the different ways in which stepfamilies perceived themselves. The different images they have reflect the circumstances in which they came into being, and in particular their family life phase, but also pattern the character of the consequent relationships which develop particularly between stepchild and step-parent (Coleman and Ganong, 1995).

Burgoyne and Clark distinguished their sample's imagery of their family life into five categories as follows:

(i)  *Not really a stepfamily* Those in this category were typically couples who had been together since the stepchild(ren) were young. Often they had subsequent children of their own and generally experienced little difficulty in their relationships with the non-residential parent(s). From an early stage, they perceived themselves as being in most important respects 'just an ordinary family' (1984, p. 191).

(ii)  *Looking forward to the departure of their children* These stepfamilies consisted of older couples who had teenage children from previous marriages. These couples often felt that up to now they had had limited opportunity to establish their own life together. The teenagers' demands on their time and resources, exacerbated by the processes of adjustment to the new household and their renegotiation of previous parental relationships, led to only a limited sense of 'family'. The couple's orientation was to the future when there would be space in their lives to devote to their own relationship.

(iii)  *The 'progressive' stepfamily* Progressive stepfamilies were ones in which the couple accepted, and even celebrated, their difference from traditional nuclear families. More conscious than most of the contemporary variations there are in household structure and organisation, they were positive about the domestic life they were constructing without necessarily expecting it to mirror conventional visions. In the main, they were materially well off and also able to manage relationships with ex-partners constructively.

(iv)  *The largely successful conscious pursuit of an ordinary family life together* As the terminology indicates, these couples were intent on constructing a 'normal' family life. The step-parent took on the parenting role quite fully, prioritising this at times over the claims of their own natural children. As Burgoyne and Clark (1984, p. 193) remark, the problems generated by doing this in the face of contradictory family pressures 'are, in the early stages, solved or successfully ignored'.

(v)  *The conscious pursuit of an ordinary family life frustrated* The final category in Burgoyne and Clark's typology is 'the conscious pursuit of an ordinary family life frustrated'. As this graphically suggests, these are couples who wish to be like those in the previous category for whom the dilemmas of stepfamily living have proved to be more insuperable. In particular, in these families (which, like the previous category consisted of a quarter of Burgoyne and Clark's sample), relationships with the non-residential parent(s) continued to generate tension. Disagreements over access, custody or financial arrangements meant that the couple's attempts to construct what they saw as a 'normal' family life were continually undermined. Their domestic life was regularly disrupted by the legacy of previous relationships in ways they were unable to resolve.

Burgoyne and Clark's schema is only one typology amongst many that could be constructed. It has the advantage, though, of highlighting that not all stepfamilies are problematic. For whatever reasons, there are some couples who do manage to resolve the dilemmas they face more successfully than others. In some ways this is easier if the non-residential parent plays no part in the children's lives, as it at least allows the new family to avoid overt conflict and disagreement about such matters as access and appropriate socialisation. Furthermore, if the stepfamily is sufficiently well off not to need financial support from the non-residential parent, another area of possible tension can be avoided. Where the non-residential parent is involved more fully in the children's lives, there is greater potential for disagreement, though, as the families in the 'progressive stepfamily' category illustrate, this is not inevitable.

Yet, avoiding tension and conflict is not simple. It does require much good will and understanding on the part of all involved and, as we saw in the previous chapter, this is not easy to achieve at times of domestic change. The emotional upheavals and material conflicts of interest cannot always be resolved in ways that allow for more positive relationships to emerge. What the adults in a stepfamily desire may not be what the children want or need. In particular, as current research and policy acknowledge that continuing contact with the non-residential parent is desirable for children's well-being, efforts by the new couple to create an 'ordinary' family life with the step-parent becoming a full 'social parent' may be inappropriate. The internal dynamics of stepfamilies are important too. While the adults may be agreed in the model of family life they seek, the children involved may be less willing participants. As the second of Burgoyne and Clark's categories suggests, children who are older when the stepfamily is formed are particularly able to influence the family's ambience. Not only can they express any antagonism they feel more forcefully, but also the new adult in the household is likely to have more impact on their lifestyle and generate more overt conflicts of loyalty than if they were younger children. As noted in Chapter 3, children from stepfamilies are more likely to leave home earlier than children in natural families (Jones, 1995).

From this, it can be recognised that within stepfamilies the interests of the different members are less uniform; the sets of relationships which need to be managed are broader; and the sense of family cohesion is less secure than in natural families. Equally, some stepfamilies 'work' much better than others. As Burgoyne and Clark (1984) demonstrate, there are clear structural characteristics behind this, but their success generally requires a high degree of sensitivity and tolerance on the part of those involved. This is most problematic when there are continuing disputes between the ex-partners. Overall, it is questionable whether the 'ordinary family' model is the most appropriate for newly forming stepfamilies. Such an ideal may well make it harder to accommodate to the different outlooks and requirements of the individuals concerned.

## Being a step-parent

As Burgoyne and Clark's (1984) typology attests, the ways that step-parents attempt to relate to their stepchildren vary a good deal. Some seek to replace the non-residential natural parent and become in all respects the child(ren)'s 'social' parent. Others do not aim for this, recognising that the natural parent remains special to the child(ren) and cannot be superseded. Here too though, there are differences in the degree to which the step-parent is involved in the children's lives and in the relationship they develop. This is hardly surprising given the variations there are in the circumstances of stepfamilies. The experience of becoming the step-parent to a child who is too young to remember is quite different compared to, say, that of becoming a step-parent to a teenager. Similarly, the issues confronted if the child's parents have recently separated are different compared to those in situations where the parent and child have been in a lone-parent household for a considerable time. This diversity of experience needs to be borne in mind throughout this section which focuses on broad issues that most step-parents need to resolve.

One key issue for step-parents is just how much of a parent they should seek to be. The answer to this is both contextual and relational (Marsiglio, 1992). Irrespective of their own feelings, the manner in which they attempt to resolve this issue will inevitably be shaped both by the wishes and behaviour of the others in the household, that is, the parent and the stepchild(ren), and by the relationship sustained between the non-residential parent and the child(ren). The extent to which they achieve full social parenthood will also be influenced by the length of time they have been in the step-parent role. Thus, what is involved needs to be understood as a social process. As the step-parent relationship becomes more established, the parameters of their 'parenting' are likely to embrace wider aspects of parenting as well as becoming more clearly defined. Of course, such accommodation does not always occur and may not always be sought, as in the case of Burgoyne and Clark's (1984) second category of stepfamily, those 'Looking forward to the departure of their children'.

While the step-parent role has become more common, there is still relatively little shared knowledge commonly available about how best to approach it. Indeed, the role is also one about which there are frequently contradictory expectations. As Giles-Sims (1984) has argued, friends and relatives, as well as the partner/parent, may in one setting encourage the step-parent to act like a parent, yet in other contexts criticise him/her for trying too hard to do so. Reflecting the normative uncertainty of step-parenting, this places step-parents 'in a classical double-bind situation, receiving pressure to become more like a parent at one level of communication and being told through other communicative means to remain at a distance' (Giles-Sims, 1984, p. 119). Essentially, this mirrors the ambiguity of the step-parent's situation. The commitment and love which is seen as the central part of parenting cannot easily be established. Yet the step-parent is involved in the day-to-day life of the child, as a member of the household helping to manage all the routine happenings which normally fall within the province of parents (Smith, 1990).

The same ambiguities are also often experienced by the stepchild(ren). The question of how much to regard the step-parent as a parent can be problematic. Such questions as how to address the step-parent, how to recognise their role within the household/family complex, how to maintain loyalty to the non-residential parent, and how to balance this with the perceived desires of the residential parent are all difficult ones for children, almost irrespective of their age. Resolution requires tolerance on their part as well as on the part of the adults. Moreover, the arrival of the step-parent disrupts the previous balance in the family. Depending on her/his age, a child may feel resentful about the time the parent is now spending with the step-parent, or that her/his involvement in family decision-making is reduced. The research literature carries numerous examples of children apparently maintaining a fine line between acceptance and rejection, at one time welcoming the involvement of the step-parent but at the next distancing themselves either through gesture or word (see, for example, Giles-Sims, 1984; Smith, 1990)

The chief contradiction is between 'family' on the one hand and 'household' on the other. The child has to accept that the step-parent, as an adult in the household, will impact on daily activities and hold a degree of authority. This, though, does not make him/her 'family' *per se*. The necessary solidarity has first to be established, a process which can frequently be precarious. Not only is there allegiance to the parent now living elsewhere, but equally the step-parent has not obviously 'chosen' the child, any more than the child has chosen the step-parent. The relationship is primarily built upon the romantic/sexual commitment between the parent and the step-parent, and, however sensitively handled, this reality colours the stepchild/step-parent relationship (Hodder, 1989). In the face of these ambiguities, it is not surprising that all involved in this relationship (step-parent, stepchild and parent) often find it a delicate one to manage (Coleman and Ganong, 1995).

Aspects of discipline provide the classic context in which these tensions become most overt. There is a acceptance that parents have the right and responsibility to control and discipline their children. This does not exclude other adults from exercising authority over them, but that authority is generally diluted when parents are present. In other words, parents are taken as being the ones who determine what is best for their children, how their children should behave in different settings, and how they are to be encouraged or coerced into acting appropriately. This relates both to occasions when active disciplining is deemed necessary (when the child has given cheek, caused damage or broken some other 'rule') and to occasions when other more passive forms of control are used (such as cajoling them to get ready for school or admonishing them to complete some household chore). Indeed in many ways the latter is the more important because it is through 'hassling' and 'nagging' rather than through direct discipline that most families persuade their children to act in acceptable ways, and maintain the order that characterises that particular household, whatever form that order may take.

Clearly, step-parents, as adults in the household can also be expected to play a significant part in the broad disciplining of children. Yet their doing so is not straightforward, often generating tension which reflects the underlying dynamics of the household. There are several elements to this. First, children may resist attempts by the step-parent to impose discipline, implicitly or explicitly denying that they have the authority to do so. The clichéd response 'You can't make me do that. You're not my mother/father.' captures this well. And even if it is soon realised that such a response is unlikely to be successful, other more subtle ways of undermining step-parental control can be utilised. In particular, children are likely to appeal to the natural parent to take their side or, at least, ameliorate the step-parent's instruction. Just as children frequently become skilled at playing their natural parents off against one another to achieve their aims, so too they are likely to try to drive a wedge between parent and step-parent.

And within this triangle, the natural parent is also likely to have mixed feelings. On the one hand, s/he will want the step-parent (that is, her/his partner) to be fully integrated into the household, and that means taking on, and being accepted in, the role of parental authority figure. On the other hand, s/he is also likely to be conscious of the child's own particular needs and may well seek to protect her/him from criticism from 'outsiders' who do not fully appreciate (that is, appreciate in the way the parent does) how the child is best handled. Quite often the natural parent feels as though s/he is a 'peace-keeper', attempting to mediate between the step-parent and the child to ensure that minor tensions do not erupt into major rows. Yet in 'protecting' each side from the other, s/he may be stifling development of an effective *modus operandi* between the two, thereby unintentionally fostering more explosive disputes as frustration builds up. Moreover, criticism of the child by the step-parent may be read as implied criticism of the parent who is culturally taken as responsible for the shaping of the child's character.

In turn, of course, the step-parent is also likely to experience ambivalence: at the same time wanting to support the natural parent, being aware of the child's resentment, yet having their own ideas about how children should be treated and what this particular child needs (Ambert, 1986). Unlike parents who have been part of the child's development since birth, step-parents do not 'naturally' have the same commitment to the child. Some step-parents, like those in Burgoyne and Clark's first category 'Not really a stepfamily', may feel great attachment to their stepchildren, but many will not, especially in the early phase of the relationship. Often uncertain of the role they should be playing, wanting acceptance but experiencing rejection in unpredictable ways, they too may feel resentment and jealousy about the manner in which childcare and child-centred activities impinge on the time they have with their partner (Smith, 1990). Moreover, just as the child(ren) might not like the step-parent, so too the step-parent might not find the child(ren) at all easy: for example, their backchat, their moods or the way they respond to criticism may grate, and these minor idiosyncrasies fester into major irritants. Yet, finding ways to handle these everyday issues can prove problematic, in part because the irritants are themselves symptomatic of the ambiguity of the relationship.

The issue of discipline thus embodies the different histories and the conflicting loyalties arising within stepfamily households. In natural families too there are disagreements over discipline. Yet these usually carry a quite different meaning, for while they may highlight the distinct perspectives of the parents, typically they do not undermine the perceived unity of the family nor imply a different level of solidarity or commitment between them and their children. In stepfamilies, especially in their early stages, this is far less certain. Unless handled sensitively, disagreements over discipline can serve to highlight divisions within the stepfamily and the lack of a shared heritage built around common commitments. More generally, a step-parent's attempts to alter disciplinary codes within the stepfamily can easily appear as criticism of the moral competence of earlier family forms, be this the natural family or the lone-parent family. Rather than simply being about a child misbehaving, it can come to be understood as an attack on the natural parent's parenting skills and symbolise a questioning of the child's moral character.

## Stepmothers and stepfathers

So far, we have discussed step-parenting in general whilst emphasising, throughout, the variation there is in the character of step-families and the way step-parenting is experienced. It is now appropriate to consider one of the major divisions within step-parenting, that between stepfathers and stepmothers. As we have argued in earlier chapters, gender divisions are central to an understanding of family life. The roles that men and women routinely play within families are clearly gendered, and highly influenced by the character of the economic and social environment experienced outside the domestic sphere. This division of responsibility colours the experiences of stepmothers and stepfathers just as it does the experiences of natural parents.

As a consequence, the issues confronting stepfathers are likely to be less problematic than those faced by stepmothers (Ambert, 1986; MacDonald and DeMaris, 1996). Indeed, stepfathers may, in some instances, play quite a limited role in their stepchildren's lives. Ferri (1984), for example, has suggested that some stepfathers define their main contribution as one of supporting the mother emotionally and providing financial security. As a member of the household they will have a direct involvement with their stepchildren, but they play a secondary role in terms of managing the children's daily activities and ensuring their well-being. Other stepfathers may feel a responsibility to act as an authority figure and become involved in discipline, whilst generally maintaining a distance from participation in routine childcare.

Yet, as we have seen, this can easily become contentious. Acting as a disciplinary figurehead may reflect traditional images of fatherhood and embrace stereotypical views of the shortcomings of lone-parent families, yet the stepfather's ambiguous position renders the right to exercise discipline problematic. Still other stepfathers play a much fuller part in their stepchildren's lives, being involved in many different aspects of their development. Crucially though, stepfathers can relatively easily avoid major responsibility for childcare. This may not be what they seek, but it does provide a way of stepping back from, and in that sense coping with if not resolving, the dilemmas of the step-parent role.

In many ways stepmothers are in a more difficult position, as being a stepmother usually entails a closer involvement with the stepchild than being a stepfather. While not always so, the standard division of labour within households applies to stepfamilies as it does to other families (Ishii-Kuntz and Coltrane, 1992; Sullivan, 1997). Consequently, stepmothers are likely to be responsible for domestic organisation and for the smooth running of the household. This will bring them into routine contact with their stepchildren far more than stepfathers' responsibilities typically require them to be involved with their stepchildren. Such tasks as preparing meals, washing and ironing clothes, getting young children dressed and older ones ready for school, tidying and cleaning rooms all fall more within the purview of mothers than fathers. Because of the impact that children of whatever age have on domestic order, it is inevitable that those responsible for that order, in this case stepmothers, are involved in overseeing the child's activities.

Moreover, stepmothers responsible for household management are also likely to be responsible for childcare: that is, it is not just through their housekeeping responsibilities that they will be involved with their stepchildren. They are also likely to assume responsibility for the day-to-day management of their stepchildren's lives. It may be, though there is little systematic evidence on this, that fathers play a more significant part than is usual here (Smith, 1990). This could be because stepmothers insist on it ('She's your daughter. You do it.'); because children in this situation turn more than usual to their fathers; or because the fathers themselves seek to be more involved, partly perhaps to ease relationships between their child(ren) and their partner. Even so, these stepmothers will frequently be involved in active mothering. They will be the ones who are primarily responsible for managing the welfare of the children, meeting their routine needs and ensuring appropriate standards of behaviour. In addition, women in families are generally taken to be the 'relationship specialists' (Hochschild, 1996; Wood, 1993). In other words, they are also expected to actively manage the relationships which develop in the household. More than men, they take responsibility for ensuring that tension and conflict are minimised and that the different needs of family members are met.

Thus the lives of most residential stepmothers are more entwined with their stepchildren than are most stepfathers. Distancing themselves from their stepchildren in the way stepfathers often can is much more difficult to negotiate. Indeed, because of the dominant ideologies about gender roles, doing so would also undermine the idea of the family being 'just a normal family'. In a sense, women are ascribed the greater responsibility for the specific 'culture' that develops within a household; it is they who are more likely to set the 'rules' and they who have most say over how the family/household is ordered. Yet they may start with little experience of mothering, especially if they do not have 'natural' children of their own. In most instances, they will not have been involved in the children's early experiences and consequently not have the sense natural parents have of shaping the child(ren)'s development. They experience all the dilemmas and ambiguities associated with step-parenthood, including hostility and rejection from the child(ren), yet are generally expected to fulfil the mothering role as though this were unproblematic. Given the standard division of labour within families, it is perhaps as well that the majority of children in stepfamilies continue to live with their natural mothers.

## Conclusion

The National Stepfamily Association (1997) recognises that there are 72 different ways in which stepfamilies can be formed. Such diversity is compounded by the different arrangements which individual stepfamilies generate in establishing their routines and relationships. Although the amount of research being undertaken on the topic of stepfamily organisation is increasing in this country and in the United States, we still know relatively little about their dynamics or the range of experiences they embrace. In particular, while step-parents' perspectives have received attention, there has been less sociological focus on the feelings, understandings and experiences of children in stepfamilies. And much of the knowledge we do have comes from asking parents about their children's well-being and adaptation rather than asking the children themselves.

One area where more research is required concerns the relationships which develop when there are step-siblings and half-siblings in the household. When two adults both bring children from previous unions into a new partnership household dynamics will evidently be more complex than when only one adult does so. And different issues will arise depending on whether or not both sets of children live in the new household, though the varied histories of parenting involved will also shape the patterns which emerge. Equally, new children born into the stepfamily will have diverse impacts on existing relationships depending on the particular circumstances of the families. In Britain there has been little research into this, though American studies have reported somewhat contradictory findings (see, for example, Ambert, 1986; Ganong and Coleman, 1988; MacDonald and DeMaris, 1996; Masiglio, 1992; White, Brinkerhoff and Booth, 1985).

The impact which the 'reconfiguring' (Coleman and Ganong, 1995) of family solidarities following divorce and remarriage has on kinship relationships outside the household warrants much more detailed research than it has so far received. We know little about the role of grandparents in stepfamilies, especially the part played by the parents of the non-residential natural parent and by the step-parent's parents (Giarrusso, Silverstein and Bengston, 1996; Henry, Ceglian and Matthews, 1992; Trygstad and Sanders, 1989). These relationships themselves become more complex as stepfamilies are formed across two (or more) generations. Simpson's (1994; 1998) research is important here for raising questions about the nature of contemporary kinship in an era of 'unclear' families, as well as for asking how cultural understandings of parenting, and in particular fathering, are altering as increasing numbers of children have experience of sustaining 'fatherhood-relevant' relationships with their mother's ex- and current partners. In other words, as more children come to have different 'father' relationships with two or more men (for example, their natural father together with one or more step-fathers), perceptions of what is involved in fatherhood, and in turn in 'parenthood' more generally, are likely to become both more complex and less uniform.

Simply raising these types of issues highlights the complexities which are involved in coming to a fuller understanding of step-families. While some stepfamilies may be no different in the eyes of their members from 'ordinary' (that is, first-time) families, many of these families have to negotiate a far more complicated accommodation. Generating solidarity between people with dif-ferent familial histories, different loyalties and different commit-ments within the one household is frequently a difficult process, made the more so by the lack of clear cultural indicators about how it can be achieved. Yet with the changing patterns of family formation and dissolution which are now part of our social struc-ture (Silva and Smart, 1999; Smart, 1997), the number of step-families formed will continue to grow. While this of itself is likely to foster fuller cultural appreciation of how the dynamics of step-families are variously organised, there is clearly a need for researchers, and indeed policy-makers, to pay greater heed to these matters than they have up to now.

# 8  Families and Households in Later Life

A frequent claim about many contemporary Western societies is that elderly people are no longer respected as they were in earlier periods of history. One strong element of this portrayal concerns the relationships between the generations and in particular the extent to which 'families' fail to give necessary support to elderly people as they age and become infirm. A major aim of this chapter is to question claims like these critically, both because they distort the reality of most family relationships in later life and because in the process they imply a frailty and passive dependence among the elderly population which does not mirror the experiences of the majority. However, before delving more deeply into the patterns of household and family relationships which elderly people sustain, it is necessary to explore the dominant trends in the social, economic and demographic characteristics of older people in contemporary Britain.

## Material realities

### Demography

The most fundamental point to make about Britain's elderly population is how much it has changed over the course of the twentieth century. As in other Western societies, these changes have been so significant that in one sense there can be no meaningful comparisons with earlier eras. The issues and dilemmas which older age generates are, from the perspective of both the individuals involved and the wider society, new ones; previous

**Table 8.1**   *Age distribution 1901–91 In thousands (UK)*

|                   | 1901   | 1951   | 1971   | 1998   |
|-------------------|--------|--------|--------|--------|
| Total population  | 38,237 | 50,225 | 55,928 | 59,237 |
| 65–74             | 1,278  | 3,689  | 4,764  | 4,965  |
| 75–84             | 470    | 1,555  | 2,160  | 3,205  |
| 85+               | 61     | 224    | 485    | 1,122  |
| All over 65       | 1,809  | 5,468  | 7,409  | 9,292  |

*Source: Annual Abstract of Statistics, 2000.*

cohorts simply did not experience old age to the extent it is now experienced. For this reason alone, ignoring all the other social and economic changes there have been, the patterns of later life emerging in contemporary society are inevitably different from the patterns characteristic of earlier eras. But, of course, the other social and economic changes occurring during the twentieth century cannot be ignored. The ways in which economic and social life developed has had major impacts on the experiences and relationships which elderly people sustain.

Consider first the extent to which the age structure has altered. Table 8.1 records the growth in the United Kingdom's elderly population in the twentieth century, comparing this to the growth in the population overall. Not only has there been a significant increase in the numbers and proportion of the population aged 65 and over but, significantly, the rate of increase is higher the older the age group. Thus while Britain's overall population has increased by 50 per cent since 1901, the population of people aged 65 or over has grown five-fold, those over 75 six-fold and those over 85 sixteen-fold. Table 8.2 expresses these same changes differently, showing the proportion of the population in given age categories over the century. As can be seen, the proportion of the population 65 or over increased by a factor of three in the twentieth century, and the proportion of those aged over 85 by a factor of nine.

Within this growth, other demographic patterns are important. In particular, women have a longer average life expectancy than men: for example, there are currently some 3.75 million men aged 65 or over in the UK, compared to 5.5 million women (*Annual Abstract of Statistics*, 1997). Moreover, there are a little

**Table 8.2**  *Proportional age distribution 1901–98 % (UK)*

|                  | 1901 | 1951 | 1971 | 1998 |
|------------------|------|------|------|------|
| 65–74            | 3.3  | 7.3  | 8.5  | 8.4  |
| 75–84            | 1.2  | 3.1  | 3.9  | 5.4  |
| 85+              | 0.2  | 0.4  | 0.9  | 1.9  |
| All over 65      | 4.7  | 10.9 | 13.2 | 15.7 |
| Total population | 100  | 100  | 100  | 100  |

*Source: Annual Abstract of Statistics, 2000.*

over a quarter of a million men aged 85 or over, but three times as many women (Grundy, 1995). In other words, 11 per cent of men aged 65 to 74 are widowed, but 35 per cent of women in this age range are. Similarly, women aged 75 or over are more than twice as likely to be widowed as men are, 64 per cent compared to 28 per cent (*Annual Abstract of Statistics*, 1997). Conversely 67 per cent of men aged 75 or older are married compared to only 22 per cent of women. (Also see Grundy, 1995; 1996.) While these differences are partly a consequence of women tending to marry men older than themselves, they still indicate the diverse experiences of men and women in old age. Employment differentials over the life course make these differences particularly significant in later life.

As would be expected, these differences in marital status are mirrored in household composition. Table 8.3 shows how much more common it is for older women to be living alone than it is for older men. While nearly three-quarters of men aged 65 or over live with a spouse, either as a couple or, in a minority of cases, with others too, fewer than two-fifths of women of this age live with a spouse. Indeed, nearly half of all women 65 or over live alone, compared with only a fifth of men. This particular differential in household circumstances reduces a little for men and women aged 80 or over, though it is still marked. Note too from Table 8.3 that only a small minority of older people live in the same household as their children. Even amongst those aged 80 and over who are not living with a spouse, only a sixth of men and a quarter of women live with their children. We will discuss the significance of this later in the chapter.

**Table 8.3**   *Older persons by type of household\* 1996 % (UK)*

|  | Males | | Females | |
|---|---|---|---|---|
| Household type | 65–74 | 75 and over | 65–74 | 75 and over |
| Alone | 21 | 34 | 40 | 68 |
| With spouse: |  |  |  |  |
| Only | 68 | 59 | 50 | 25 |
| And child(ren) | 9 | 4 | 5 | 1 |
| Without spouse and with child(ren) | 2 | 3 | 4 | 5 |

\**Living in private households*
*Source*: Social Trends, 1997.

## Retirement

In contemporary Western societies, later life is now strongly associated with retirement. Very few people aged over 65 are expected
to be in employment. Indeed, with the economic restructuring
Britain experienced at the end of the twentieth century, retirement
age has become younger than this for many. What is often forgotten in this is just how recent in historical terms the experience of
retirement actually is. In the 1930s, for example, only around half
the male population over 65 were retired. By 1971, this figure was
close to 80 per cent, and rose steeply to 94 per cent by 1981 in
response to the sharp decline in employment opportunities as the
economy went into recession. It has continued to rise, albeit more
slowly, since then (Phillipson, 1982, 1998).

   Throughout the century, retirement has entailed different transitions for the majority of men and women. For men and most
single women, it has meant a loss of their main adult activity, paid
work; consequently for many it represents a major shift in their
social location and in their identity. For many married women,
the social implications of retirement *per se* have been less
significant. For much of this century, 'retirement' age has not
signified a radical break with the past for wives, as employment
has been less central in their lives. Reaching the official age of
'retirement' did not of itself represent a significant transition; they
carried on with their domestic responsibilities much as before,
though of course the nature of these responsibilities altered over

the life course. For many, the main social change around retirement arose when their husbands, rather than they themselves, reached retirement age. Their husbands typically spent more time around the home, disrupting their wives' previous routines and often requiring higher levels of emotional support from them in adjusting to their own changed circumstances (Mason, 1987).

The situation is different for the current cohort of married women reaching retirement age. Paid work has been a more significant element in their lives, so that retirement carries many of the same connotations as it does for men, and other women active in the labour force. Even though these women have often been employed in low-paid, routine, unfulfilling work, retirement represents a change in their day-to-day lives and in their self-identity. The continuation of their housewife/domestic-service role mitigates some of the impact of retirement but, as we saw in earlier chapters, this role is not highly valued. Having previously been incorporated into routines which also involved employment, it cannot really act as a replacement activity for that employment. As with redundancy, the first few weeks or months of retirement may be experienced very positively as a time to 'catch up' with tasks that have previously been neglected, but in the long run, domestic labour is a poor substitute for the benefits of even part-time and low-status employment (Bernard, Itzin, Phillipson and Skucha, 1995).

*Pensions*

In large part, retirement became a more established phase of life in the second half of the twentieth century because of the institutionalisation of pension arrangements. Without some form of alternative income, most people could not afford to retire from paid work. Ultimately the development of retirement as a recognised phase of life is also a consequence of the greater efficiency of modern forms of production and a declining demand for labour. But if older workers were to be retired from the active labour force, then pension facilities needed to be established. The Welfare State promised an adequate and secure income in retirement, but this was never fully realised in practice and concern over poverty amongst older people remains (Phillipson, 1998). The state continues to grapple with the most appropriate ways of funding pension arrangements, especially given the rise in the number of elderly people in the population and the changing patterns of political commitment to tackling pensioner poverty. In recent years, there has been heavy promotion of private and occupational pensions as the major form of provision, with the standard state pension increasingly being seen as a 'safety net' rather than the major component of income in older age.

This is not the place to go into the details of pension policy. However, there are some aspects of pension provision which are key to understanding the different experiences of older people, and which consequently impinge on household organisation and the character of their family relationships. In particular, pension arrangements reflect strongly the divisions which arise in earlier life phases. For the great majority of people, economic standing in later life is a direct result of their lifelong location within the occupational structure. As in other areas of activity, class and gender are especially significant in determining elderly people's living standards. By itself, the state pension at best keeps people out of poverty, though many who are solely dependent on it also qualify for income support. Their income, in other words, is at what the state normally defines as the minimum level necessary. Consequently, access to private and, more frequently, occupational pensions is crucial if higher living standards are to be achieved. But the distribution of occupational and private pensions is highly skewed.

Currently, middle-class employees are more likely than working-class employees to belong to occupational pension schemes. Moreover, the conditions of the schemes to which most non-manual personnel belong are considerably more generous than those to which manual workers belong, tending, for example, to be based on the years of highest earnings rather than on average earnings. In their analysis of data from the 1985 General Household Survey, Ginn and Arber (1991) report that nearly 90 per cent of men over 65 who had been in professional and senior management positions were in receipt of an occupational or other non-state pension, as were over three-quarters of other male non-manual staff. In contrast, only a half of unskilled male manual workers and two-thirds of male skilled manual workers were. Moreover, Ginn and Arber's (1991) data also indicate the differences there are in the amount of non-state pensions received by men with different class histories. The upper-quartile (the point separating the top 25 per cent from the bottom 75 per cent in each category) non-state pension income for senior managers and professionals was then some £80 per week, compared to approximately £30 for supervisory and skilled manual workers. The upper quartile for state benefits at the time for men was close to £45, so this variation in non-state pension represented a significant difference.

However, these differences are relatively small compared to the differences between men and women. Because of their very different employment histories, far fewer women than men of retirement age have a non-state pension. As Ginn and Arber (1996, p. 469) point out in a later paper, 'Research has established women's very substantial income disadvantage in later life compared with men's and has shown how this gender inequality arises from older women's earlier domestic roles and the constraints these place on employment and the acquisition of occupational and personal pensions.' A number of factors are involved here.

First, many of the cohort of women now in later old age were not employed after marriage and so had no prospect of belonging to an occupational pension scheme. Although those reaching retirement age more recently are more likely to have been employed, relatively few were involved in pension schemes. Thus, as we saw in Chapter 5, these women were typically employed in less skilled and less well-paid occupations. Even in those rare instances where this employment offered an occupational pension scheme, the generally lower level of their earnings in comparison to men's meant that the amount of pension due on retirement was less, even when they had been employed throughout their adult life. Importantly though, many married women were not employed for the length of time necessary to acquire full pension rights. The period they spent as full-time housewives and mothers reduced their years of contribution below that required for a full pension. In addition, many of these women returned to part-time jobs. Many of these do not offer membership of occupational pension schemes, and even where they do, contributions made as a part-time employee result in a reduced pension on retirement. A further point is that while their husbands are alive, older women may benefit from the occupational pensions derived from their employment. Once they are widowed, however (bearing in mind that wives do typically outlive their husbands by up to a decade), a wife's pension rights are often reduced very significantly, frequently leaving them in relative poverty.

In their later study, using data from the OPCS Retirement and Retirement Plans Survey collected in 1988/9, Ginn and Arber (1996) were able to provide more detailed information about differences in men's and women's pension entitlements. The study focuses on women aged 60–69 and men aged 65–69 and so includes fewer women who were never employed after marriage (17 per cent) than the elderly population overall. Yet gender differences remain substantial. Only a quarter of women in the sample had a non-state pension of their own, whereas nearly three-quarters of the men did. The median amount of this non-state pension for these 25 per cent of women was £17 per week, compared to £31 for the men. Overall, the median income for the men in the study was approximately £80 per week, compared to a median for the women of less than £45. From these data Ginn and Arber are also able to compare the pension experiences of women with different work histories. As Table 8.4 shows, differences between those employed full-time and and those employed part-time are significant, as are differences between those with disrupted work histories and those employed for at least 30 years between the ages of 20 and 55. The median amount of non-state pension for those women with one who had been employed full-time for 30 or more years was £34 per week, differing only slightly from the median amount for men with such a pension (though the differences became more significant at the top end of the distribution). However, women with non-state pensions who had other employment histories, predominantly part-time work and/or fewer years spent in employment, received on average less than £20 per week from this source (Ginn and Arber, 1996, pp. 478–82).

The key issue here is the degree to which the material conditions of later life are linked to earlier experiences in the labour force. As a result, class and gender continue to be key variables in determining people's lifestyles in older age (Vincent, 1995). Other factors, including marital status, ethnicity and disabilities, are also important but it is gender and class which dominate because of their impact on pensions. However, pension arrangements are not static. Current cohorts of employees have different work histories and different pension rights from earlier cohorts,

**Table 8.4**  *Percentage of women with different employment histories in receipt of non-state pensions (women 60–69)*

| Years of employment between different ages | % |
|---|---|
| 30+ years between 20 and 55 with at least 90% full-time | 62 |
| 30+ years between 20 and 55 with less than 90% full-time | 25 |
| Less than 30 years between 20 and 55, but at least 12 years between 40 and 55, at least 50% of which was full-time | 49 |
| Less than 30 years between 20 and 55, but at least 12 years between 40 and 55, at least 50% of which was part-time | 14 |
| Less than 12 years between 40 and 55, but at least 10 years between 30 and 55, at least 50% of which was full-time | 29 |
| Less than 12 years between 40 and 55, but at least 10 years between 30 and 55, at least 50% of which was part-time | 9 |
| All other employment histories | 5★ |

★ Approximate
Derived from Ginn and Arber, 1996.

though with the continuing importance of occupational pensions in pension policies, the major differences identified here are likely to continue to pattern people's experience of old age in the foreseeable future.

## The transition to later life

With this brief mapping of older people's social and material circumstances, we can now turn more directly to consider the main concern of this chapter: the patterns of family and household relationships which develop in later life. In analysing these, it needs always to be remembered that the transitions involved in later life are not uniform. There is no simple progression to old age that people inevitably follow. Their experiences are patterned by a wide range of factors. Indeed, in examining the impact of older age on household and family relationships, three conceptual elements, central to all domestic experience, need highlighting: *diversity*, *continuity* and *change*. Just as these elements are present in earlier life and family transitions, so they characterise later phases of life as well.

It is particularly important to recognise continuity. Our cultural portrayals and common-sense understandings of old age often emphasise change: a move from being economically active to inactive; from being able-bodied to being infirm; from independence to a greater dependency. In reality, continuity is just as important. Certainly, radical changes do occur which have major consequences for some: retirement from employment, widowhood and disabling illnesses are among the more obvious examples. Yet the experience of ageing at this phase of life also entails continuity, just as it does in earlier life phases: for instance, while retirement undoubtedly represents a significant shift for many older people, other relationships in which they are involved continue much as before. The patterning of their marriages and the domestic division of labour may change little despite the extra time now spent in the home (Askham, 1995). Similarly, their leisure interests may alter only slowly, and their relationships with their children continue much as before.

Indeed in terms of family and household relationships, some of the impact of old age will be the result of the changes that others in their family networks are experiencing rather than anything to do with their own ageing *per se*. For example, the character of grandparent–grandchild relationships is likely to alter not because of (the grandparent's) retirement or their reaching some benchmark age (65, 70 or whatever) but more because of the changes the younger generation experience as they become independent. These processes are likely to affect the latter's relationships with their grandparents, and arguably, by altering their parents' responsibilities and freedoms, also modify the tie between their parents and their grandparents. Understanding familial and domestic aspects of older age requires that the experience is seen within a broad context and not just in the light of the biological ageing process.

From a conceptual angle, the impact of later-life ageing on domestic and familial relationships, and indeed on lifestyle more generally, is no different from the impact of ageing at other periods of life. As one ages, the relationships in which one is involved and the pattern of rights, responsibilities and commitments entailed, evolves, sometimes slowly, sometimes more rapidly. We saw this in Chapter 3 in the discussion of the transition to early adulthood, but it applies equally to other life phases, though often awareness of changes in these other phases is more muted. At issue here is how individuals' current activities and relationships are patterned by the social and economic constraints and opportunities they experience and includes this the continuing impact of the network of familial and other relationships built up over time. These are also dynamic: for example, the process of older people migrating to 'retirement areas' provides a good illustration of how individuals' social networks can evolve. The concentration of retired populations on the south coast of England, the Mediterranean coasts of various European states, and in Florida in the USA has important implications for those involved and for their wider societies (Laslett, 1996). It is because different people's lives are differentially patterned, by their past and current social and economic location, that ideas of continuity, change and diversity are key for understanding the domestic and familial experiences of later life.

Somewhat similarly, the relationships people maintain in later life with their wider family also depend, in part, on the forms which these relationships took in earlier life phases. They too have a history which is likely to influence how they are currently patterned. Despite cultural concerns about the extent to which elderly people are isolated from their families, numerous studies have demonstrated that this is rarely so. In particular, the great majority of adult children continue to have active ties with their parents. Those elderly people who are more isolated tend to be people who either had no children or whose children have died (Scott and Wenger, 1995). Some children also lose contact with their parents through divorce, being taken into care or as a result of a history of childhood abuse. In most cases too, siblings continue to be involved with one another, though once again the degree and extent of this is coloured by the character of these ties in earlier life phases.

To consider the issues involved here, let us focus on parent–child relationships. In examining the culture of American kinship a generation ago, Schneider (1968) coined the term 'diffuse, enduring solidarity'. While applied to kin ties generally, it is a particularly apt characterisation of many contemporary parent–child relationships. These ties are certainly enduring. They rarely break down completely; some form of contact is generally maintained, though there can be great variation within as well as between sibling groups. Secondly, the sense of commitment that parents and (adult) children feel towards one another is diffuse. There are no set rules about the responsibilities each owes the other or about what should be included as pertinent to the relationship. Each is concerned for the other's welfare in a general sense without the 'content' of this concern being specified (Finch and Mason, 1993). Moreover, unlike other types of relationship, issues of reciprocity are rarely to the fore. There are cultural norms about gratitude for the help and support provided, but there is no direct equivalence of exchange built into the tie. Whether help is given and what form this takes depends very much on the specific support needed at different times, as well as the other responsibilities of each party.

Consequently there is a good deal of leeway in the expression of solidarity between parents and adult children. Very different relationships can emerge which nonetheless fit within this cultural format of 'diffuse, enduring solidarity'. In a sense each relationship has its own logic, with that logic being structured over time by the different configuration of interests and commitments both sides have. One way of perceiving this is to think of each relationship as having its own 'trajectory' with its future patterning depending in part on the 'route' it has taken earlier. The trajectory may alter quite radically as circumstances change, but routinely its individual history influences its future pathway.

Within this, each relationship is part of a wider network which also shapes its form. In this, kinship can be seen as a social network, with each link being embedded in a wider set of ties which affect its ordering (Allan, 1996). The relationship, for instance, that develops between an individual's partner and her/his parents will have a bearing on the character of the parent – adult–child tie. Where they get on well with each other, interaction is likely to be more frequent and probably closer. Conversely where there is conflict between them, this too will spill over into the relationship between the parents and child. Equally, when grandchildren are born, they often provide a fresh focus for the parent–adult–child tie that reinforces the solidarity between them, especially as the previous period is often one in which independence between the two generations is being established. Similarly, an individual's relationship with her or his parents can be influenced by the nature of the ties which exist between the parents and their other children. If one sibling lives close by and sees their parents regularly, other siblings living further afield may feel less need to be as actively involved with their parents as they would if they were, say, an only child.

Just as the idea of 'diffuse, enduring solidarity' represents a strong cultural theme in parent – adult–child relationships, so does the notion of 'independence'. As we saw in Chapter 3, independence is an important signifier of adult status. In this regard, Parsons' (1949) arguments about the structural isolation of the nuclear family within Western kinship systems are right despite the criticisms they have received. In describing the nuclear family as structurally isolated, Parsons was asserting that the responsibilities an individual has in adulthood to her/his partner and dependent children overrode their responsibilities to other kin, including their parents and siblings. This does not mean that there is no responsibility felt towards these other kin: studies have consistently shown that there are (see Allan, 1996). What it does mean, quite simply, is that the demands made by the nuclear family are given precedence over other kin solidarities (Harris, 1983; 1990).

This is not so clearly the case with ethnic minority kinship systems. Among some of Britain's Asian population in particular, greater priority is given to parental ties in adulthood (Afshar, 1989; Blakemore and Boneham, 1994; Phillipson *et al.*, 1998). There is more sharing of the home across three generations for some, and this often entails a common housekeeping. There also seems to be a greater deference to parental views throughout adulthood than is the case within the mainstream British kinship system. Whether such patterns will be maintained with future generations – with increased social mobility, conflicting cultural claims and a reliance on individual wages rather than common family property – remains to be seen (Blakemore and Boneham, 1994; Fennell, Phillipson and Evers, 1988).

Within the dominant kinship system though, maintaining a level of independence from non-nuclear family remains impor-tant throughout adulthood. In contrast to the ethnic minority pattern just discussed, it is expected that adult children will maintain separate households from their parents and to be free of too much 'parental interference' in making significant decisions. Yet, as we saw in Chapter 3, the notion of 'independence' is far more complex than it appears, not being an 'either/or' concept. Baltes (1996) captures this well in her reference to 'the many faces of dependency in old age'. It is doubtful where the boundaries are drawn between dependence, interdependence and independence, or what counts as 'interference' in different spheres. It is moot whether, for example, receiving money from adult children, confiding in them about personal problems or regularly relying on them as carers, compromises one's independence.

What matters is the way the relationships are balanced and the understandings by those involved of their exchanges. As mentioned above, reciprocity, especially short- to middle-term reciprocity, appears less significant in these relationships than it does in many non-kin ties. Yet overall, if a sufficient degree of independence is to be sustained, then there must be an acceptable balance in the support each side gives the other. Too much of a one-way flow over time is likely to generate a sense of dependency. Clearly there are ways of managing the relationships so that independence is not undermined; for example, financial transfers can be accomplished through purchases for grandchildren or through generous presents at ceremonial times like birthdays and Christmas. Similarly, mechanisms can be constructed so that concern over and advice about grandchildren are not represented overtly as 'interfering', thereby sustaining the imagery of independence alongside an active involvement.

These issues of independence and autonomy are highly salient to people in later life. While the great majority of older people lead as independent (or more accurately, as inter-dependent) lives in later life as they have done earlier, the spectre of infirmity – increasing dependence as people age – is a very powerful one. Cultural images of ageing encourage a perception of later life as a period in which individuals have less control over their lives. And, as researchers like Phillipson (1982) and Phillipson and Walker (1986) have argued so well, the institutionalisation of old age within Western society fostered a structural dependency that was absent in earlier adulthood, though recent developments in care policies have begun to alter this (Phillipson, 1998). Against this backcloth, many elderly people are fiercely protective of their independence, guarding it as strongly as possible. Even if over time they do begin to require assistance from others for tasks they could previously achieve for themselves – and of course this is not inevitable, least of all in early 'old age' – they will seek ways of managing this that do not indicate dependency.

For some, their developing needs will be met principally by others living in the household, in particular a spouse or adult child. Minor forms of assistance are likely to be viewed as part of the normal patterning of household organisation, though this imagery is harder to sustain if more personal forms of care are needed. Another way in which independence can be protected is through buying whatever services are necessary through the market. Such exchanges are usually taken as a form of self-management rather than as an indicator of dependency. However, this is obviously an option which is more open to those with higher pensions than others. For many older people who find they are no longer so able to do all the tasks necessary for daily living, support is received informally from others living inside or outside their households, and in particular from their spouse or one or more of their adult children.

In many respects, such support is simply a further manifestation of the diffuse solidarity of kinship. Gradually, when children visit, they may begin to do more for their parent(s) than they previously did. They may fix things in the house, do some cleaning of more inaccessible areas or bring some shopping with them. Such activities are routine and largely unproblematic. They are part of the long-term and broad-based exchanges which characterise most parent–child relationships. They are treated as part of the normal support each gives the other. Just as in earlier life phases when the support that parents give to their children is often disguised so as to maintain the younger generation's image of independence, the practical and other support activities children begin to give their ageing parents are also represented without too much difficulty as unremarkable elements within the natural order typifying these family ties.

However, if the need for support grows, it can become more difficult to portray the assistance given as simply an element within the normal exchanges of familial ties. Instead it highlights the increasing dependence of the older generation because it represents such a clear transformation of past patterns. At such times, issues of reciprocity remain important, though they are not always easy to resolve. It may be that the parent can still provide some services for their children, especially if they have financial resources available for this. Alternatively they may seek to limit the help the younger generation provides, in part by disguising their degree of need and the time it takes them to complete particular activities. The child involved may also be active in 'managing' reciprocity by downplaying the degree of support they provide and the inconvenience it causes. Most importantly, perhaps, the discourse constructed by the child around the support may emphasise the inappropriateness of considering short-term reciprocity significant: that is, the help currently provided by the child may be contrasted with the history of support received from the parent(s) across the life course.

A further issue that arises here with regard to the assistance children provide for their parents is how that support is divided within the sibling set. Is it shared equally? And if not, are there identifiable patterns in its distribution? As we shall see, in most cases there is not an equal division between siblings; generally, one particular child carries a disproportionate responsibility for providing support. The idea of relationship trajectories introduced above is important for understanding the processes involved here. However, as we have been emphasising, parent – adult–child relationships are both diffuse and enduring. There are no strong norms delineating exactly what obligations a child has towards her/his parents or what s/he should do in particular circumstances, a point Finch and Mason (1993) make forcefully on the basis of their research into kinship obligations. Instead, Finch and Mason argue, a process of 'negotiation' occurs through which responsibility is either assumed or assigned. Often this negotiation is tacit rather than explicit, building on the actions, reputations and circumstances of the different siblings. Consequently within these negotiations, the character of the relationship which each child has built up in adulthood with their parent(s), the relationship trajectory, is significant.

While this may imply that emotional closeness is the key to siblings' differential support, in reality this is not necessarily the case. What generally matters more are the practicalities of people's circumstances. Two influences seem to be operating. The first of these is gender. Largely because of the standard division of domestic labour combined with the distinct pattern of participation of many married women in the labour force, daughters (and in some cases, daughters-in-law) are often more readily available to help out with mundane tasks as necessary. While this may start out as quite limited and relatively undemanding, as circumstances alter, this very help may become a rationale for providing more extensive support. In contrast, the help sons provide tends to be more piece-meal and linked to their traditional gender roles. They may help with aspects of household maintenance or provide financial advice and management. But other modes of support, such as help with cleaning the house, doing shopping, and running errands, as well as more personal forms of care (all of which are usually more time-consuming, as they are required more frequently) are usually pro-vided disproportionately by daughters.

The second influence is propinquity. Where there is an adult child living in the same household as the parent(s), other things being equal, they are likely to take major responsibility for the parent's welfare. Of course, other things are not always equal. Some of those who share a house with their elderly parents do so because of their own disabilities, and so may not be able to provide appropriate forms of support. Moreover, resident sons may provide less support if they have a sister living nearby whose circumstances are such that she can cater for the parents' emerg-ing needs (Qureshi and Walker, 1989). Gender here 'competes' with household membership as the key factor. Where there is no child living with the parent(s), then the geographical location of the siblings often impacts on the distribution of tasks. Clearly some activities require proximity, particularly those that need to be performed frequently. However, it is not just a case of avail-ability, for often a sibling who lives near to their parent(s) has, over time, developed a different relationship, typified by more regular exchanges, from those developed by siblings living further away. This history of routine involvement makes it likely also that that sibling is the one 'obviously' drawn into providing help as this becomes necessary. This in turn can have repercussions if the support required becomes more extensive.

The main points here are, first, that most elderly people do not need particular support from their adult children, over and above the routine exchanges on which their relationship is based; and second, that the ethic of independence and managing for oneself is an extremely powerful one, in old age as in other times. Children typically are concerned for their parents' welfare, but

188 Families, Households and Society

that concern is patterned by the emphasis placed by all on independence. In a sense, it is only when parents are 'failing to thrive' (to use the language applied in childcare) on their own that children are likely to move much beyond the broad matrix of exchange found at other adult life phases. Similarly, if one sibling is providing the support necessary to ensure the relative well-being of the parents, other siblings are likely to play a small part, especially if they live some distance away. However, it is worth noting that the recent changes in family formation and dissolution outlined in Chapter 2 are likely to affect these processes. In particular, the increasing levels of divorce and remarriage are bound to make the provision of support for 'parents' more complex and possibly more contentious.

## Infirmity and later life

As we have noted, the dominant image of elderly people requiring high levels of assistance is misleading. The great majority of elderly people are in comparatively good health and well able to manage for themselves. Of course, some, perhaps especially those who have been widowed and whose social networks have shrunk through the death of others, are likely to experience episodes of loneliness and depression, but the majority have relatively active lifestyles, at least to the extent their material resources permit. Even if some tasks gradually become more difficult, they require little, if any, additional support beyond that entailed in the normal exchanges and cooperations of everyday adult life. Bury and Holme's (1991) study of people in their nineties shows that, even for this group, age and dependence are not linked in any straightforward way. However, a minority of elderly people do become far more infirm and experience great difficulty in managing the routine activities of everyday living.

Measuring disability is not easy as there are so many dimensions involved with it. While sophisticated methods of measurement have been produced (Duckworth, 1983), applying them is labour-intensive and consequently expensive. For large-scale studies simpler measurements have to be applied. One of the most straightforward is that devised for use with the General Household

Survey, a nationally representative survey of households which focuses on aspects of everyday living. It periodically includes questions about disability based on the extent to which people are able to accomplish a small number of routine tasks. Together these provide a general measure of the extent to which infirmity limits people's activities. (Note that because the survey is one of households, it excludes people living in institutions including care and nursing homes. Fewer than 5 per cent of the population aged 65 or over are living in institutional care though many of these will have severe disabilities (Social Trends, 1997).) In all, there are six distinct tasks about which questions are asked in the G.H.S. These concern the individual's ability to: bathe and wash all over; cut toe nails; walk outside; get around the house; get up and down stairs; and get in and out of bed. There are three alternative answers allowed for each of these questions: 'no help required'; 'can do with difficulty'; and 'cannot manage without help'. Each task is then given a score of between 0 and 2: 0 if a task can be done unaided; 1 if it can only be done with difficulty; and 2 if help is required (Arber and Ginn, 1992; Green, 1988; O.P.C.S., 1992). Thus across the six items, each individual could score a maximum of 12 (that is, cannot manage any of the activities without help) and a minimum of 0 (that is, requires no help with any of them).

In their analysis, Arber and Ginn (1992) concern themselves with elderly people who are severely disabled, by which they mean people who score 6 or more on this scale, irrespective of the permutation by which that total is reached. They further distinguish those who are very severely disabled, whom they define as those scoring between 9 and 12. Overall, half of those aged 65 or over in the study reported having no disability (a score of 0), with a further quarter having only a mild disability (score 1–2, mainly being unable to cut their own toe nails) (Arber and Ginn, 1992, p. 94). Of those 65 or over, 11 per cent had a severe disability (scoring 6 or over). As indicated in Table 8.5, there is a definite correlation between age and having severe disabilities, but note how for all age categories the majority are not within the 'severely disabled' category. As importantly, gender differences are significant, with men at every age being less likely than women to have a score of 6 or more.

In the same study, Arber and Ginn also examine older people's living arrangements and the relationship between these and dis-

**Table 8.5**  *Percentage of men and women in different age categories with severe disability*

| Age | Severe (6–8) | | Very severe (9–12) | |
|---|---|---|---|---|
| | *Men* | *Women* | *Men* | *Women* |
| 65–69 | 3 | 4 | 2 | 2 |
| 70–74 | 3 | 5 | 1 | 2 |
| 75–79 | 5 | 10 | 6 | 5 |
| 80–84 | 7 | 15 | 4 | 9 |
| 85+ | 14 | 22 | 10 | 21 |

*Source*: Arber and Ginn, 1992, p. 95.

ability. Table 8.6 outlines their results. As can be seen, a high proportion of the relatively small number of older people with significant disabilities lived alone or with their spouse only. Thus, of the men with a disability score of 6 or more, over a fifth lived alone and nearly two-thirds lived with their wives. The situation is rather different for women. Of those with serious levels of disability, over 40 per cent lived alone and some 30 per cent with their husbands. Overall, only around a fifth of the elderly people with high levels of disability in this survey lived in other forms of household, the great majority of these with adult children either in their own homes or in their children's.

Such statistics as these could be taken to indicate that relatives, especially adult children, provide comparatively little care. The evidence of so many elderly people with severe disabilities living on their own might be read as indicative of a breakdown of family support. Undoubtedly some of these elderly people are living some distance from their children; others have no surviving children; while relationships between a small number of others have broken down through abuse, marital separation or for some other reason. However, there is another, more accurate way of interpreting these figures. Many elderly people desire very strongly to remain in their own homes, and in reality their adult children frequently play a significant part in enabling them to do so (Evandrou, 1996; St Leger and Gillespie, 1991). Innovations associated with 'Care in the Community' policies are also working towards meeting people's preference for staying in their own

**Table 8.6** *Living arrangements of elderly men and women with different levels of disability*

| | Not disabled (Score: 0–5) | | Severe disability (Score: 6–8) | | Very severe disability (Score: 9–12) | |
|---|---|---|---|---|---|---|
| | *Men* | *Women* | *Men* | *Women* | *Men* | *Women* |
| Lives alone | 20 | 48 | 26 | 52 | 14 | 29 |
| Lives in own household with spouse | 71 | 37 | 58 | 31 | 69 | 27 |
| Lives in own household with others (mainly children) | 6 | 8 | 9 | 9 | 7 | 18 |
| Not in own household: with children | 2 | 3 | 6 | 6 | 5 | 21 |
| Not in own household: with others | 2 | 3 | – | 2 | 5 | 4 |
| Number of respondents | 1370 | 1853 | 65 | 189 | 42 | 113 |

*Source*: Arber and Ginn, 1992, p. 99.

home (Walker and Warren, 1996). Rather than being a sign of family pathology, the numbers of severely disabled elderly people living alone is a symbol of family effectiveness.

As we have argued above, most elderly people wish to remain independent as fully and for as long as possible. Within the dominant culture, having one's own home is a powerful signifier of such independence. Moving to a child's house, or of course to residential care of some sort, however sensible that may appear on 'objective' grounds, is often an action of last resort. It symbolises dependence, an inability to control one's own affairs and a reliance on others. Staying in one's own home, on the other hand, is an indicator of independence, a sign that one is still capable of managing and being in control. Symbolically, in your own home, you are able to set the 'rules', maintain privacy and determine your own timetable, rather than having to fit in with others. For such reasons many older people experiencing severe difficulties in managing on their own nonetheless remain determined to stay in their own home as long as possible.

Enabling them to do so has become state policy in recent years. The 1990 National Health and Community Care Act emphasises that resources should be spent on helping people to remain living at home rather than in institutionalised care. Both social services and health services have been encouraged to promote independence through domiciliary provision, though financing this adequately has proved difficult. But more important than formal provision, informal support plays the major part in enabling many older people to sustain independent living. And research has demonstrated repeatedly that informal support from outside the household is most typically provided by close kin. Neighbours and friends can undoubtedly be important at times, but the great majority of routine informal care is provided either by others in the household or by adult children and their partners (Clarke, 1995; Qureshi and Walker, 1989).

Thus in many instances, elderly people with severe disabilities living alone are able to do so only because of the support they receive from family members. Without this, managing would be exceedingly difficult. The actual support provided will vary a great deal depending on the circumstances of those involved, but as disability becomes more limiting, the demands placed on those providing support can become very heavy. In an analysis based on the same data which Arber and Ginn used in the study discussed above, Green (1988) reported that 83 per cent of those providing some degree of care for others (estimated as 6.8 million people in total) were doing so for someone in another household. While on average co-resident carers provide significantly more support than those living elsewhere, the demands of providing care in another household can be extensive (Clarke, 1995).

As the need for support increases, it becomes more difficult to provide it at times chosen solely by the carer. Like many aspects of domestic servicing, informal care provision, especially in its more personal forms, is by its nature piecemeal. It cannot always be easily consolidated into a specific block of time: for example, an individual may need help with getting in and out of bed, with preparing meals, and with aspects of toileting and personal hygiene, as well as with shopping, laundry, and house cleaning. While the latter tasks can be done at convenient times, the former, despite being regular activities, require that people are available at the appropriate times throughout the day. Thus providing care becomes onerous not just because of its scope, but also because of its propensity to interfere with the range of other activities in which the individual is involved. Many studies have shown the high physical, emotional and financial costs that caring for a disabled elderly person within your own home can have (Briggs and Oliver, 1985; Bury and Holme, 1991; Evandrou, 1996; Nissel and Bonnerjea, 1982; Ungerson, 1987): it frequently leaves the principal carer exhausted physically and isolated socially. Fewer studies have focused on the consequences for carers of helping to maintain two separate households, though undoubtedly this too can be extremely onerous (Allen, Hogg and Peace, 1992).

Frequently the provision of informal support falls disproportionately on one individual. In recent decades there has been much rhetoric about the existence of 'informal networks of carers', involving neighbours and friends as well as family. The reality is different. While neighbours and friends do at times provide assistance, they tend mainly to do so when the level of support needed is quite low. As infirmity and the level of support required increases, so the tasks more frequently fall to kin. And as family become more fully involved, so neighbours and others are likely to play a smaller part, not wishing to interfere in what is seen as predominantly a family matter. Of course, this depends to some degree on how close a person's family is geographically, but typically the character and dominant exchange basis of neighbour and friend relationships renders them less suitable than family ties for providing support as disability becomes more severe (Allan, 1991; Clarke, 1995).

Yet it is equally a mistake to view the care that is provided as 'family' care. Certainly informal care does tend to be provided by family members more than it is by non-family, but it is rarely shared equally between different family members. Rather, it falls on a particular individual who carries much, if not all, of the responsibility. Often this is the spouse, where there is one (Arber and Gilbert, 1989; Clarke, 1995). But whether or not there is, once one member of the family network is perceived as the principal carer, others tend to take more of a back seat. As Finch and Mason (1993) argue, the person acting as principal carer emerges through a process of implicit or explicit 'negotiation' within the kin group. Nonetheless, there are certain regularities in this which structure the negotiations. We have already discussed how the character of the previous relationship existing between people patterns future involvement. It is not just issues of compatibility that matter, but also how the circumstances and other commitments of those involved are recognised as patterning the assistance they can provide (Jordan, Redley and James, 1994). An interesting issue for the future is how current demographic changes, particularly concerning patterns of cohabitation, divorce and remarriage, will impact on the readiness of children to provide support for their different natural and social parents (Clarke, 1995; Qureshi, 1996).

While Finch and Mason (1993) show that the provision of informal support to elderly parents does not follow set norms agreed by all as 'right and proper', there is nonetheless a patterning behind who does become most fully involved as need arises. Qureshi and Walker's (1989) research into the support received by elderly people living in Sheffield is particularly pertinent here. On the basis of their data, they produced a broad hierarchy of helpers most likely to become involved in providing support. This is shown in Table 8.7.

In practice, not all cases fitted this model, though once allowance had been made for distance and ill-health, they found it applied to 75 per cent of their sample who were receiving some level of support from others. Essentially, their model highlights both the importance of household membership and of gender.

Other studies have also emphasised these factors, with gender especially being seen as crucial in determining who it is who, aside from a spouse, becomes most involved in providing high

**Table 8.7**  *Model of principal helper*

1   Spouse
2   Relative in life-long joint household
3   Daughter
4   Daughter-in-law
5   Son
6   Other relative
7   Non-relative

*Source*: Qureshi and Walker, 1989, p. 126.

levels of personal and domestic care (Dalley, 1996). Because the 'negotiations' which develop are built around people's availability, current responsibilities and differential abilities, as well as their previous involvement with the person in need of support, aspects of gender inevitably play a significant part in them. Through socialisation and experience, women are typically seen as more appropriate carers than men and also as being more readily available because of their perceived lesser commitment to employment. As a result, it is not children in general who provide support for elderly infirm parents and help them sustain a level of independence, any more than it is children in general who do most of the domestic and caring labour if a parent moves in to live with them. Rather it is daughters who do most of the 'tending' (Parker, 1981) that is necessary; and if there are only sons available, it is often their female partners who become most actively involved in the care process on a day-to-day level. As research has now convincingly demonstrated, when children rather than spouses are involved as providers, family care is most frequently female care. Comparative studies, such as that by Waerness (1990), show that many of the issues about care raised by ageing are common to all societies with a mature demographic profile, even though the details of how they are tackled vary.

## Conclusion

There have been several themes in this chapter. The first is that Britain's elderly population is far fitter and more self-reliant than popular stereotypes suggest. The large majority of elderly people require no more personal support to sustain their routine life than do other age groups. A second theme is that there is much diversity in later-life experiences. The resources elderly people have differ significantly, with the impact of both class and gender over the life course being important in shaping people's lifestyles as they age. In particular, the availability and extent of people's entitlement to occupational pensions is important in patterning their social activities and participation. Thirdly, and again contrary to popular mythology, elderly people are not in the main, ignored or neglected by their families. Most older people who have children do have regular contact with them, without old age of itself altering the previous balance or dynamics of the tie.

In this chapter, as elsewhere in the book, we have emphasised the significance of 'independence'. Certainly, for many older people maintaining independence rather than becoming (or being seen as) dependent is very important, whether the prime unit here is the individual or the household. Managing and coping within your own resources, without requiring additional unreciprocated help from others, remains a key signifier of full adult status and citizenship. In reality, this refers more to interdependence than independence as such; what matters is that the exchanges occurring in a relationship are perceived as balanced. It is important that the cultural dimensions of these relationships are acknowledged alongside the economic ones, as Vincent (1995) argues on the basis of his comparative research. In most of old age this is relatively unproblematic. Relationships with adult children continue to be patterned as they have been in the past. However, with increased frailty new patterns emerge, often requiring a degree of subtlety in the management of dependency issues. What is evident from the now quite extensive research literature is that if there is no spouse or other household member able to meet the emerging needs that infirmity creates, it is typically 'family' (usually a daughter, less often daughter-in-law or son) who acts to provide informal support. Thus, far from neglecting older people at times of need, children are more often key in helping them sustain independent living. This issue of independence and family support is one which we will take up further in the concluding chapter.

# 9 Households and Families: Commonality and Differentiation

The changing patterns of household and family relationships described in the preceding chapters are open to numerous competing sociological interpretations. Some accounts stress the novelty of phenomena such as cohabitation and emphasise the growth of diversity in domestic arrangements, while others focus greater attention on the essential continuities which are present in the norms underlying family life. Approaches which emphasise variation in contemporary domestic patterns are generally based on theoretical frameworks which highlight the growing opportunities for individual control over personal life and the scope which exists to be different. In contrast, those emphasising continuities are more mindful of the constraints which operate to limit people's ability to construct their home lives according to individual preferences. These constraints take a variety of forms, ranging from informal pressures to conform to established conventions of family life to more formal regulation of behaviour through the various agencies which work to implement social policies. In turn, writers giving prominence to social change have demonstrated how social policies affecting families are themselves subject to continual pressure for modification due to demographic trends which are largely beyond the control of policy-makers. Striking the appropriate balance in explanations of continuity and change in domestic life is a difficult task, itself calling for regular updating.

The growing diversity of family and household types has become a well-established theme in the sociology of domestic life. Chester's (1977) suggestion that lone-parent households are a variant rather than a deviant family form is merely an early example of the progressive recognition of the heterogeneous

197

nature of how people now live. Previous chapters have charted how the family type once taken as a norm, that of the male breadwinner married to a full-time housewife with responsibility for dependent children, has become increasingly abnormal, at least in a statistical sense. The declining proportion of the population living at any time in such conventional households reflects a number of factors, including the growth of married women's employment, the spread of cohabitation and the rising numbers of lone-parent, stepfamily, childless and single person households (McRae, 1999). It is, of course, important not to read too much into this heterogeneity of forms: for example, it does not follow that diverse patterns of household composition will necessarily generate equally diverse patterns in the domestic lives people construct. The desire of many stepfamilies to live as 'normal' families, reported by Burgoyne and Clark (1984), and the construction of 'pretended family relationships' within the homosexual communities described by Weeks (1991; see also Weeks, Heaphy and Donovan, 1999a, b) both serve to illustrate the power of familial ideology to limit variation in patterns of domestic life (Beechey, 1985).

Yet the change there has been indicates that family practices are not reproduced unaltered across the generations. Moreover, individual conformity to conventional roles is not an automatic outcome of socialisation processes. A degree of choice is involved in the extent to which the patterns of preceding generations are reproduced: for example, the active nature of striving to be 'good' parents has been demonstrated in several studies (Backett, 1982; Baker, 1989; Boulton, 1983; Everingham, 1994; Ribbens, 1994; Segal 1990), and in the process, such research has shown the scope which exists for individuals to put their own personal stamp on the performance of domestic roles. At the same time, other research, such as Graham's (1987a, b) investigations into lone mothers' poverty, has sought to place individual agency in the context of wider structures which limit the scope for personal autonomy. It is against this background that concepts such as 'negotiation' and 'strategy' have come to be used extensively in analyses of how people relate to others in their households and families (Finch and Mason, 1993; Wallace, 1993).

Discussions of family negotiations and household strategies highlight both the flexibility and fluidity of domestic relationships and the ways in which wider social forces operate to open up some possibilities but close off others. It is precisely because domestic arrangements are *not* fixed that so much potential for misunderstanding and tension exists between family members. Families and households require a basic level of agreement over the rights and responsibilities of their members if they are to be sustainable, as discussions in earlier chapters of financial arrangements, the domestic division of labour and caring relationships have demonstrated. These discussions noted how norms in these areas are subject to change over time at the household level as people move into new life course positions. Norms change at a societal level too, as Lewis, Clark and Morgan's (1992) study of evolving ideals of marriage illustrates. While norms relating to marriage, divorce and remarriage have been relaxed, there remains a surprising degree of conformity at the more fundamental level of people's domestic arrangements; there exists here a 'paradox of "choice" where almost everyone is "choosing" marriage or a marriage-type relationship' (Lewis, Clark and Morgan, 1992, p. 17). Burgoyne has also noted the problematic nature of 'choice' in her critique of writers who suggest, simplistically, 'that household structures and domestic lifestyles and strategies are individually and freely chosen' (1987, p. 85). Choices need to be understood in context, and people's choices are constrained by structural factors and by cultural and policy settings in which alternatives to the conventional family continue to be treated as second best options.

## Change and continuity in the norms of domestic life

Examination of Bernardes's (1985) question, 'Do we really know what "the family" is?', provides some idea of the degree to which patterns of domestic life have changed in recent decades. Around the middle of the twentieth century, sociologists conveyed far greater certainty about family practices than they do now. During this period, family sociology tended to revolve around functionalist analyses which idealised the operation of the nuclear family. Cheal suggests that such analyses, exemplified by the writings of Parsons (1955) and Goode (1964), then comprised a 'standard theory of the family' (1991, p. 3). Subsequent decades have seen previously unquestioned ideas about the normality and function- ality of the nuclear family subjected to critical scrutiny. Change in domestic life is not only a matter of shifting demographic pat- terns; relationships within households and families also change. The roles of husband, wife, father, mother, son and daughter have all been subject to substantial modification and extension over time, so that what is expected of men, women and children in domestic relationships, and what they themselves expect of these relationships, are remarkably different from the picture con- tained in the formerly standard theory of the family. For example, notions of what constitutes a 'good father' have shifted away from the rational and financially responsible but emotionally distant paternalistic ideal towards a model in which men's expressive side is given greater prominence, embodied in greater involvement in childcare activities. There are, of course, many reasons to be sceptical about how far the ideals of this 'new fatherhood' are actually put into practice in everyday domestic life (Gillis 1997; Segal 1990). As Lewis and O'Brien observed, 'discussion about the "new father" far outweighs evidence to demonstrate his exis- tence' (1987, p. 3). Even so, the very fact that the discussion is happening at all is indicative of the point that family relationships are neither fixed nor natural, but are better understood as shaped by the social and economic context in which they occur.

It is somewhat ironic that this last point was one of the central thrusts of what Cheal has called the standard theory of the family. One of Parsons's purposes in developing his account of the modern American family was to show that family relationships change along with the societies in which they are located. Yet it is now widely accepted that there is no straightforward 'fit' between families and households and the societies in which they are located (Harris, 1983). The standard theory of the family made the mistake of treating family forms as simply a dependent variable which altered in response to changing socio-economic requirements. Such ideas have a tendency to exaggerate the extent of uniformity to be found in patterns of change. Suggestions that a logical connection exists between industrialisa- tion and the spread of the nuclear family form have generally been confounded by the growing awareness of diverse counter cases. The debate about the 'privatisation' of family life illuminates many of the issues at stake here. Numerous writers including Donzelot (1979), Harris (1980), Morgan (1985) and Rodger (1996) have noted how state agencies have been actively involved in the development, promotion and regulation of the 'private' family, while the upshot of other research has been to challenge the picture of family life becoming progressively cut off from wider kin and community ties (Allan and Crow, 1991; Bell and Ribbens, 1994; Devine, 1992). Indeed, there are good reasons for supposing that while men's lives may have become more 'privatised' as their working weeks have been shortened, women's growing involvement in the labour market has propelled them in the opposite direction, suggesting that family members are subject to contradictory pressures which are in practice often difficult to reconcile.

Other examples of the contradictory nature of trends in domestic life cast further doubt on the notion of family relationships adapting smoothly to changing socio-economic contexts. Harris (1980) has pointed out how structurally-isolated nuclear families are vulnerable to 'implosion' because of the excessive pressures which the absence of wider support networks places on family members, particularly mothers. Furthermore, the social processes, like geographical and social mobility, which promote the spread of the nuclear family form may also, paradoxically, contribute to the disintegration of such families. Alternatively, Harris suggests, child-centred families may be formed 'in which the parents' lives are given meaning and purpose primarily through their children' (1980, p. 400). In turn, Jamieson (1998) has cast doubt on the view that child-centredness is the inevitable outcome of a long-term trend, while detailed studies of parent–child relationships such as those by Everingham (1994), Ribbens (1994) and Sharpe (1994) show that it is far from clear to contemporary parents precisely how to behave in appropriately child-centred ways.

The unfolding trends in family relationships are strongly influenced by ideas of the 'naturalness' of patterns of domestic life, despite the fact that these relationships have been subject to progressively closer scrutiny, direction and regulation. The role of state agencies in structuring family relationships has been touched on at various points in this book, including the discussion in Chapter 6 of the impact of divorce legislation and the analysis in

Chapter 8 of policies relating to the care of older people. As Morgan (1996, p. 196) notes, 'The links between state and family have a long and complex history'. The state's involvement in controlling women's fertility provides a good illustration of how certain outcomes are encouraged while others are discouraged, with assessments of 'fitness' for motherhood being affected by political considerations (Hanmer, 1993; Richardson, 1993). If some state bodies have come to be increasingly involved in the regulation of reproductive technologies, other agencies of the state are equally active in setting limits to how families function (Knowles, 1996). The surveillance of mothers by health visitors is just one example of how public regulation reaches into the private sphere of domestic life although, as Bloor and McIntosh (1990, p. 163) note, such regulation is more likely to be effective where health professionals and their clients operate with shared notions of 'acceptable standards of child development, "good" and "bad" parenting, healthy and unhealthy lifestyles, and appropriate and inappropriate childcare practice'. A similar point could be made that the actions of officials involved in dealing with divorcing parents are more likely to have an impact where they can find some common ground over definitions of the best interests of the child and parental responsibility (Piper, 1993).

Whatever the rhetoric in which they are dressed up, there are significant disagreements about precisely how benevolent and how controlling state intervention into domestic life is. Growth in the regulation of domestic life has been facilitated by the proliferation of guidance from 'experts' on the parameters of 'good' parenting. Particularly striking in this respect are the models of 'good' mothering contained in the many childrearing manuals now available (Marshall, 1991; Richardson, 1993). In these discourses, notions of 'good' mothering are drawn from medical and psychological theories in which 'motherhood is constructed as being an unquestionably positive experience' (Marshall, 1991, p. 72), with experts and professionals playing a crucial role in guiding mothers towards appropriately 'natural' and 'normal' behaviour. Several commentators have pointed out the oppressive effects of idealising motherhood and of portraying women who have negative experiences of being a mother or who choose not to have children as somehow 'unnatural' (Gordon, 1990; Hanmer 1993; Marshall, 1991).

There is, of course, nothing new about the observation that notions of what constitutes a 'good' mother is socially-constructed and frequently contested. The same point could be made about notions of 'good' fathers, children, husbands and wives. This said, notions of normal family life are not infinitely flexible, and norms of appropriate behaviour do exert a powerful influence on how individuals perform domestic roles, as studies like Voysey's (1975) sensitive account of how parents of disabled children strive to be 'normal' families illustrates. While such norms have undoubtedly changed over time, it remains the case that moral notions like those of 'putting the family first' and 'respectability' continue to affect the choices made by individuals in the construction of their domestic lives.

## Strategies and negotiations: the construction of families and households

The variability of patterns of domestic organisation has rightly been interpreted as running counter to the view of families and households as natural entities with a fixed unity of purpose. Much recent research has been concerned with exploring in more detail how particular relationships between family and household members come to take the forms that they do and why they vary. In addressing this problem, Finch and Mason (1993) propose that the concept of 'negotiation' has the potential to provide insights into how individuals' actions involve more than simply acting out roles according to general rules of obligation. In contrast to the standard theory of the family in which positions are more or less predetermined by wider social structures, 'the concept of negotiation emphasises that individuals do have some room for manoeuvre, though it is never entirely open-ended and sometimes it can be quite tightly constrained' (Finch and Mason, 1993, p. 60). Consideration of the negotiated character of domestic relations can thus be seen to be closely connected to the discussion of strategies which has also featured prominently in recent research into how families and households operate in patterned but not overly determined ways. Pahl's (1984) analysis highlights that different work strategies are available to households at any time, and that over the life course there can be considerable change. All households face the problem of resolving how best to get by, but in doing so they do not always act in the uniform ways which standard theories of family responsibilities and obligations would lead us to expect.

The domestic division of labour provides an instructive example of how domestic relations can be seen to be the product of negotiation. In couple relationships, who does what within the home is something which evolves out of the developing bonds between partners and is affected by changing circumstances. As discussed in Chapters 4 and 5, Mansfield and Collard's (1988) research into the lives of newly-married couples suggests that some patterns established early in a relationship become embedded in routines and, consequently, have an enduring significance. Mansfield and Collard found that several standpoints were available for wives and husbands to draw upon as they entered into negotiations about who performed various tasks such as cooking and cleaning. Traditional ideas about the allocation of duties according to each partner's 'natural' aptitudes and abilities were often in tension with more egalitarian thinking in which other commitments (most obviously, paid work) were brought into the equation. Similarly, negotiations around the domestic division of labour occur in dual-earner households (Brannen and Moss, 1991; Gregson and Lowe, 1994; Hochschild, 1990; Jamieson, 1998; Potuchek, 1997; Sharpe, 1984), in households where husbands are unemployed (Harris, 1987; Pahl, 1984; Wheelock, 1990), among couples where wives are in better-paid jobs than their husbands (McRae, 1986), and in marriages where one partner has a disability (Parker, 1993). The evidence of such extensive 'domestic bargaining' points to the conclusion that 'relatively harmonious co-existence is not something which just happens. It must be actively produced by family members' (Hutson and Jenkins, 1989, p. 52). In other words, the unity of household members is always vulnerable to conflicts of interest between individuals undermining their sense of collective identity and endeavour.

Negotiations over who does what are frequently not negotiations between parties of equal bargaining strength. As we have argued in previous chapters, relations between partners do not develop in isolation. They are influenced by numerous factors, not least of which is the greater earning capacity which men generally enjoy. Men's higher earnings continue to exert a strong influence on domestic inequalities when decisions are made about childcare. Once women have taken a spell out of the labour market to devote themselves full-time to motherhood, the pattern is reinforced. This does not mean that women are compelled to devote themselves primarily to the care of young children, though mothers choosing to return to work after maternity leave do not always receive much support from husbands and others (Brannen and Moss, 1991). Negotiating from a position of relative weakness, any difficulties which arise from juggling the competing demands of home and work are taken to be part of the choice made by women, with their employment (rather than the limited nature of their husbands' contribution to housework) identified as the main cause of any difficulties which develop.

Women's responsibility for ensuring that domestic life runs smoothly is a consistent finding of researchers investigating other potentially conflictual situations. According to McKee and Bell (1986), husbands' unemployment becomes a problem which wives have to learn to manage, and in similar fashion Hutson and Jenkins (1989) emphasise that it is mothers who 'take the strain' of unemployed youths living at home. Further examples of women engaging in emotional labour for the good of the family can be found in the literature on food in families, where it has been observed that 'as well as cooking the proper family meal it also falls to women to ensure that mealtimes are a happy family occasion' (Charles and Kerr, 1988, p. 85). A related theme of women putting their families before themselves runs through the literature on caring. It is also instructive that several of the respondents in Brannen and Moss's (1991) study of women returning to work stated that they were doing it for the good of the whole household and not just for themselves. In general these women 'did not appear to want to calculate whether each partner was receiving fair and equal shares of household resources' (Brannen and Moss, 1991, p. 47). Thus, marital partnerships are quite frequently understood by wives and husbands to be characterised by fairness where contributions to the household are adjudged to be appropriately complementary, even where outcomes in terms of the amount of money available for individual spending, or the performance of housework, are far from equal.

Dempsey's (1997) consideration of the reasons why what appears 'unfair' in the eyes of outside observers can be perceived as 'fair' by household members makes the important point that much hinges on the basis of comparison. The sense that things are not as bad as they used to be was captured in a female respondent's comment: 'Can't complain. Look how hard my mother had it.' (1997, p. 159). Similarly selective standpoints make it possible for individuals to reconcile what Bittman and Pixley (1997, p. 145) refer to as 'the disjunction between domestic inequality and the idea of equality'. More generally, they argue that myths about family life have a profound influence on our perceptions. This helps to explain why claims of a long-term trend towards the greater democratisation of family relations remain popular, despite the evidence being at best partial. Certainly, women and to a lesser extent children have come to have more of a voice in domestic decision-making than they had in 'traditional' family arrangements, yet it is not clear how far such changes have dislodged the processes whereby male advantages are 'tied up with being the breadwinner: with "keeping" their families' (Delphy and Leonard, 1992, p. 191). The finding that all but one of the 36 couples interviewed in Jordan, Redley and James's study of middle-class households 'accounted for their decisions within strongly gendered requirements of family responsibility – men as main providers of income, women as primarily responsible for childcare and domestic organisation' (1994, p. 5) has particular significance in this context because it is in precisely such higher-income households that one would expect to find more egalitarian ideologies and practices.

What all of these studies reveal is that there is no easy way for family members to determine how best to use the resources available to them. Even in families in which decision-making processes are closer to the consensual ideal, knowledge of how to deal with the opportunities and constraints which they face is necessarily imperfect because engagement in work and expenditure activities inevitably involves uncertainty and risk. Anderson, Bechhofer and Kendrick (1994) argue that the difficulties of devising household strategies are particularly acute for poorer households on the grounds that a lack of resources makes it difficult to plan. In addition they point out that poorer people are often more vulnerable to unemployment and ill-health. Wallman, however, disputes the view that success in managing household resources can be attributed to 'having a better job, more money, more kin, more education, or a higher general status than the people next door', preferring to see it as depending 'on combinations of style and circumstance' (1984, p. 213). Thus, her account attaches as much importance to moral values as it does to economic issues. Disagreements over the extent to which emphasis should be placed on either choice or constraint are at the heart of the debate about household strategies (Wallace, 1993), which in turn can shed light on the issue of how household diversity might be explained.

While some of the diversity in contemporary domestic arrangements can be attributed to active negotiations between family members, it is clear that there are limits to how far these negotiations can be taken. To begin with, the class contexts in which these negotiations take place matter, because poor families find many options closed off to them (Cheal, 1996; Warde, 1990). Gregson and Lowe's (1994) research into how middle-class families make use of the option of employing nannies and cleaners illustrates the impact which class differences can have. A further demonstration of the salience of class differences to household negotiations can be found in Brannen *et al.*'s (1994) analysis of parent–child relationships in which middle-class parents are more likely to adopt 'communicative strategies', while their working-class counterparts more frequently apply 'normative rules'. Further instances of material and cultural forces beyond the individual household could be cited in relation to factors such as ethnic differences, like the expectation among the East African Sikh women in Britain studied by Bhachu that they should work for a living even when they are quite old, a norm enforced by other women's preparedness to criticise them for 'sitting at home doing nothing' (1985, p. 68). Overall, a focus on negotiations may help in opening up the 'black box' (Brannen and Wilson, 1987) of family and household relationships by highlighting their active construction. At the same time, it is important not to lose sight of the influences which limit the extent to which individuals can exercise choice over how they construct their domestic lives.

## Household change, family change and social change

Two of the central purposes of this book have been to chart and explain the growing diversity of domestic arrangements. Neither of these tasks is as easy as it might at first appear. Describing the changing patterns of family and household relations raises all sorts of questions about the adequacy of the concepts and the measures used. Earlier chapters provide many instances of the difficulties of studying domestic life: for example, the category 'lone-parent household' is defined by a boundary which is blurred rather than fixed, there being no agreement on precisely which households are appropriately classified thus (Crow and Hardey, 1992). Similar observations have been made of cohabiting couples and stepfamilies, all of which serve to illustrate the more general point that classifications are inevitably somewhat arbitrary. At one level, the arbitrariness of the household types to which people are allotted is an abstract academic issue. However, it is also one with very real consequences for people in relation to the operation of welfare state agencies such as the Department of Social Security, since entitlement to various benefits hinges on such classifications. Likewise, the analysis of change in domestic relations may also have serious practical effects, as is shown by Neale and Smart's (1997) investigation into how new ideas about fatherhood have come to be embodied in post-divorce arrangements.

While there is certainly more diversity in domestic arrangements at the beginning of the twenty-first century than there was for most of the twentieth, precisely how much more diversity there is and why this has come about remain open to dispute. Many comparisons look back to the 1950s when, as noted above, the standard theory of the family was being promulgated. However, there are good reasons for treating this time, with its peculiar economic, social and political circumstances, as an exceptional period rather than taking it as a benchmark against which to compare subsequent developments (Finch and Summerfield, 1991). Stacey (1998, p. 10) refers to the 1960s as an 'aberrant' decade, in terms of its family and household trends, rather than a norm. Social historians and others have drawn appropriately sceptical conclusions about accounts which treat the years of mid-century as a golden age of orderly family life (Gillis, 1997; Gordon, 1994; Jamieson, 1998), pointing out that the standard theory of the family was at odds with the findings of many empirical studies of the time as well as being theoretically suspect. The greater emphasis which sociologists in recent years have come to place on the negotiated nature of family relationships appears to offer a more adequate account of the diversity of domestic relations than the standard theory of the family could. Indeed Cheal has referred to the '*destandardisation* of the family' (1991, p. 133, emphasis in original), with individuals now more able to construct alternative arrangements according to their personal preferences and objectives. Yet as we have argued, in some respects patterns of domestic life retain a surprising degree of uniformity.

The labour market provides a good example of how structural factors external to the household nevertheless have a profound effect on the nature of domestic life. Changing patterns of employment and unemployment have affected the domestic division of labour and decision-making processes, as has been discussed above (for example, in discussions of youth unemployment in Chapter 3 and of the growth of married women's paid work in Chapter 5). This said, the general conclusion of studies in these areas is that domestic relations have been modified rather than revolutionised by changing patterns of work, though in the process they have also led to challenges to what was conventionally perceived as 'natural'. According to Morris (1990a), the fact that rates of male unemployment and female employment have risen in recent decades without there being correspondingly fundamental changes in gender relations in households needs explanation, the problem being to explain not how much but how little variation there is in who contributes what to the household. Her explanation in relation to the United States and the United Kingdom refers to the 'normative constraints reinforcing and maintaining established gender roles, and the inequitable distribution of power within the household that enhances male power to resist change' (Morris, 1990a, p. 190). Equally importantly she emphasises how the labour market reproduces differential opportunities for women and men, as well as the enduring gendered assumptions on which the agencies of the welfare state operate.

Other writers have also emphasised the potential of comparative studies to highlight the uneven effects of labour market organisation and state policies on who contributes what to households, and the interconnected nature of these processes. Noting that France has operated policies relating to maternity leave and pre-school childcare which are more supportive of women's full-time employment than equivalent British policies, Beechey and

Perkins go on to observe that 'The state plays a central role in determining what form the division of labour in the household takes and how this affects women's participation in the labour market' (1987, p. 147). In like fashion, Duncan and Edwards (1997a) have observed that the policies adopted towards single mothers by governments in different welfare states have an important bearing on the extent to which such mothers are involved in paid work. In some welfare states, policies towards single mothers treat them as primarily responsible for caring for their children at home, while in welfare states at the other end of the spectrum, policies are adopted which encourage single mothers to take up employment. On the basis of such comparisons, Duncan and Edwards conclude that British welfare state policies occupy an intermediate position, embodying ambiguities which reveal policy makers to be unsure as to whether single mothers are better treated primarily as mothers or workers. Similar observations have been made more generally about how among welfare states there are varying degrees of tolerance of and support for households other than those founded on the male breadwinner model (Sainsbury, 1994).

Writers like Duncan and Edwards (1997a, b) have also been concerned to draw attention to more local influences on people's behaviour in households, including the cultures of the neighbourhoods and social networks in which they live. Aspects of the sub-national contexts in which people live include the extent to which informal networks of childcare support are available to parents locally which can enable them to take up paid work. Duncan and Edwards (1997b) found significant variation between local cultures in this respect. They argue that the fact that employment rates are higher among black single mothers and lower among white working-class single mothers can be linked to the greater acceptability of lone-mother employment in the inner-city neighbourhoods in which their black respondents lived, while their white working-class respondents lived in areas where mothers were expected to be at home with their children. In the absence of the informal support which would be necessary for them to take up paid work, this latter group of single mothers faced an uphill struggle to establish and maintain identities as workers. Examples such as this and those considered in Wallman's (1984) study of London households indicate that the growing diversity of family relationships does not refer only to the secular shift away from the domestic arrangements embodied in the standard theory of the family. Certainly, household types have become more heterogeneous, but diversification relates also to the presence of important differences in how individual cases of any one type of household actually operate.

In this context, Wallman's consideration of the purpose of studying household types is instructive. She notes that classification is a necessary part of understanding any subject, but she observes too that 'any typology is tidier than real life' (1984, p. 18). While static analyses like those generated by the decennial census tell us a great deal about people's household situations at one moment in time, they are of only limited value in capturing household processes. At various points in this book it has been apparent that there is great value in looking at the dynamic nature of family and household relationships as a complementary perspective to that arising from snap-shot statistics, since the boundaries around families and households and the nature of the relationships which take place within these boundaries are regularly shifting. It will also have been apparent that these shifts are frequently hard to describe and even harder to explain. As a result, there is a time lag between developments in domestic relations and the ability to account adequately for these developments.

While this has not deterred sociologists from attempting to interpret longer-term trends in domestic life, a good deal of caution is required if the pitfalls encountered by earlier attempts are to be avoided. The fate of models like Young and Willmott's (1973) symmetrical family serves as a warning against the pitfalls of over-generalisation and unwarranted extrapolation of current trends into the future, as Finch (1983) amongst others has noted. Similar points have been made about Giddens's more recent theory of the 'pure relationship' which Jamieson (1998, p. 40) has criticised for the way in which its 'vision of a possible future draws selectively from the range of available evidence and only briefly discusses aspects of the wider context which perpetuate inequalities between men and women'. All such general theories are questionable to the extent that they overlook what Lewis, Clark and Morgan (1992, p. 15) refer to as the 'scope for considerable variation according to class, religion and ethnic group' which exists in marriage-type relationships. Nevertheless, some element of speculation is unavoidable if accounts of domestic arrangements are to be explanatory as well as descriptive, since explanation involves comparison, which in turn requires that consideration be given to how things might be otherwise. In the study of family and household relationships as in other parts of the discipline, the sociological imagination leads us to look to alternatives and to the future, to which our knowledge of the past and the present is an imperfect yet indispensable guide.

# Bibliography

Afshar, H. (1989) 'Gender Roles and the "Moral Economy of Kin" Among Pakistani Women in West Yorkshire', *New Community*, 15, pp. 211–25.

Ainley, P. (1991) *Young People Leaving Home* (London: Cassell).

Alcock, P. (1997) *Understanding Poverty* (Basingstoke: Macmillan).

Allan, G. (1985) *Family Life* (Oxford: Blackwell).

Allan, G. (1989) *Friendship* (Hemel Hempstead: Harvester Wheatsheaf).

Allan, G. (1991) 'Social Work, Community Care, and Informal Networks', in M. Davies (ed.) *The Sociology of Social Work* (London: Routledge).

Allan, G. (1996) *Kinship and Friendship in Modern Britain* (Oxford: Oxford University Press).

Allan, G. (ed.) (1999) *The Sociology of the Family: A Reader* (Oxford: Blackwell).

Allan, G. and Crow, G. (1991) 'Privatisation, Home-Centredness and Leisure', *Leisure Studies*, 10, pp. 19–32.

Allan G. and Crow, G. (eds) (1989) *Home and Family* (London: Macmillan).

Allatt P. and Yeandle, S. (1986) '"It's Not Fair, Is It?": Youth Unemployment, Family Relations and the Social Contract', in S. Allen *et al.* (eds) (1986) *The Experience of Unemployment*, (Basingstoke: Macmillan).

Allatt, P. and Yeandle, S. (1992) *Youth Unemployment and the Family* (London: Routledge).

Allatt, P., Keil, T., Bryman, A. and Bytheway, B. (eds) (1987) *Women and the Life Cycle* (Basingstoke: Macmillan).

Allen, I. and Bourke Dowling, S. (1999) 'Teenage Mothers: Decisions and Outcomes', in S. McRae (ed.) *Changing Britain*.

Allen, I., Hogg, D. and Peace, S. (1992) *Elderly People: Choice, Participation and Satisfaction* (London: Policy Studies Institute).

Allen, I. and Perkins, E. (eds) (1995) *The Future of Family Care for Older People* (London: HMSO).

Allen, S., Waton, A. Puecell, K. and Wood, S. (eds) *The Experience of Unemployment* (Basingstoke: Macmillan).

Amato, P. (1993) 'Children's Adjustment to Divorce; Theories, Hypotheses and Empirical Support', *Journal of Marriage and the Family*, 55, pp. 23–38.

Amato, P. and Booth, A. (1996) 'A Prospective Study of Divorce and Parent–Child Relationships', *Journal of Marriage and the Family*, 58, pp. 356–65.

Ambert, A.-M.(1986) 'Being a Stepparent: Live-In and Visiting Stepchildren', *Journal of Marriage and the Family*, 48, pp. 795–804.

Ambert, A.-M. (1988) 'Relationships with Former In-Laws After Divorce: A Research Note', *Journal of Marriage and the Family*, 50, pp. 679–86.

Anderson, M. (1980) *Approaches to the History of the Western Family, 1500–1914* (London: Macmillan).

Anderson, M., Bechhofer, F. and Kendrick, S. (1994) 'Individual and Household Strategies' in M. Anderson, F. Bechhofer and J. Gershuny (eds) *The Social and Political Economy of the Household*.

Anderson, M., Bechhofer, F. and Gershuny, J. (eds) (1994) *The Social and Political Economy of the Household* (Oxford: Oxford University Press).

Andersson, G. (1998) 'Trends in Marriage Formation in Sweden 1971–1993', *European Journal of Population*, 14, pp. 157–78.

*Annual Abstract of Statistics* (1997) (London: Office for National Statistics).

*Annual Abstract of Statistics* (2000) (London: Office for National Statistics).

Arber, S. and Gilbert, N. (1989) 'Men: The Forgotten Carers', *Sociology*, 23, pp. 111–18.

Arber, S. and Ginn, J. (1991) *Gender and Later Life* (London: Sage).

Arber, S. and Ginn, J. (1992) '"In Sickness and in Health": Care-Giving, Gender and the Independence of Elderly People', in C. Marsh and S. Arber (eds), *Families and Households*.

Arber, S. and Ginn, J. (eds) (1995) *Connecting Gender and Ageing* (Buckingham: Open University Press).

Aron, E. and Aron, A. (1996) 'Love and Expansion of Self: The State of the Model', *Personal Relationships*, 3, pp. 45–58.

Askham, J. (1995) 'The Married Lives of Older People', in S. Arber and J. Ginn (eds), *Connecting Gender and Ageing*.

Babb, P. and Bethune, A. (1995) 'Trends in Births Outside Marriage', *Population Trends*, 81, pp. 17–22.

Backett, K. (1982) *Mothers and Fathers* (London: Macmillan).

Baker, D. (1989) 'Social Identity in the Transition to Motherhood', in S. Skevington and D. Baker (eds) *The Social Identity of Women* (London: Sage).

Baker, M. and Phipps, S. (1997) 'Family Change and Family Policies: Canada', in S. Kamerman and A. Kahn (eds) *Family Change and Family Policies.*

Ballard, R. (ed.) (1994) *Desh Pardesh: The South Asian Presence in Britain* (London: Hurst).

Baltes, M. (1996) *The Many Faces of Dependency in Old Age* (Cambridge: Cambridge University Press).

Barker, D. and Allen, S. (eds) (1976) *Dependence and Exploitation in Work and Marriage* (London: Longmans).

Barnes, H. (1996) 'Losers in Love? The Legal Rights of Cohabiting Couples in Comparative Perspective', Paper presented at the British Society of Population Studies seminar on Family and Household Formation.

Barrett, M. and McIntosh, M. (1982) *The Anti-Social Family* (London: Verso).

Beall, A. and Sternberg, B. (1995) 'The Social Construction of Love', *Journal of Social and Personal Relationships*, 12, pp. 417–38.

Beck, U. (1992) *Risk Society* (London: Sage).

Beck, U. (1997) *The Reinvention of Politics* (Cambridge: Polity).

Beck, U. and Beck-Gernsheim E. (1995) *The Normal Chaos of Love* (Cambridge: Polity).

Beechey, V. (1985) 'Familial Ideology' in V. Beechey and J. Donald (eds) *Subjectivity and Social Relations* (Milton Keynes: Open University Press).

Beechey, V. (1986) 'Women's Employment in Contemporary Britain', in V. Beechey and E. Whitelegg (eds) *Women in Britain Today* (Milton Keynes: Open University Press).

Beechey, V. and Perkins, T. (1987) *A Matter of Hours* (Cambridge: Polity).

Bell, C. (1968) *Middle Class Families* (London: Routledge & Kegan Paul).

Bell, L. and Ribbens, J. (1994) 'Isolated Housewives and Complex Maternal Worlds', *Sociological Review*, 42, pp. 227–62.

Bernard, J. (1976) *The Future of Marriage* (Harmondsworth: Penguin).

Bernard, M., Itzin, C., Phillipson, C. and Skucha, J. (1995) 'Gendered Work, Gendered Retirement', in S. Arber and J. Ginn (eds) *Connecting Gender and Ageing.*

Bernardes, J. (1985) 'Do We Really Know What "the Family" Is?' in P. Close and R. Collins (eds) *Family and Economy in Modern Society* (London: Macmillan).

Bernardes, J. (1997) *Family Studies* (London: Routledge).

Berrington, A. (1994) 'Marriage and Family Formation Among the White and Ethnic-Minority Populations in Britain', *Ethnic and Racial Studies*, 17, pp. 517–46.

Berrington, A. and Diamond, I. (1999) 'Marital Dissolution Among the 1958 British Birth Cohort: the Role of Cohabitation', *Population Studies*, 53, pp. 19–38.

Berrington, A. and Diamond, I. (2000) 'Marriage or Cohabitation? A Competing Risks Analysis of First Partnership Formation Amongst the 1958 British Birth Cohort', *Royal Statistical Society Series A*, 163, pp. 127–52.

Berrington, A. and Murphy, M. (1994) 'Changes in the Living Arrangements of Young Adults in Britain During the 1980s', *European Sociological Review*, 10, pp. 235–57.

Berscheid, E. and Meyers, S. (1996) 'A Social Categorical Approach to a Question About Love', *Personal Relationships*, 3, pp. 19–43.

Beuret, K. and Makings, L. (1987) "I've Got Used to Being Independent Now": Women and Courtship in a Recession', in P. Allatt *et al.* (eds), *Women and the Life Cycle*.

Bhachu, P. (1985) *Twice Migrants* (London: Tavistock).

Bhatti-Sinclair, K. (1994) 'Asian Women and Violence from Male Partners' in C. Lupton and T. Gillespie (eds) *Working with Violence*.

Bhopal, K. (1997) 'South Asian Women Within Households: Dowries, Degradation and Despair', *Women's Studies International Forum*, 20, pp. 483–92.

Binney, V., Harkell, G. and Nixon, J. (1985) 'Refuges and Housing for Battered Women', in J. Pahl (ed.) *Private Violence and Public Policy*.

Bittman, M. and Pixley J. (1997) *The Double Life of the Family* (St Leonards, NSW: Allen & Unwin).

Blakemore, K. and Boneham, M. (1994) *Age, Race and Ethnicity* (Buckingham: Open University Press).

Blood, R. and Wolfe, D. (1960) *Husbands and Wives* (Glencoe: Free Press).

Bloor, M. and McIntosh, J. (1990) 'Surveillance and Concealment', in S. Cunningham-Burley and N. McKeganey (eds) *Readings in Medical Sociology* (London: Routledge).

Boulton, M. (1983) *On Being a Mother* (London: Tavistock).

Bornat, J., Dimmock, B., Jones, D. and Peace, S. (1999) 'The Impact of Family Change on Older People: The Case of Stepfamilies', in S. McRae (ed.) *Changing Britain*.

Bowlby, S., Gregory, S. and McKie, L. (1997) '"Doing Home": Patriarchy, Caring and Space', *Women's Studies International Forum*, 20, pp. 343–50.

Bradshaw, J. (1990) *Child Poverty and Deprivation in the UK* (London: National Children's Bureau).

Bradshaw J. and Millar, J. (1991) *Lone-Parent Families in the UK* (London: HMSO).

Brannen, J. (1995) 'Young People and Their Contribution to Household Work', *Sociology*, 29, pp. 317–38.

Brannen, J. (1999) 'Reconsidering Children and Childhood', in E. Silva and C. Smart (eds) *The New Family?*

Brannen, J. and Moss, P. (1991) *Managing Mothers* (London: Unwin Hyman.

Brannen, J., Dodd, K., Oakley, A. and Storey, P. (1994) *Young People, Health and Family Life* (Buckingham: Open University Press).

Brannen, J. and O'Brien, M. (eds) (1996) *Children in Families* (London: Falmer).

Brannen, J. and Wilson, G. (eds) (1987) *Give and Take in Families* (London: Allen & Unwin).

Briggs, A. and Oliver, J. (1985) *Caring* (London: Routledge and Kegan Paul).

Brown, S. and Booth, A. (1996) 'Cohabitation Versus Commitment', *Journal of Marriage and the Family*, 58, pp. 668–78.

Bryman, A., Bytheway, B., Allatt, P. and Keil, T. (eds) (1987) *Rethinking the Life Cycle* (Basingstoke: Macmillan).

Buchanan, C., Maccoby, E. and Dornbusch, S. (1996) *Adolescents After Divorce* (London: Harvard University Press).

Buck, N. and Ermisch, J. (1995) 'Cohabitation in Britain', *Changing Britain* (ESRC) 3, pp. 3–6.

Bumpass, L., Raley, R. K. and Sweet, J. (1995) 'The Changing Character of Stepfamilies', *Demography*, 32, pp. 425–36.

Burgess, E. and Locke, H. (1953) *The Family: From Institution to Companionship* (New York: American Book Co.).

Burghes, L. (1993) *One-Parent Families* (London: Family Policy Studies Centre).

Burghes, L. (1994) *Lone Parenthood and Family Disruption* (London: Family Policy Studies Centre).

Burghes, L. (1996) 'Debates on Disruption: What Happens to the Children of Lone-Parents?', in E. Silva (ed.) *Good Enough Mothering*.

Burghes, L. with Brown, M. (1995) *Single Lone Mothers* (London: Family Policy Studies Centre).

Burgoyne, C. (1990) 'Money in Marriage', *Sociological Review*, 38, pp. 634–65.

Burgoyne, J. (1987) 'Rethinking the Family Life Cycle' in A. Bryman *et al.* (eds) *Rethinking the Life Cycle*.

Burgoyne, J. and Clark, D. (1984) *Making a Go of It* (London: Routledge & Kegan Paul).

Bury, M. and Holme, A. (1991) *Life After Ninety* (London: Routledge).

Campbell, E. (1985) *The Childless Marriage* (London: Tavistock).

Cancian, F. (1987) *Love in America* (Cambridge: Cambridge University Press).

Carmichael, G. and Mason, C. (1998) 'Consensual Partnering in Australia', *Journal of the Australian Population Association*, 15, pp. 131–53.

Charles, N. (1990) 'Food and Family Ideology', in C. C. Harris (ed.) *Family Economy and Community*.

Charles, N. and Kerr, M. (1988) *Women, Food and Families* (Manchester: Manchester University Press).

Cheal, D. (1991) *Family and the State of Theory* (London: Harvester Wheatsheaf.

Cheal, D. (1996) *New Poverty: Families in Postmodern Society* (Westport, Connecticut: Greenwood Press).

Cherlin, A. (1978) 'Remarriage as an Incomplete Institution', *American Journal of Sociology*, 84, pp. 634–50.

Cherlin, A. (1992) *Marriage, Divorce, Remarriage* (Cambridge, Mass.: Harvard University Press).

Cherlin, A. and Furstenberg, F. (1994) 'Stepfamilies in the United States: A Reconsideration', *American Review of Sociology*, 20, pp. 359–81.

Cherlin, A., Kiernan, K. and Chaselansdale, P. (1995) 'Parental Divorce in Childhood and Demographic Outcomes in Young Adulthood', *Demography*, 32, pp. 299–318.

Chester, R. (1977) 'The One Parent Family: Deviant or Variant?' in R. Chester and J. Peel (eds) *Equalities and Inequalities in Family Life*.

Chester, R. and Peel, J. (eds) (1977) *Equalities and Inequalities in Family Life* (London: Academic Press).

Clark, D. (ed.) (1991) *Marriage, Domestic Life and Social Change* (London: Routledge).

Clarke, L. (1995) 'Family Care and Changing Family Structure', in I. Allen and E. Perkins (eds) *The Future of Family Care for Older People*.

Coffield, F., Borrill, C. and Marshall, S. (1986) *Growing Up at the Margins* (Milton Keynes: Open University Press).

Cohen, A. (1985) *The Symbolic Construction of Community* (London: Tavistock).

Coleman, M. and Ganong, L. (1990) 'Remarriage and Stepfamily Research in the 1980s', *Journal of Marriage and the Family*, 52, pp. 925–40.

Coleman, M. and Ganong, L. (1995) 'Family Reconfiguring Following Divorce', in S. Duck and J. Wood (eds) *Confronting Relationship Challenges* (Thousand Oaks California: Sage).

Coyle, A. (1984) *Redundant Women* (London: The Women's Press).

Crompton, R. and Sanderson, K. (1990) *Gendered Jobs and Social Change* (London: Unwin Hyman).

Cromwell, R. and Olsen, D. (1975) *Power in Families* (New York: Wiley).

Crow, G. (1989a) 'The Post-War Development of the Modern Domestic Ideal', in G. Allan and G. Crow (eds) *Home and Family* (London: Macmillan).

Crow, G. (1989b) 'The Use of the Concept of "Strategy" in Recent Sociological Literature', *Sociology*, 23, pp. 1–24.

Crow, G. and Allan, G. (1994) *Community Life* (Hemel Hempstead: Harvester-Wheatsheaf).

Crow, G. and Hardey, M. (1991) 'The Housing Strategies of Lone-Parents', in M. Hardey and G. Crow (eds) *Lone Parenthood.*

Crow, G. and Hardey, M. (1992) 'Diversity and Ambiguity Among Lone-Parent Households in Modern Britain', in C. Marsh and S. Arber (eds) *Families and Households.*

CSA (1997) Child Support Agency web site at: http://www. dss.gov.uk/csa/

Dahl, R. (1961) *Who Governs?* (London: Yale University Press).

Dalley, G. (1996) *Ideologies of Caring* (London: Macmillan) (2nd edn).

Daly, K. (1996) *Families and Time* (London: Sage).

Davies, R., Elias, P. and Penn, R. (1994) 'The Relationship Between a Husband's Unemployment and his Wife's Participation in the Labour Force', in D. Gallie *et al.* (eds) *Social Change and the Experience of Unemployment.*

de Acosta, M. (1997) 'Single mothers in the USA', in S. Duncan and R. Edwards (eds) *Single Mothers in an International Context.*

Delphy, C. (1976) 'Continuities and Discontinuities in Marriage and Divorce', in D. Barker and S. Allen (eds) *Sexual Divisions and Society* (London: Tavistock).

Delphy, C. and Leonard, D. (1992) *Familiar Exploitation* (Cambridge: Polity).

DeMaris, A. and Rao, K. V. (1992) 'Premarital Cohabitation and Subsequent Marital Stability in the United States', *Journal of Marriage and the Family*, 54, pp. 178–90.

Demo, D. (1992) 'Parent–Child Relations: Assessing Recent Changes', *Journal of Marriage and the Family*, 54, pp. 104–17.

Demo, D. (1993) 'The Relentless Search for Effects of Divorce', *Journal of Marriage and the Family*, 55, pp. 42–45.

Demo, D. and Acock, A. (1988) 'The Impact of Divorce on Children', *Journal of Marriage and the Family*, 50, pp. 619–48.

Dempsey, K. (1997) *Inequalities in Marriage: Australia and Beyond* (Melbourne: Oxford University Press).

Dennis, N. and Erdos, G. (1993) *Families Without Fatherhood* (London: Institute of Economic Affairs).

Devine, F. (1992) *Affluent Workers Revisited* (Edinburgh: Edinburgh University Press).

Dion K. and Dion K. (1996) 'Cultural Perspectives on Romantic Love', *Personal Relationships*, 3, pp. 5–17.

Dobash, R. and Dobash, R. (1980) *Violence Against Wives* (London: Open Books).

Dobash, R. and Dobash, R. (1987) 'The Response of the British and American Women's Movements to Violence Against Women' in J. Hanmer and M. Maynard (eds) *Women, Violence and Social Control.*

Dobash, R. and Dobash, R. (1992) *Women, Violence and Social Change* (London: Routledge).

Dobash, R., Dobash, R., Wilson, M. and Daly. M. (1992) 'The Myth of Sexual Symmetry in Marital Violence', *Social Problems*, 39, pp. 71–91.

Donzelot, J. (1979) *The Policing of Families* (London: Hutchinson).

Doucet, A. (1996) 'Encouraging Voices', in L. Morris and E. S. Lyon (eds) *Gender Relations in Public and Private.*

Duckworth, D. (1983) *The Classification and Measurement of Disablement*, DHSS Research Report No. 10 (London: HMSO).

Duncan, S. and Edwards, R. (1997a) 'Introduction: A Contextual Approach to Single Mothers and Paid Work' in S. Duncan and R. Edwards (eds) *Single Mothers in an International Context.*

Duncan, S. and Edwards, R. (1997b) 'Single Mothers in Britain' in S. Duncan and R. Edwards (eds) *Single Mothers in an International Context.*

Duncan, S. and Edwards, R. (eds) (1997) *Single Mothers in an International Context* (London: UCL Press).

Duncombe, J. and Marsden, D. (1993) 'Love and Intimacy', *Sociology*, 27, pp. 221–41.

Duncombe, J. and Marsden, D. (1995) '"Workaholics and Whingeing Women": Theorising Intimacy', *Sociological Review*, 43, pp. 150–169.

Dunne, G. (1996) *Lesbian Lifestyles* (Basingstoke: Macmillan).

Edgell, S. (1980) *Middle-Class Couples* (London: George Allen & Unwin).

Edwards, R. and Duncan, S. (1996) 'Rational Economic Man or Lone Mothers in Context?', in E. Silva (ed.) *Good Enough Mothering.*

Elliot, F. R. (1996) *Gender, Family and Society* (London: Macmillan).

Elliott, J. and Richards, M. (1991) 'Parental Divorce and the Life Chances of Children', *Family Law*, 21, pp. 481–4.

Ermisch, J. (1989) 'Divorce: Economic Antecedents and Aftermath', in H. Joshi (ed.) *The Changing Population of Britain* (Oxford: Blackwell).

Ermisch, J. and Francesconi, M. (1996) 'Partnership Formation and Dissolution in Great Britain', *Working Papers of the ESRC Research Centre on Micro-Social Change*, Paper 96–10 (Colchester: University of Essex).

Evandrou, M. (1996) 'Unpaid Work, Carers and Health', in D. Blane, E. Brunner and R. Wilkinson (eds) *Health and Social Organisation* (London: Routledge).

Everett, C. (1991) *The Consequences of Divorce* (New York: Haworth Press).

Everingham, C. (1994) *Motherhood and Modernity* (Buckingham: Open University Press).

Farber, B. (1973) *Family and Kinship in Modern Society* (Brighton: Scott, Foresman).

FASTATS (1999) http://www.cdc.gov/nchswww/fastats/divorce.htm

Feld, S. and Carter, W. (1998) 'Foci of Activity as Changing Contexts for Friendship', in R. Adams and G. Allan (eds) *Placing Friendship in Context* (Cambridge: Cambridge University Press).

Fennell, G., Phillipson, C. and Evers, H. (1988) *The Sociology of Old Age* (Milton Keynes: Open University Press).

Ferri, E. (1984) *Stepchildren* (Windsor: NFER – Nelson).

Finch, J. (1983) *Married to the Job* (London: George Allen & Unwin).

Finch, J. (1987) 'Family Obligations and the Life Course', in A. Bryman *et al.* (eds) *Rethinking the Life Cycle*.

Finch, J. (1989) *Family Obligations and Social Change* (Cambridge: Polity).

Finch, J. and Mason, J. (1990) 'Divorce, Remarriage and Family Obligations', *British Journal of Sociology*, 38, pp. 219–46.

Finch, J. and Mason, J. (1993) *Negotiating Family Responsibilities* (London: Routledge).

Finch, J. and Morgan, D. (1991) 'Marriage in the 1980s', in D. Clark (ed.) *Marriage, Domestic Life and Social Change*.

Finch, J. and Summerfield, P. (1991) 'Social Reconstruction and the Emergence of Companionate Marriage, 1945–59' in D. Clark (ed.) *Marriage, Domestic Life and Social Change*.

Fletcher, R. (1973) *The Family And Marriage in Britain* (Harmondsworth: Penguin).

Foreman, S. and Dallos, R. (1993) 'Domestic Violence', in R. Dallos and E. McLaughlin (eds) *Social Problems and the Family* (London: Sage).

Furstenberg, F. (1990) 'Divorce and the American Family', *Annual Review of Sociology*, 16, pp. 379–403.

Furstenberg, F. and Nord, C. (1985) 'Parenting Apart: Patterns of Childbearing after Divorce', *Journal of Marriage and the Family*, 47, pp. 898–904.

Furstenberg, F. and Spanier, G. (1987) *Recycling the Family* (Newbury Park, California: Sage).

Furstenberg, F. and Teitler, J. (1994) 'Reconsidering the Effects of Marital Disruption', *Journal of Family Issues*, 15, pp. 173–90.

Gallie, D., Gershuny, J. and Vogler, C. (1994) 'Unemployment, the Household and Social Networks', in D. Gallie *et al.* (eds) *Social Change and the Experience of Unemployment*.

Gallie, D., Marsh, C. and Vogler, C. (eds) (1994) *Social Change and the Experience of Unemployment* (Oxford: Oxford University Press).

Ganong, L. and Coleman, M. (1988) 'Do Mutual Children Cement Bonds in Stepfamilies?', *Journal of Marriage and the Family*, 50, pp. 687–98.

Gardner, K. and Shukur, A. (1994) '"I'm Bengali, I'm Asian, I'm Living Here": the Changing Identity of British Bengalis', in R. Ballard (ed.) *Desh Pardesh*.

Gershuny, J. Godwin, M. and Jones, S. (1994) 'The Domestic Labour Revolution: A Process of Lagged Adaptation', in M. Anderson *et al.* (eds) *The Social and Political Economy of the Household*.

G. H. S. (1997) *Living in Britain: Results from the 1995 General Household Survey* (London: Stationery Office).

Giarrusso, R., Silverstein, M. and Bengston, V. (1996) 'Family Complexity and the Grandparent role', *Generations*, 20, pp. 17–23.

Gibson, C. (1994) *Dissolving Wedlock* (London: Routledge).

Giddens, A. (1991) *Modernity and Self-Identity* (Cambridge: Polity).

Giddens, A. (1992) *The Transformation of Intimacy* (Cambridge: Polity).

Giddens, A. (1998) *The Third Way* (Cambridge: Polity).

Gilding, M. (1991) *The Making and Breaking of the Australian Family* (North Sydney: Allen & Unwin).

Giles-Sims, J. (1984) 'The Stepparent Role', *Journal of Family Issues*, 5, pp. 116–30.

Gillespie, N., Lovett, T. and Garner, W. (1992) *Youth Work and Working Class Youth Culture* (Buckingham: Open University Press).

Gillis, J. (1997) *A World of Their Own Making* (Oxford: Oxford University Press).

Ginn, J. and Arber, S. (1991) 'Gender, Class and Income Inequality in Later Life', *British Journal of Sociology*, 42, pp. 369–96.

Ginn, J. and Arber, S. (1996) 'Patterns of Employment, Gender and Pensions', *Work, Employment and Society*, 10, pp. 469–90.

Glover, J. and Arber, S. (1995) 'Polarisation in Mothers' Employment', *Gender, Work and Organisation*, 2, pp. 165–79.

Goldthorpe, J. (1988) 'Intellectuals and the Working Class in Modern Britain' in D. Rose (ed.) *Social Stratification and Economic Change*.

Goldthorpe, J., Lockwood, D., Bechhofer, F. and Platt, J. (1969) *The Affluent Worker in the Class Structure* (Cambridge: Cambridge University Press).

Goode, W. J. (1959) 'On the Theoretical Importance of Love', *American Sociological Review*, 24, pp. 38–47.

Goode, W. J. (1964) *The Family* (Englewood Cliffs, NJ: Prentice Hall).

Goode, W. J. (1993) *World Changes in Divorce Patterns* (New Haven: Yale University Press).

Gordon, T. (1990) *Feminist Mothers* (Basingstoke: Macmillan).

Gordon, T. (1994) *Single Women* (Basingstoke: Macmillan).

Graefe, D. and Lichter, D. (1999) 'Life Course Transitions of American Children', *Demography*, 36, pp. 205–17.

Graham, H. (1987a) 'Women's Poverty and Caring', in C. Glendinning and J. Millar (eds) *Women and Poverty in Britain* (Brighton: Wheatsheaf).

Graham H. (1987b) 'Being Poor: Perceptions and Coping Strategies of Lone Mothers', in J. Brannen and G. Wilson (eds) *Give and Take in Families*.

Graham, H. (1993) *Hardship and Health in Women's Lives* (Hemel Hempstead: Harvester Wheatsheaf).

Green, E., Hebron, S, and Woodward, D. (1990) *Women's Leisure, What Leisure?* (Basingstoke: Macmillan).

Green, H. (1988) *Informal Carers*, Series GHS 15 (London: OPCS).

Gregson, N. and Lowe, M. (1994) *Servicing the Middle Classes* (London: Routledge).

Griffin, C. (1993) *Representations of Youth* (Cambridge: Polity Press).

Grundy, E. (1995) 'Demographic Influences on the Future of Family Care', in I. Allen and E. Perkins (eds) *The Future of Family Care for Older People.*

Grundy, E. (1996) 'Population Review: The Population Aged 60 and Over', *Population Trends*, 84, pp. 14–20.

Hague, G. and Malos, E. (1993) *Domestic Violence* (Cheltenham: New Clarion Press).

Halsey, A. (1993) 'Changes in the Family', *Children and Society*, 7, pp. 125–36.

Hanmer, J. (1993) 'Women and Reproduction', in D. Richardson and V. Robinson (eds) *Introducing Women's Studies* (Basingstoke: Macmillan).

Hanmer, J. and Saunders, S. (1993) *Women, Violence and Crime Prevention* (Aldershot: Avebury).

Hanmer, J. and Maynard, M. (eds) (1987) *Women, Violence and Social Control* (Basingstoke: Macmillan).

Hantrais, L. and Letablier, M.-T. (1996) *Families and Family Policies in Europe* (Harlow: Addison Wesley Longman).

Hardey, M. and Crow, G. (eds) (1991) *Lone Parenthood* (Hemel Hempstead: Harvester Wheatsheaf).

Hareven, T. K. (1978) 'Family Time and Historical Time' in A. S. Rossi, J. Kagan and T. K. Hareven (eds) *The Family* (New York: Norton).

Hareven, T. K. (1982) *Family Time and Industrial Time* (Cambridge: Cambridge University Press).

Hareven, T. (1991) 'Synchronising Individual Time, Family Time and Historical Time', in J. Bender and D. Wellbery (eds) *Chronotypes* (Stanford, California: Stanford University Press).

Harris, C. C. (1969) *The Family* (London: Allen & Unwin).

Harris, C. C. (1980) 'The Changing Relation Between Family and Societal Form in Western Society' in M. Anderson (ed.) *Sociology of the Family* (Harmondsworth: Penguin) 2nd edn.

Harris, C. C. (1983) *The Family and Industrial Society* (London: Allen & Unwin).

Harris, C. C. (1987) *Redundancy and Recession in South Wales* (Oxford: Blackwell).

Harris, C. C. (1994) 'The family in Post-War Britain', in J. Obelkevich and P. Catterall (eds) *Understanding Post-War British Society*.

Harris, C. C. (ed.) (1990) *Family, Economy and Community* (Cardiff: University of Wales Press).

Haskey, J. (1991) 'Lone Parenthood and Demographic Change' in M. Hardey and G. Crow (eds) *Lone Parenthood*.

Haskey, J. (1992) 'Pre-Marital Cohabitation and the Probability of Subsequent Divorce', *Population Trends*, 68, pp. 10–19.

Haskey, J. (1994a) 'Stepfamilies and Stepchildren in Great Britain', *Population Trends*, 76, pp. 17–28.

Haskey, J. (1994b) 'Estimated Numbers of One-Parent Families and their Prevalence in Great Britain in 1991', *Population Trends*, 78, pp. 5–19.

Haskey, J. (1995) 'Trends in Marriage and Cohabitation', *Population Trends*, 80, pp. 5–15.

Haskey, J. (1996a) 'The Population of Married Couples Who Divorce', *Population Trends*, 83, pp. 25–36.

Haskey, J. (1996b) 'Population Review: (6) Families and Households in Great Britain', *Population Trends*, 85, pp. 7–24.

Haskey, J. (1997) 'Children who Experience Divorce in their Family', *Population Trends*, 87, pp. 5–10.

Haskey, J. (1998) 'One-Parent Families and their Dependent Children in Great Britain', *Population Trends*, 91, pp. 5–14.

Haskey, J. and Kiernan, K. (1989) 'Cohabitation in Great Britain', *Population Trends*, 58, pp. 23–32.

Hawkes, G. (1996) *A Sociology of Sex and Sexuality* (Buckingham: Open University Press).

Heaphy, B., Donovan, C. and Weeks, J. (1999) 'Sex, Money and the Kitchen Sink: Power in Same-Sex Couple Relationships', in J. Seymour and P. Bagguley (eds) *Relating Intimacies*.

Heath, S. and Dale, A. (1994) 'Household and Family Formation in Great Britain: An Ethnic Dimension', *Population Trends*, 77, pp. 5–13.

Hendrix, H. (1990) *Getting the Love You Want* (New York: Harper Perennial).

Henry, C., Ceglian C. and Matthews, W. (1992) 'The Role Behaviors, Role Meanings, and Grandmothering Styles of Grandmothers and Stepgrandmothers', *Journal of Divorce and Remarriage*, 17, pp. 1–22.

Hester, M., Kelly, L. and Radford, J. (eds) (1996) *Women, Violence and Male Power* (Buckingham: Open University Press).

Hetherington, E. (1979) 'Divorce: A Child's Perspective', *American Psychologist*, 34, pp. 851–8.

Hey, V. (1986) *Patriarchy and Pub Culture* (London: Tavistock).

Hill, M. and Tisdall, K. (1997) *Children and Society* (London: Longmans).

Hines, A. (1997) 'Divorce-Related Transitions, Adolescent Development, and the Role of the Parent–Child Relationship', *Journal of Marriage and the Family*, 59, pp. 375–88.

Hochschild, A. (1983) *The Managed Heart* (Berkeley: University of California Press).

Hochschild, A. (1990) *The Second Shift* (London: Piatkus).

Hochschild, A. (1996) 'The Emotional Geography of Work and Family Life' in L. Morris and E. S. Lyon (eds) *Gender Relations in Public and Private*.

Hochschild, A. (1997) *The Time Bind* (New York: Metropolitan Books).

Hockey, J. and James, A. (1993) *Growing Up and Growing Old* (London: Sage).

Hodder, E (1989) *Stepfamilies Talking* (London: Macdonald).

Holme, A. (1985) *Housing and Young Families in East London* (London: Routledge & Kegan Paul).

Homer, M, Leonard, A. and Taylor, P. (1985) 'Personal Relationships: Help and Hindrance', in N. Johnson (ed.) *Marital Violence*, Sociological Review Monograph No. 31 (London: Routledge & Kegan Paul).

Hughes, C. (1994) 'From Field Notes to Dissertation: Analyzing the Stepfamily', in R. Burgess (ed.) *Analyzing Qualitative Data* (London: Routledge).

Hunt, G. and Saterlee, S. (1987) 'Darts, Drinks and the Pub: The Culture of Female Drinking', *Sociological Review*, 35, pp. 575–601.

Hunt, P. (1978) 'Cash Transactions and Household Tasks', *Sociological Review*, 26, pp. 555–71.

Hutson, S. and Cheung, W. (1992) 'Saturday Jobs', in C. Marsh and S. Arber (eds) *Families and Households*.

Hutson, S. and Jenkins, R. (1989) *Taking the Strain* (Milton Keynes: Open University Press).

Illouz, E. (1997) *Consuming the Romantic Utopia* (Berkeley: University of California Press).

Ineichen, B. (1977) 'Youthful Marriage: The Vortex of Disadvantage', in R. Chester and J. Peel (eds) *Equalities and Inequalities in Family Life*.

Irwin, S. (1995) *Rights of Passage* (London: UCL Press).

Ishii-Kuntz, M. and Coltrane, S. (1992) 'Remarriage, Stepparenting, and Household Labor', *Journal of Family Issues*, 13, pp. 215–33.

Jackson, S. (1993) 'Even Sociologists Fall in Love: an Exploration in the Sociology of Emotions', *Sociology* 27, pp. 201–20.

Jacobs, S. (1997) 'Employment Changes over Childbirth: A Retrospective View', *Sociology*, 31, pp. 577–90.

James, N. (1989) 'Emotional Labour: Skill and Work in the Social Regulation of Feeling', *Sociological Review*, 37, pp. 15–42.

Jamieson, L. (1998) *Intimacy* (Cambridge: Polity).

Jensen, A-M. (1998) 'Partnership and Parenthood in Contemporary Europe', *European Journal of Population*, 14, pp. 157–78.

Jenks, C. (1996) 'The Postmodern Child', in J. Brannen and M. O'Brien (eds) *Children in Families*.

Jerrome, D. (1984) 'Good Company: The Sociological Implications of Friendship', *Sociological Review*, 32, pp. 696–718.

Johnson, C. (1988) 'Active and Latent Functions of Grandparenting During the Divorce Process', *The Gerontologist*, 28, pp. 185–91.

Johnson, M. (1995) 'Patriarchal Terrorism and Common Couple Violence', *Journal of Marriage and the Family*, 57, pp. 283–94.

Jones, G. (1995) *Leaving Home* (Buckingham: Open University Press).

Jones, G. and Wallace, C. (1992) *Youth, Family and Citizenship* (Buckingham: Open University Press).

Jordan, B., Redley, M. and James, S. (1994) *Putting the Family First* (London: UCL Press).

Jordan, B., James, S., Kay, H. and Redley, M. (1992) *Trapped in Poverty?* (London: Routledge).

Kamerman, S. and Kahn, A. (1997) 'Family Change and Family Policies: United States', in S. Kamerman and A. Kahn (eds) *Family Change and Family Policies in Great Britain, Canada, New Zealand and the United States*.

Kamerman, S. and Kahn, A. (eds) (1997) *Family Change and Family Policies in Great Britain, Canada, New Zealand and the United States* (Oxford: Clarendon).

Keith, L. and Morris, J. (1996) 'Easy Targets: A Disability Rights Perspective on the "Children as Carers" Debate', in J. Morris (ed.) *Encounters with Strangers* (London: The Women's Press).

Kerckhoff, A. (1990) *Getting Started* (Boulder, Colorado: Westview Press).

Kerr, M. (1958) *The People of Ship Street* (London: Routledge & Kegan Paul).

Kiernan, K. (1996) 'Partnership Behaviour in Europe', in D. Coleman (ed.) *Europe's Population in the 1990s* (Oxford: Oxford University Press).

Kiernan, K. (1997) 'Becoming a Young Parent', *British Journal of Sociology*, 48, pp. 406–28.

Kiernan, K. (1999) 'Cohabitation in Western Europe', *Population Trends*, 96, pp. 25–32.

Kiernan, K. and Estaugh, V. (1993) *Cohabitation* (London: Family Policy Studies Centre).

Kiernan, K. and Lelièvre, E. (1995) 'Great Britain', in H.-P. Blossfeld (ed.) *Family Formation in Modern Societies and the New Role of Women*, (Boulder, Colorado: Westview Press).

Kiernan, K. and Mueller, G. (1999) 'Who Divorces?', in S. McRae (ed.) *Changing Britain*.

Kiernan, K., Land, H. and Lewis, J. (1997) *Lone Motherhood in Twentieth Century Britain* (Oxford: Oxford University Press).

Klein, J. (1965) *Samples from English Cultures* (London: Routledge & Kegan Paul) vol. 1.

Knowles, C. (1996) *Family Boundaries* (Peterborough, Ontario: Broadview Press).

Kurz, D. (1995) *For Richer, For Poorer: Mothers Confront Divorce* (London: Routledge).

Land, H. (1978) 'Who Cares for the Family?', *Journal of Social Policy*, 7, pp. 257–84.

Land, H. (1996) 'The Crumbling Bridges Between Childhood and Adulthood', in J. Brannen and M. O'Brien (eds) *Children in Families*.

Laslett, P. (1996) *A Fresh Map of Life* (Basingstoke: Macmillan) (2nd edn).

Lawson, A. (1988) *Adultery* (New York: Basic Books).

Lefaucheur, N. and Martin, C. (1997) 'Single Mothers in France', in S. Duncan and R. Edwards (eds) *Single Mothers in an International Context*.

Leonard, D. (1980) *Sex and Generation* (London: Tavistock).

Leonard, D. (1990) 'Persons in their Own Right: Children and Sociology in the UK', in Chisholm, L., Büchner, P., Krüger, H.-H. and Brown, P. (eds) *Childhood, Youth and Social Change* (London: Falmer).

Leslie, L. and Grady, K. (1985) 'Changes in Mothers' Social Networks and Social Support Following Divorce', *Journal of Marriage and the Family*, 47, pp. 663–73.

Lewis, C. and O'Brien, M. (1987) 'Constraints on Fathers: Research, Theory and Clinical Practice', in C. Lewis and M. O'Brien (eds) *Reassessing Fatherhood*.

Lewis, C. and O'Brien, M. (eds) (1987) *Reassessing Fatherhood* (London: Sage).

Lewis, J. (1992) *Women in Britain Since 1945* (Oxford: Blackwell).

Lewis, J. and Kiernan, K. (1996) 'The Boundaries Between Marriage, Non-Marriage, and Parenthood', *Journal of Family History*, 67, pp. 372–87.

Lewis, J. and Meredith, B. (1988) *Daughters Who Care* (London: Routledge).

Lewis, J., Clark, D. and Morgan, D. (1992) *Whom God Hath Joined Together* (London: Routledge).

Liddiard, M. and Hutson, S. (1990), 'Youth Homelessness in Wales', in C. Wallace and M. Cross (eds) *Youth in Transition* (London: Falmer).

Lillard, L., Brien, M. and Waite, L. (1995) Premarital Cohabitation and Subsequent Marital Dissolution', *Demography*, 32, pp. 437–57.

Litwak, E. (1960a) 'Occupational Mobility and Extended Family Cohesion', *American Sociological Review*, 25, pp. 9–21.

Litwak, E. (1960b) 'Geographic Mobility and Extended Family Cohesion', *American Sociological Review*, 25, pp. 385–94.

Luhmann, N. (1986) *Love as Passion* (Cambridge: Polity).

Lukes, S. (1974) *Power* (London: Macmillan).

Lund, M. (1987) 'The Non-Custodial Father', in C. Lewis and M. O'Brien (eds) *Reassessing Fatherhood*.

Lupton, C. and Gillespie, T. (eds) (1994) *Working With Violence* (Basingstoke: Macmillan).

MacDonald, R. and Coffield, F. (1991) *Risky Business?* (London: Falmer).

MacDonald, W. and DeMaris, A. (1995) 'Remarriage, Stepchildren, and Marital Conflict', *Journal of Marriage and the Family*, 57, pp. 387–98.

MacDonald, W. and DeMaris, A. (1996) 'Parenting Stepchildren and Biological Children', *Journal of Family Issues*, 5, pp. 17–25.

Macfarlane, A. (1987) *The Culture of Capitalism* (Oxford: Blackwell).

Macintyre, S. (1976) 'Who Wants Babies: The Social Construction of Instincts', in D. Barker and S. Allen (eds) *Sexual Divisions and Society* (London: Tavistock).

Maclean, M. (1987) 'Households After Divorce', in J. Brannen and G. Wilson (eds) *Give and Take in Families*.

Maclean, M. (1991) *Surviving Divorce* (Basingstoke: Macmillan).

McCrone, D. (1994) 'Getting By and Making Out in Kirkaldy', in M. Anderson, F. Bechhofer and J. Gershuny (eds) *The Social and Political Economy of the Household*.

McGregor, O. R. (1957) *Divorce in England* (London: Heinemann).

McHugh, M. and Millar, J. (1997) 'Single Mothers in Australia', in S. Duncan and R. Edwards (eds) *Single Mothers in an International Context*.

McKee, L. (1987) 'Households During Unemployment', in J. Brannen and G. Wilson (eds) *Give and Take in Families*.

McKee, L. and Bell, C. (1986) 'His Unemployment, Her Problem: The Domestic and Marital Consequences of Male Unemployment', in S. Allen *et al.* (eds) *The Experience of Unemployment*.

McLaughlin, E. and Rodgers, P. (1997) 'Single Mothers in the Republic of Ireland', in S. Duncan and R. Edwards (eds) *Single Mothers in an Internation Context*.

McRae, S. (1986) *Cross-Class Families* (Oxford: Clarendon Press).

McRae, S. (1993a) *Cohabiting Mothers* (London: Policy Studies Institute).

McRae, S. (1993b) 'Returning to Work After Childbirth: Opportunities and Inequalities', *European Sociological Review*, 9, pp. 125–37.

McRae, S. (ed.) (1999) *Changing Britain* (Oxford: Oxford University Press).

Malos, E. and Hague, G. (1997) 'Women, Housing, Homelessness and Domestic Violence', *Women's Studies International Forum*, 20, pp. 397–410.

Mansfield, P. and Collard, J. (1988) *The Beginning of the Rest of Your Life?* (Basingstoke: Macmillan).

Marsden, D. (1978) 'Sociological Perspectives on Family Violence', in J. P. Martin (ed.) *Violence and the Family* (Chichester: Wiley).

Marsh, A., Ford, R. and Finlayson, L. (1997) *Lone Parents* (London: The Stationery Office).

Marsh, C. and Arber, S. (eds) (1992) *Families and Households* (London: Macmillan).

Marshall, H. (1991) 'The Social Construction of Motherhood', in A. Phoenix, A. Woollett and E. Lloyd (eds) *Motherhood*.

Marsiglio, W. (1992) 'Stepfathers with Minor Children Living at Home', *Journal of Family Issues*, 13, pp. 195–214.

Marx, K. (1934) *The Eighteenth Brumaire of Louis Bonaparte* (Moscow: Progress Publishers).

Mason, J. (1987) 'A Bed of Roses? Women, Marriage and Inequality in Later Life', in P. Allatt, *et al.* (eds) *Women and the Life Cycle*.

Mason, J. (1989) 'Reconstructing the Public and the Private: The Home and Marriage in Later Life', in G. Allan and G. Crow (eds) *Home and Family*.

Medick, H. (1976) 'The Proto-Industrial Family Economy', *Social History*, 1, pp. 291–315.

Milardo, R. (1987) 'Changes in Social Networks of Women and Men Following Divorce', *Journal of Family Issues*, 8, pp. 78–96.

Millar, J. (1989) *Poverty and the Lone-Parent Family* (Avebury: Gower).

Millar, J. (1992) 'Lone Mothers and Poverty' in C. Glendinning and J. Millar (eds) *Women and Poverty in Britain: The 1990s* (Hemel Hempstead: Harvester Wheatsheaf).

Millar, J. (1994) 'State, Family and Personal Responsibility', *Feminist Review*, 48, pp. 24–39.

Mills, C. W. (1970) *The Sociological Imagination* (Harmondsworth: Penguin).

Mitchell, A. (1985) *Children in the Middle* (London: Tavistock).

Mooney, J. (1996) 'Researching Domestic Violence' in L. Morris and E. S. Lyon (eds) *Gender Relations in Public and Private*.

Morgan, D. (1985) *The Family, Politics and Social Theory* (London: Routledge & Kegan Paul).

Morgan, D. (1996) *Family Connections* (Cambridge: Polity).

Morgan, D. (1999) 'Risk and Family Practices', in E. Silva and C. Smart (eds) *The New Family?*

Morris, J. (1993) *Independent Lives?* (Basingstoke: Macmillan).

Morris, L. (1985) 'Renegotiation of the Domestic Division of Labour', in B. Roberts, R. Finnegan and D. Gallie (eds) *New Approaches to Economic Life* (Manchester: Manchester University Press).

Morris, L. (1990a) *The Workings of the Household* (Cambridge: Polity).

Morris, L. (1990b) 'The Household and the Labour Market', in C. C. Harris (ed.) *Family, Economy and Community*.

Morris, L. (1994) *Dangerous Classes* (London: Routledge).

Morris, L. and Lyon, E. S. (eds) (1996) *Gender Relations in Public and Private* (London: Macmillan).

Mullan, B. (1984) *The Mating Trade* (London: Routledge & Kegan Paul).

Mullender, A. (1996) *Rethinking Domestic Violence* (London: Routledge).

Murray, C. (1994) *Underclass: The Crisis Deepens* (London: Institute of Economic Affairs).

National Stepfamily Association (1997) National Stepfamily Association web site at: http://www.webcreations.co.uk/nsa/index.html

Nazroo, J. (1995) 'Uncovering Gender Differences in the Use of Marital Violence', *Sociology*, 29, pp. 475–94.

Neale, B. and Smart, C. (1997) 'Experiments with Parenthood?' *Sociology*, 31, pp. 201–19.

New Earnings Survey (1999) (London: Department of Employment).

Nissel, M. and Bonnerjea, L. (1982) *Family Care of the Handicapped Elderly* (London: Policy Studies Institute).

Nock, S. (1995) 'A Comparison of Marriage and Cohabiting Relationships', *Journal of Family Issues*, 16, pp. 53–76.

Noller, P. (1996) 'What is this Thing Called Love?', *Personal Relationships*, 3, pp. 97–115.

Oakley, A. (1974) *The Sociology of Housework* (London: Martin Robertson).

Oakley, A. (1976) *Housewife* (Harmondsworth: Penguin).

Obelkevich, J. and Catterall, P. (eds) (1994) *Understanding Post-War British Society* (London: Routledge).

O'Brien, M. (1987) 'Patterns of Kinship and Friendship Among Lone Fathers', in C. Lewis and M. O'Brien (eds) *Reassessing Fatherhood*.

Oerton, S. (1997) '"Queer Housewives?" Some Problems in Theorising the Division of Domestic Labour in Lesbian and Gay Households', *Women's Studies International Forum*, 20, pp. 421–30.

O.P.C.S. (1992) *General Household Survey: Carers in 1990*, OPCS Monitor SS 92/2 (London: OPCS).

Pahl, J. (1980) 'Patterns of Money Management Within Marriage', *Journal of Social Policy*, 9, pp. 313–35.

Pahl, J. (1983) 'The Allocation of Money and the Structuring of Inequality Within Marriage', *Sociological Review*, 31, pp. 237–62.

Pahl, J. (1989) *Money and Marriage* (Basingstoke: Macmillan).

Pahl, J. (ed.) (1985) *Private Violence and Public Policy* (London: Routledge & Kegan Paul).

Pahl, R. (1984) *Divisions of Labour* (Oxford: Blackwell).

Pahl, R. and Wallace, C. (1988) 'Neither Angels in Marble Nor Rebels in Red: Privatisation and Working-Class Consciousness', in D. Rose (ed.) *Social Stratification and Economic Change*.

Parker, G. (1993) *With This Body* (Buckingham: Open University Press).

Parker, R. (1981) 'Tending and Social Policy', in E. Goldberg and S. Hatch (eds) *A New Look at the Personal Social Services* (London: Policy Studies Institute).

Parsons, T. (1949) 'The Social Structure of the Family' in R. Ashen (ed.) *The Family* (New York: Haynor).

Parsons, T. (1955) 'The American Family', in T. Parsons and R. Bales, *Family: Socialisation and Interaction Process* (Glencoe, Illinois: Free Press).

Peace, H. (1993) 'The Pretended Family: A Study of the Division of Domestic Labour in Lesbian Families', *Discussion Papers in Sociology*, 93/3 (University of Leicester).

Peng, I. (1997) 'Single Mothers in Japan', in S. Duncan and R. Edwards (eds) *Single Mothers in an International Context*.

Peplau, A., Venigas, R. and Miller Campbell, S. (1996) 'Gay and Lesbian Relationships' in R. Savin-Williams and K. Cohen (eds) *The Lives of Lesbians, Gays and Bisexuals* (New York: Harcourt Brace).

Phillipson, C. (1982) *Capitalism and the Construction of Old Age* (London: Macmillan).

Phillipson, C. (1998) *Reconstructing Old Age* (London: Sage).

Phillipson, C. and Walker, A. (eds) (1986) *Ageing and Social Policy* (Aldershot: Gower).

Phillipson, C., Bernard, M., Phillips, J. and Ogg, J. (1998) 'The Family and Community Life of Older People', *Ageing and Society*, 18, pp. 259–89.

Phoenix, A. (1991) *Young Mothers?* (Cambridge: Polity).

Phoenix A., Woollett A. and Lloyd, E. (eds) (1991) *Motherhood* (London: Sage).

Pickvance, C. and Pickvance, K. (1994) 'Towards a Strategic Approach to Housing Behaviour' *Sociology* 28, pp. 657–77.

Piper, C. (1993) *The Responsible Parent* (Hemel Hempstead: Harvester Wheatsheaf).

Popay, J. and Jones, G. (1991) 'Patterns of Health and Illness Amongst Lone-Parent Families', in M. Hardey and G. Crow (eds), *Lone Parenthood*.

Potuchek, J. (1997) *Who Supports the Family?* (Stanford, California: Stanford University Press).

Prinz, C. (1995) *Cohabiting, Married, or Single* (Aldershot: Avebury).

Procter, M. (1990) 'The Privatisation of Working-Class Life', *British Journal of Sociology*, 41, pp. 157–80.

Qureshi, H. (1996) 'Obligations and Support Within Families', in A. Walker (ed.) *The New Generational Contract* (London: UCL Press).

Qureshi, H. and Walker, A. (1989) *The Caring Relationship* (Basingstoke: Macmillan).

Radford, J. and Stanko, E. (1996) 'Violence Against Women and Children', in M. Hester, L. Kelly, and J. Radford (eds) *Women, Violence and Male Power*.

Rands, M. (1988) 'Changes in Social Networks Following Marital Separation and Divorce', in R. Milardo (ed.) *Families and Social Networks* (Newbury Park, California: Sage).

Ravanera, Z. and Rajulton, F. (1996) 'Stability and Crisis in the Family Life Course', *Canadian Studies in Population*, 23, pp. 165–84.

Ribbens, J. (1994) *Mothers and Their Children* (London: Sage).

Ribbens, J., Edwards, R. and Gillies, V. (1996) 'Parenting and Step-Parenting After Divorce/Separation: Issues and Negotiations', *Changing Britain* (ESRC) 5, pp. 4–6.

Richards, L. (1990) *Nobody's Home* (Oxford: Oxford University Press).

Richards, M. (1982) 'Do Broken Marriages Affect Children?', *Health Visitor*, 55, pp. 152–3.

Richards, M. (1999) 'The Interests of Children at Divorce' in G. Allan (ed.) *The Sociology of the Family*.

Richardson, D. (1993) *Women, Motherhood and Childrearing* (Basingstoke: Macmillan).

Risman, B. and Johnson-Sumerford, D. (1998) 'Doing It Fairly: A Study of Postgender Marriages', *Journal of Marriage and the Family*, 60, pp. 23–40.

Roberts, E. (1984) *A Woman's Place* (Oxford: Blackwell).

Roberts, K., Parsell, G. and Connolly, M. (1991) 'Young People's Transitions into the Labour Market', in M. Cross and G. Payne (eds) *Work and the Enterprise Culture* (London: Falmer).

Robinson, M. (1991) *Family Transformation Through Divorce and Remarriage* (London: Routledge).

Robinson, M. and Smith, D. (1993) *Step by Step* (Hemel Hempstead: Harvester Wheatsheaf).

Rodger, J. (1996) *Family Life and Social Control* (Basingstoke: Macmillan).

Rose, D. (ed.) (1988) *Social Stratification and Economic Change* (London: Hutchinson).

Roseneil, S. and Mann, K. (1996) 'Unpalatable Choices and Inadequate Families', in E. Silva (ed.) *Good Enough Mothering*.

Rosser, C. and Harris, C. (1965) *The Family and Social Change* (London: Routledge & Kegan Paul).

Rowlingson, K. and McKay, S. (1998) *The Growth of Lone Parenthood* (London: Policy Studies Institute).

Rutter, M. and Madge, N. (1976) *Cycles of Disadvantage* (London: Heinemann).

Safilios-Rothschild, C. (1969) 'Family Sociology or Wives' Family Sociology', *Journal of Marriage and the Family*, 31, pp. 290–301.

Sainsbury, D. (ed.) (1994) *Gendering Welfare States* (London: Sage).

Sarsby, J. (1983) *Romantic Love and Society* (Harmondsworth: Penguin).

Schneider, D. (1968) *American Kinship: A Cultural Account* (Englewood Cliffs, New Jersey: Prentice Hall).

Schofield, M. (1968) *The Sexual Behaviour of Young People*, (Harmondsworth: Penguin).

Schofield, M. (1971) *The Sexual Behaviour of Young Adults* (London: Allen Lane).

Scott, A. and Wenger, G. (1995) 'Gender and Social Support Networks in Late Life', in S. Arber and J. Ginn (eds) *Connecting Gender and Ageing*.

Scott, J. (1997) 'Changing Households in Britain', *Sociological Review*, 45, pp. 591–620.

Segal, L. (1990) *Slow Motion* (London: Virago).

Seymour, J. and Bagguley, P. (eds) (1999) *Relating Intimacies* (Basingstoke: Macmillan).

Sharpe, S. (1984) *Double Identity* (Harmondsworth: Penguin).

Sharpe, S. (1994) *Fathers and Daughters* (London: Routledge).

Shaw, A. (1994) 'The Pakistani Community in Oxford', in R. Ballard (ed.) *Desh Pardesh*.

Shorter, E. (1975) *The Making of the Modern Family* (London: Fontana).

Silva, E. and Smart, C. (1999) 'The "New" Practices and Politics of Family Life', in E. Silva and C. Smart (eds) *The New Family*.

Silva, E. (ed.) (1996) *Good Enough Mothering* (Routledge: London).

Silva, E. and Smart, C. (eds) (1999) *The New Family?* (London: Sage).

Simpson, B. (1994) 'Bringing the Unclear Family into Focus' *Man*, 29, pp. 831–51.

Simpson, B. (1998) *Changing Families* (Oxford: Berg).
Simpson, B., McCarthy, P. and Walker, J. (1995) *Being There: Fathers After Divorce* (Newcastle: Relate Centre for Family Studies).
Sinfield, A. (1981) *What Unemployment Means* (London: Martin Robertson).
Sly, F., Price, A. and Risdon, A. (1997) 'Women in the Labour Market', *Labour Market Trends*, 105, pp. 99–120.
Smart, C. (1984) *The Ties That Bind* (London: Routledge & Kegan Paul).
Smart, C. (1996) 'Deconstructing Motherhood', in E. Silva (ed.) *Good Enough Mothering.*
Smart, C. (1997) 'Wishful Thinking and Harmful Tinkering', *Journal of Social Policy*, 26, pp. 301–21.
Smart, C. and Neale, B. (1999) *Family Fragments?* (Cambridge: Polity).
Smith, D. (1990) *Stepmothering* (Hemel Hempstead: Harvester Wheatsheaf).
Social Trends (1997) (London: ONS).
Social Trends (1998) (London: ONS).
Song, M. and Edwards, R. (1997) 'Comment: Raising Questions about Perspectives on Black Lone Motherhood', *Journal of Social Policy*, 26, pp. 233–44.
Spencer, A. and Podmore, D. (1987) *In a Man's World* (London: Tavistock).
St Leger, F. and Gillespie, N. (1991) *Informal Welfare in Belfast: Caring Communities?* (Aldershot: Avebury).
Stacey, J. (1998) *Brave New Families* (Berkeley: University of California Press) (2nd edn).
Stanley, L. (1992) 'Changing Households? Changing Work?', in N. Abercrombie and A. Warde (eds) *Social Change in Contemporary Britain* (Cambridge: Polity).
Stephens, L. (1996) 'Will Johnny See Daddy This Week?: An Empirical Test of Three Theoretical Perspectives of Post-Divorce Contact', *Journal of Family Issues*, 17, pp. 466–94.
Stone, L. (1979) *The Family, Sex and Marriage in England 1500–1800* (Harmondsworth: Penguin).
Stone, L. (1988) 'Passionate Attachments in the West in Historical Perspective', in W. Gaylin and E. Person (eds) *Passionate Attachments* (New York: Free Press).
Straus, M., Gelles, R. and Steinmetz, S. (1980) *Behind Closed Doors* (New York: Anchor).
Straus, M., Hamby, S., Boney-McCoy, S. and Sugarman, D.(1996) 'The Revised Conflict Tactics Scales (CTS2)', *Journal of Family Issues*, 17, pp. 283–316.
Sullivan, O. (1996) 'Time Co-ordination, the Domestic Division of Labour and Affective Relations', *Sociology*, 30, pp. 79–100.

Sullivan, O. (1997) 'The Division of Housework Among "Remarried" Couples', *Journal of Family Issues*, 18, pp. 205–23.

Summerfield, P. (1994) 'Women in Britain since 1945', in J. Obelkevich and P. Catterall (eds) *Understanding Post-War British Society*.

Taylor, M., Keen, M., Buck, N. and Corti, L. (1994) 'Income, Welfare and Consumption', in N. Buck, J. Gershuny, D. Rose and J. Scott (eds) *Changing Households* (Colchester, Essex: ESRC Research Centre on Micro-Social Change.)

Thomson, E. and Colella, U. (1992) 'Cohabitation and Marital Stability', *Journal of Marriage and the Family*, 54, pp. 259–67.

Tivers, J. (1985) *Mothers Attached* (London: Croom Helm).

Townsend, P. (1979) *Poverty in the United Kingdom* (Harmondsworth: Penguin).

Trygstad, D. and Sanders, G. (1989) 'The Significance of Stepgrandparents', *International Journal of Aging and Human Development*, 29, pp. 119–34.

Ungerson, C. (1987) *Policy is Personal* (London: Tavistock).

Vaughan, D. (1987) *Uncoupling* (London: Methuen).

Vincent, J. (1995) *Inequality and Old Age* (London: UCL Press).

Vogler, C. (1994) 'Money in the Household', in M. Anderson *et al.* (eds) *The Social and Political Economy of the Household*.

Vogler, C. and Pahl, J. (1994) 'Money, Power and Inequality Within Marriage', *Sociological Review*, 42, pp. 263–88.

Voysey, M. (1975) *A Constant Burden* (London: Routledge & Kegan Paul).

Waddington, D., Wykes, M. and Critcher, C. (1991) *Split at the Seams?* (Buckingham: Open University Press).

Waerness, K. (1990) 'Informal and Formal Care in Old Age', in C. Ungerson (ed.) *Gender and Caring* (Hemel Hempstead: Harvester-Wheatsheaf).

Walker, A. and Walker, C. (eds) (1997) *Britain Divided* (London: Child Poverty Action Group).

Walker, A. and Warren, L. (1996) *Changing Services for Older People* (Buckingham: Open University Press).

Walker, J. (1993) 'Cooperative Parenting Post-Divorce: Possibility or Pipe-Dream?', *Journal of Family Therapy*, 15, pp. 273–93.

Walker, K. and Messenger, L. (1979) 'Remarriage After Divorce', *Family Process*, 18, pp. 185–92.

Wallace, C. (1987) *For Richer, for Poorer* (London: Tavistock).

Wallace, C. (1993) 'Reflections on the Concept of "Strategy"' in D. Morgan and L. Stanley (eds) *Debates in Sociology* (Manchester: Manchester University Press).

Wallace, C. and Kovatcheva, S. (1998) *Youth in Society* (Basingstoke: Macmillan).

Wallman, S. (1984) *Eight London Households* (London: Tavistock).

Ward, C., Dale, A. and Joshi, H. (1996) 'Income Dependency Within Couples', in L. Morris and E. S. Lyon (eds) *Gender Relations in Public and Private*.

Warde, A. (1990) 'Household Work Strategies and Forms of Labour', *Work, Employment and Society*, 4, pp. 495–515.

Warrier, S. (1994) 'Gujarati Prajapatis in London: Family Roles and Sociability Networks', in R. Ballard (ed.) *Desh Pardesh*.

Weeks, J. (1991) 'Pretended Family Relationships' in D. Clark (ed.) *Marriage, Domestic Life and Social Change*.

Weeks, J., Heaphy, B. and Donovan, C. (1999a) 'Partners by Choice: Equality, Power and Commitment in Non-Heterosexual Relationships', in G. Allan (ed.) *The Sociology of the Family*.

Weeks, J., Heaphy, B. and Donovan, C. (1999b) 'Partnership Rites: Commitment and Ritual in Non-Heterosexual Relationships', in J. Seymour and P. Bagguley (eds) *Relating Intimacies*.

Wheelock, J. (1990) *Husbands at Home* (London: Routledge).

White, L., Brinkerhoff, D. and Booth, A. (1985) 'The Effect of Marital Disruption on Children's Attachment to Parents', *Journal of Family Issues*, 6, pp. 5–22.

Whitehead, A. (1976) 'Sexual Antagonism in Herefordshire' in D. Barker and S. Allen (eds) *Dependence and Exploitation in Work and Marriage*.

Wilson, E. (1980) *Only Halfway to Paradise* (London: Tavistock).

Wilson, G. (1987) *Money in the Family* (Aldershot: Avebury).

Wilson, W. J. (1987) *The Truly Disadvantaged* (Chicago: University of Chicago Press).

Wood, J. (1993) 'Engendered Relations', in S. Duck (ed.) *Social Context and Relationships* (Newbury Park, California: Sage).

Wrong, D. (1979) *Power* (Oxford: Blackwell).

Wyn, J. and White, R. (1997) *Rethinking Youth* (St Leonards, NSW: Allen & Unwin).

Young, M. and Willmott, P. (1957) *Family and Kinship in East London* (London: Routledge & Kegan Paul).

Young, M. and Willmott, P. (1973) *The Symmetrical Family* (London: Routledge & Kegan Paul).

# Index

237